The Echo Chamber Evangelists
Beyond the Vanishing Point of Belief

by
Padraig D. Lydon

Persuasion Dynamics

The Echo Chamber Evangelists
Beyond the Vanishing Point of Belief
© 2025 by Padraig D. Lydon
All rights reserved.
No part of this publication may be reproduced, stored in a retrieval system, or transmitted in any form or by any means—electronic, mechanical, photocopying, recording, or otherwise—without the prior written permission of the publisher, except in the case of brief quotations used for purposes of review or scholarly analysis.
Published by **Persuasion Dynamics**
www.persuasiondynamics.net

ISBN: 979-8-9942863-0-2

First Edition
This work of nonfiction examines rhetorical patterns, belief systems, and persuasive techniques as cultural phenomena. Some names, descriptions, and scenarios have been altered or combined for clarity and illustrative purposes. Any resemblance to actual persons, living or dead, is coincidental and unintentional.
The views expressed in this book are those of the author and are presented for the purposes of analysis, education, and critical inquiry.
Printed in the United States of America

ABOUT THE PUBLISHER

Persuasion Dynamics is an independent nonfiction imprint dedicated to the study of rhetoric, belief formation, and the mechanics of persuasion in modern culture.

Its focus is not on debating conclusions, but on examining how narratives are constructed, how language shapes identity, and how persuasive systems influence what people come to accept as true. Through cultural analysis, historical context, and careful attention to rhetorical technique, Persuasion Dynamics publishes work that aims to make persuasion visible—so it can be examined rather than absorbed unnoticed.

www.persuasiondynamics.net

DEDICATION

To my father, who passed down a deep disdain for lies dressed as truth.
And to my mother, who gave me the love of words that led me here.

AUTHOR'S NOTE

This book was not written to ridicule belief, nor to score points in a culture war. It was written to understand how certain ideas take hold, how they persist, and why they can feel convincing even when the evidence beneath them is thin or absent.

Flat Earth belief is often treated as a joke, a curiosity, or a harmless oddity. That dismissal misses the point. The real subject of this book is not the shape of the Earth, but the persuasive systems that allow demonstrably false ideas to survive, spread, and profit in a modern, connected world. Flat Earth serves here as a case study—an unusually clear one—through which broader patterns of rhetoric, identity, and belief formation can be examined.

Throughout these pages, I focus less on *what* people believe and more on *how* belief is constructed and defended. Language, narrative framing, repetition, community reinforcement, and appeals to certainty matter as much as facts—often more. Evidence alone rarely changes minds. Stories do.

This work approaches its subject with care. Many who encounter Flat Earth ideas are not foolish, malicious, or intellectually lazy. They are responding to persuasive messages that speak to genuine human needs: belonging, certainty, control, and meaning. Understanding those forces is not an act of endorsement, but a prerequisite for honest engagement.

At the same time, this book does not pretend that all claims are equally valid. Scientific knowledge is not a belief system in the rhetorical sense explored here; it is a method—imperfect, self-correcting, and grounded in evidence and open to revision. Distinguishing between methods of inquiry and methods of persuasion is central to the analysis that follows.

If this book has a purpose beyond explanation, it is this: to make persuasion visible. Once rhetorical mechanisms are seen clearly, they lose much of their power. Certainty becomes something to examine rather than surrender to, and belief becomes something we can hold thoughtfully instead of defensively.

This is not a book about winning arguments. It is a book about understanding how arguments win us.

TABLE OF CONTENTS

AUTHOR'S NOTE i
TABLE OF CONTENTS iii
The Curious Case of a Flat World viii
Chapter 1 — In the Beginning: The Flat Earth Story 1

    Horizons of Belief: Ancient Cosmologies 1
    The Zetetic Rebellion: 19th Century Doubt 16
    A Revival in the Digital Age 22
    When Stories Outlast the Stars 26

Chapter 2: The Gospel of Certainty — The Bonds of Belief, Faith, and Firmament 27

    The Firmament's Echo: When Faith Shapes the Horizon 28
    Whose Bible? Whose Words? The Flat Earth's Scriptural
    Foundation 34
    Which Bible? Whose words? And why were those words
    chosen? 35
    The Language of Belonging: Forging Unity Through a
    Narrowed Lens 49
    Belief Under Duress: Fear and Damnation 53
    Inside the Bubble: Language, Conformity, and the Self 58
    Certainty as Salvation 64
    The Allure of Absolute Certainty 65
    Simplicity's Hidden Costs 67
    Courage in Complexity 68

Chapter 3: Narrative by Design: Crafting a Flat World 71

    Every Story Needs a Villain: The Power of a Clear Enemy .. 71
    Casting NASA and Science as the Deceivers 73
    Government as the Puppet Master 76
    The Comfort of Blame 78
    When the Villain Becomes the Proof 80

The Hero's Journey: Framing the Believer as the Protagonist 81
Standing Against the World: Contrast as Persuasion.............83
The Confident Truth-Teller: Performing Ethos 84
Doubt as the Villain, Certainty as the Weapon 86
The Ego Hook 87
Being 'In the Know': Exclusive Ethos....................................90
The Hook of the Unknown...92
Forbidden Knowledge as Proof..93
The Thrill of Discovery 94
Presentism: Framing the Past to Serve the Present.................96
Cherry-Picking and Anachronisms...97
The Authority of the Ancients 98
Rewriting as Legitimizing 100
The Comfort of a Simple Storyline 101
The Seductive Power of Simplicity 102
Clarity vs. Complexity 104
Stripping Away Nuance 106
The Comfort of Clean Lines..107
Us vs. Them: The Narrative Need for Sides........................110
Turning Belief Into Belonging 111
Language as a Boundary Line 113
When the Story Becomes the Community 114
Foreshadowing the Chamber...115
The Frame as Proof 116

Chapter 4: The Stage of Echoes - The Theater of Belief 118

Inside the Chamber..119
Ritual and Repetition...120
Identity Inside the Walls 122
Language as a Barrier..123
The Chamber as a Constructed Reality 125
Voices in Unison..126
Memes as Mini-Arguments 128
The Power of Short Phrases 129
Chorus and Refrain..131

    Repetition as Construction 132
    Weaponized Mockery 134
    Center Stage... 135
    The Language of Absolutes 137
    Rehearsed Monologue 138
    Charisma vs. Content.. 140
    Confidence as Contagion... 142
    The Actor's Mask 143
    Holding the Walls 145
    Language of Exclusion 146
    Fear of Contamination 148
    The Sound of Silence.. 149
    Ritual Defense 151
    The Walls as Comfort 152
    Carrying the Echo... 154
    Amplified by Design 155
    Echoes Beyond Believers 157
    The Feedback Loop 159
    Voices Made Viral 160
    Resonance vs. Noise... 162
    Curtain Call 164

Chapter 5 — Rhetorical Sleight of Hand: Tricks, Tropes, and Tactics 166

    Emotional Appeals: Fear, Pride, and Belonging.................. 167
    Logical Fallacies in Plain Sight... 174
    Why Fallacies Feel Persuasive Anyway 184
    The Gish Gallop: Drowning in Details................................ 185
    Owning the Stage 188
    Data Mining and Cherry-Picking 192
    Question-Framing and Shifting the Burden of Proof 199
    Visual Rhetoric: Memes, Maps, and Diagrams 204
    The Residue of Persuasion 216

Chapter 6 — The Grift Beneath the Globe: Flat Earth as a Business 217

v

The Psychology of the Grift 218
Crafting the Face of the Movement 222
Building the Marketplace 228
Buying Into Belief 232
The Martyr Narrative: Silenced or Selling? 239

Chapter 7 — Beyond the Vanishing Point: What This Teaches Us 246

Why Flat Earth Persists 247
Rhetoric, Not Evidence, Wins Hearts 253
The Emotional Architecture of a Lie 255
The Theater of Certainty 258
Repetition as Identity Reinforcement 259
Engaging Without Reinforcing 261
Breaking the Spell: Case Studies in Doubt and Departure ... 266
Why Doubt Is Both Fragile and Powerful 269
Lessons for Communicators 270
The Risks of Underestimating Persuasive Language 272
Persuasion loses much of its force when it is dragged into the light 278

Holding the Thread 280
Epilogue: On Transparency, Doubt, and the Use of Tools .. 281
The Lens We Choose 283
Glossary 285
Appendix A: The Scientific Method and Proper Research — A Primer 290

Introduction: Why This Matters 290
Understanding the Scientific Method 291
Inside a Real Experiment 292
What Proper Research Looks Like 294
Patience and Process 299
Final Thoughts 300

Appendix B: Eric Dubay's "200 Proofs" — A Rhetorical Analysis 301

Introduction 301
The Illusion of Quantity 301
Thematic Repetition and Claim Recycling 303
Padding the List with Tricks, Not Evidence 304
Why This Matters 306
Final Thoughts 306

Appendix C – Visual Rhetoric and Flat Earth Media 308

Why the Visual Works 308
Common Visual Tactics 309
Spot the Trick 312
Final Thoughts 315

Appendix D: Cognitive Biases and Psychological Influences 316

Why We Believe — Even When It Makes No Sense 316
The Biases Behind the Belief 317
The Levers They Pull 318
Tactics That Tap into Bias 320
Why It Works So Well 321
Final Thoughts 322

Appendix E: How to Talk to a Flat Earther Without Losing Your Mind – A Quick Reference Guide 323

Before You Begin 323
Final Thought 326

Appendix F: Suggested Readings and References 327

Introduction: Keep Learning 327
Books on Rhetoric and Persuasion 327

References 330

The Curious Case of a Flat World

Some ideas endure not because they are true, but because they are told well. Flat Earth belief is one of the clearest examples of how a story — told with conviction, repeated often enough, and wrapped in the right words — can take on a life of its own.

This book does not aim to ridicule or dismiss those who believe differently — nor does it settle for simply calling their claims "wrong" and moving on. Instead, it examines both the evidence and the rhetoric behind Flat Earth belief, showing why the scientific case for a globe holds — and how language, story, and strategy have kept the Flat Earth narrative alive despite that evidence.

At first glance, the idea seems strange — even laughable. After all, a flat, stationary Earth defies both what we've learned and what we can see with our own eyes. Yet beneath the smirks and eye-rolls lies something harder to ignore: a growing movement, passionately defended, skillfully argued, and more influential than it might first appear.

The gravity of belief isn't always rational. People don't cling to the Flat Earth because they've carefully weighed the evidence — they cling to it because it feels right to them. Identity, emotion, and mistrust pull harder than proof. Many find in this belief a sense of control, a place to belong, and a narrative that feels simpler than the messy, complicated truth.

Belief does not have to be true to be persuasive — and that is what makes it worth studying. By seeing how Flat Earth language works, we can begin to see how all kinds of ideas, good and bad, can take hold and endure. Sometimes, the map distorts the territory — and what feels like discovery turns out to be delusion.

In The Echo Chamber Evangelists: Beyond the Vanishing Point of Belief, we'll uncover how this belief is built — not by accident, but through a deliberate mix of language, narrative, and repetition. We'll see how it spreads — not despite our modern world, but because of how we connect, share, and persuade today. And along the way, we'll see what this phenomenon reveals about our shared human need for meaning, belonging, and certainty.

Throughout these pages, we will explore questions like:
Why are some people drawn to ideas that promise a deeper, hidden understanding of the world?
How do words and community create a sense of who we are — and where we belong?
What makes stories that clearly define good and bad feel more compelling?
How do familiar phrases and shared spaces — online and off — turn doubt into certainty?
And how does belief become a business — and what does that reveal about those who sell it?

Words have power — more than we often realize. They can comfort or divide, inspire or mislead, reveal or obscure. In the chapters ahead, we'll see how Flat Earth has become something much larger than a question of maps or models: a story that persuades, endures, and even profits. By understanding its rhetoric, you may begin to recognize the same strategies at work all around you — and gain a clearer view of how language quietly shapes the way we believe.

Let's step carefully, and critically, beyond the vanishing point.

Chapter 1 — In the Beginning: The Flat Earth Story

Every belief begins as a story. To understand the belief, we must first hear the story.

Before we can understand how Flat Earth belief persists today, we must first know where it began — and how it evolved over the centuries. This chapter traces the story of how people have imagined the Earth's shape, from ancient myths to modern movements. It shows how powerful narratives of meaning and belonging often outweigh the slow accumulation of evidence. By seeing how these stories took hold and endured, we can better understand why they still resonate — and why the shape of the Earth remains, for some, a matter of identity rather than fact.

Horizons of Belief: Ancient Cosmologies

From humanity's earliest recorded stories, the cosmos was imagined as a vast, orderly stage—flat, stable, and profoundly meaningful. In ancient Mesopotamia, as early as the 3rd millennium BCE, inscriptions and myths described a level Earth encircled by a cosmic ocean (the Apsu) and covered by a solid dome that held back the celestial waters above (Krupp, 1997; Nardo, 2004). This model, supported by unseen pillars or floating atop primordial waters, was more than a map of geography; it was a sacred structure, giving shape to the divine order of gods and mortals alike (Long, 2011).

Egyptian thought in the 2nd millennium BCE envisioned a similar but uniquely personified world. The sky arched overhead as the goddess Nut, her star-strewn body spanning the flat land represented by Geb, while the sun god Ra sailed his boat across the heavens each day (Hart, 1990; Pinch, 2004). Here too the Earth stood firm and contained, held aloft by Shu or resting on pillars, and always surrounded by waters—a recurring motif that gave comforting boundaries to an otherwise infinite unknown (Frankfort et al., 1949).

Among the Hebrews, early biblical texts echoed this shared Near Eastern vision. Genesis, Job, and Psalms describe the Earth resting on foundations or pillars, overarched by the firmament, a solid vault separating the "waters above" from the "waters below" (Walton, 2009; Young, 1995). Though clothed in distinct theological meaning, this cosmology shared the structural simplicity of its neighbors: a stable plane beneath the feet, heaven above, the deep below (Heidel, 1949).

These ancient models were not the products of ignorance, but of observation, imagination, and the universal human desire for meaning. The flat horizon, the dome of stars, the predictability of celestial cycles—all suggested order and stability to the naked eye. And in cultures where the cosmos was as much moral story as physical space, these stories resonated as deeply true. Rhetorically, they appealed to what Aristotle later called pathos—affirming identity, belonging, and trust in the wisdom of the ancestors (Burke, 1969).

That resonance came not from scientific proof, but from what rhetoricians call narrative fidelity. These stories aligned beautifully with daily experience, sensory observation, and cultural expectations (Fisher, 1987). In eras when measurement was rudimentary and meaning inseparable from myth, a flat, ordered Earth "made sense" in a way modern scientific abstractions often do not (Livingstone, 2007).

It is no wonder, then, that even today, modern Flat Earth advocates selectively cite these ancient cosmologies as "proof" of their timeless validity. They commit a rhetorical fallacy known as appeal to tradition, mistaking ancient resonance for eternal truth (Walton, 2008). What they overlook is that these models were never intended as testable scientific theories, but as stories imbued with ethos—credible because they came from the priests, scribes, and elders who spoke for the gods and the community (Conley & Cain, 2006).

To understand these beliefs on their own terms, we must set aside modern assumptions of falsifiability and instead hear them as their makers intended: stories of identity and place, of firmaments and pillars, offering comfort, order, and belonging in a world still largely mysterious (Eliade, 1959; Toulmin, 1958).

By the 6th century BCE, the story of the cosmos began to shift. Among the Greek philosophers, a new kind of questioning emerged—one that saw the Earth not just as a backdrop for divine drama, but as a puzzle that could be measured, reasoned about, and explained through abstract principles (Grant, 1996; Guthrie, 1962). This intellectual pivot marked a profound departure from cosmologies rooted in myth and common sense, turning instead toward speculation and rational inquiry.

Pythagoras (c. 570–c. 495 BCE) is often remembered as the first to propose that the Earth was not flat but spherical. Yet his reasoning was not empirical in the modern sense. For Pythagoras and his followers, the sphere was the most perfect and harmonious of all shapes, the natural expression of a universe governed by proportion and order (Guthrie, 1962; Lloyd, 1970). In a cosmos believed to sing with mathematical harmony, it seemed only fitting that the Earth, too, should take the most elegant possible form. Though this was philosophy, not proof, it planted a conceptual seed that would grow in the minds of later thinkers like Aristotle (Krupp, 1997).

This turn to abstraction was a hallmark of logos—a rational appeal to internal consistency and logic, even without direct observation. It reflected what rhetorician Walter Fisher would later call narrative coherence: the power of a story that hangs together plausibly within its own framework (Fisher, 1987). For the Greeks, the spherical Earth fit perfectly into their growing sense of a cosmos that was orderly, symmetrical, and governed by unseen mathematical truths (Cornford, 1937).

Parmenides (c. 515–c. 450 BCE) added his own voice to the idea of a spherical Earth, positing a finite, unmoving globe at the center of a similarly spherical universe (Furley, 1987). His reasoning, like Pythagoras's, sprang from philosophical principles of symmetry and perfection rather than direct observation. Later, Plato (c. 428–c. 348 BCE) would develop the idea further. In his dialogue Timaeus, he described the Earth as the handiwork of a divine craftsman who chose the sphere as the most perfect possible shape for the world—a form that was whole, balanced, and self-sufficient (Plato, Timaeus, 33b; Taylor, 1928).

These early arguments for a spherical Earth were philosophical and aesthetic rather than empirical. Yet they signaled a crucial shift: a growing willingness to frame the Earth's shape as a clue to the universe's underlying logic. For the first time, reason and speculation began to challenge inherited myth. Among the intellectual elite, the notion of a spherical Earth began to take hold—not yet proven beyond doubt, but persuasive in its symmetry and consistency with the rationalist worldview (Raven, 1957).

Even here, rhetoric worked quietly alongside reason. The sphere was more than a possible fact—it was a metaphor, a persuasive image of harmony, perfection, and cosmic order. Its elegance resonated with Greek aesthetic and intellectual sensibilities, lending the idea a power that went beyond mere argument (Kennedy, 1963).

For centuries, philosophers had speculated about Earth's shape, weaving arguments from harmony, symmetry, and perfection. In the 4th century BCE, Aristotle (384–322 BCE) turned speculation into something more concrete—showing that the answer could be seen in the world around us. His arguments for a spherical Earth, laid out in On the Heavens, remain some of the earliest systematic, evidence-based reasoning in recorded history (Dreyer, 1953; Grant, 1996).

Aristotle's method was simple and brilliant: point to what anyone could see, if they cared to look closely enough. He described how ships disappeared over the horizon—not shrinking uniformly, as they would on a flat plane, but with their hulls vanishing before their masts (Aristotle, On the Heavens, II.14, 297b). He noted how the Earth's shadow during a lunar eclipse was always curved, no matter the angle of the Moon, which only a sphere could produce. And he observed that travelers moving north or south saw different stars rise and set, a phenomenon that only made sense on a curved surface (Aristotle, On the Heavens, II.14, 298a).

These arguments did more than sound plausible—they felt undeniable. Aristotle invited his audience to see for themselves, grounding his case in shared, ordinary experience rather than philosophical ideals. This was logos at its most accessible: logical reasoning that spoke directly to what people could witness with their own eyes. But his brilliance lay not only in what he observed, but in how he framed those observations. By choosing vivid, relatable examples—the vanishing ship, the round eclipse shadow, the shifting constellations—he shaped a narrative that was intuitive, memorable, and convincing (Kennedy, 1963; Goffman, 1974).

That framing was crucial. Each observation fit neatly into a larger story, one that felt coherent and internally consistent—what Walter Fisher would later call narrative coherence (Fisher, 1987). Together, they painted a picture of the world that was both empirically grounded and rhetorically powerful, a story that could stand up against the enduring pull of tradition and appearances.

In Aristotle's hands, the question of Earth's shape moved decisively from the realm of speculative philosophy to the domain of evidence and observation. Yet even here, rhetoric was doing its quiet work—reminding us that truth is rarely just about what is true, but also about how it is told.

When Aristotle showed that Earth's shape could be reasoned from observation, he opened the door for a new kind of argument—one grounded not only in what could be seen but in what could be measured. In the 3rd century BCE, Eratosthenes of Cyrene (c. 276–195/194 BCE), chief librarian of Alexandria, walked through that door with brilliance and precision. Using nothing more than sunlight, shadows, and geometry, he calculated the circumference of the Earth with astonishing accuracy—one of the most elegant scientific achievements of the ancient world (Sagan, 1980; van Helden, 1989).

Eratosthenes began with a striking observation. At noon on the summer solstice in Syene (modern Aswan), vertical columns cast no shadow. At that same moment in Alexandria, directly north, vertical rods did cast measurable shadows. From this difference, he reasoned, one could determine the angle of Earth's curvature between the two cities. Careful measurement of the Alexandrian shadow gave him an angle of about 7.2 degrees—one-fiftieth of a full circle (Cleomedes, On the Circular Motions of the Celestial Bodies, I.10; Dutka, 1993). If that segment represented one-fiftieth of Earth's total circumference, then multiplying the distance between Syene and Alexandria by fifty would yield the planet's full size.

He estimated the distance between the cities at roughly 5,000 stadia (about 800 kilometers) based on survey records and professional pacers. His final figure for the Earth's circumference was around 250,000 stadia—remarkably close to modern measurements and perhaps off by only 1–2% (Fischer, 1975; Rawlins, 1982).

This was more than a clever calculation. Eratosthenes demonstrated logos in its purest form: a logical, replicable method rooted in geometry and observation, which others could follow step by step. His experiment also showed the rhetorical power of framing. By contrasting a shadowless Syene with a shadowed Alexandria at the very same moment, he turned the Earth's curvature from an abstraction into something vivid, almost visible (Goffman, 1974; Entman, 1993). The simplicity of his setup—two sticks, two cities, one sun—made the curvature of the Earth feel as real and undeniable as the sun overhead.

Even today, his experiment stands as one of history's most compelling arguments against a flat Earth—not because it silenced all critics, but because it told a clear, elegant story. Careful observation, rigorous reasoning, and a touch of rhetorical craft combined to show how truth can emerge from simple tools and sharp thinking. Eratosthenes didn't just measure the Earth—he showed how the universe could be known.

As Greek ideas spread westward, the Roman Republic and Empire absorbed and normalized the notion of a spherical Earth. What began as speculation and measurement among philosophers became, for Roman thinkers, almost a given—more assumed than argued. Writers like Cicero and Pliny the Elder treated Earth's roundness not as a question to be debated but as an obvious fact, seamlessly integrated into their understanding of the cosmos (Grant, 1996; Roller, 2006).

Cicero, the statesman and philosopher, often referenced the Earth's curvature in his writings. In On the Republic, particularly in the famous "Dream of Scipio" passage, he described the Earth as a small globe, dwarfed by the vastness of the heavens—a perspective as philosophical as it was humbling (Cicero, De Re Publica, VI.16.16). Similarly, Pliny the Elder, compiling his monumental Natural History, confidently recounted Aristotle's and Eratosthenes' arguments for a spherical Earth, describing the evidence as obvious and well-attested (Pliny the Elder, Natural History, II.64–66). To these Roman thinkers, the spherical Earth fit perfectly into the larger Roman ideal of a harmonious, ordered universe—a cosmos that reflected their cultural values of gravitas, stability, and ratio (Carey & Warmington, 1929).

This ready acceptance illustrates what rhetoricians call narrative coherence: the idea of a spherical Earth aligned beautifully with the Roman worldview. The model was orderly, rational, and elegant—qualities that resonated with Roman sensibilities. It was no longer just a clever theory; it had become a cultural assumption among the educated, woven into their stories about the natural world and humanity's place within it (Fisher, 1987).

Yet outside of intellectual circles, belief was less uniform. Many ordinary Romans, relying on daily experience and inherited stories, likely still imagined the Earth as flat and solid beneath their feet. For farmers, merchants, and soldiers, the curvature of the Earth was irrelevant to their immediate lives and invisible to their senses. Here, the ancient flat-Earth narrative persisted, not as doctrine but as a familiar, intuitive frame of reference—one that felt true because it matched what they saw day to day (Russell, 1991; Goffman, 1974).

This period shows that belief rarely changes all at once, nor evenly across society. Among the educated elite, the spherical model, supported by logos—reason, measurement, and logic—dominated. Among the broader population, the older flat-Earth imagery endured, carried by its narrative fidelity and the comfort of its simplicity. The two beliefs coexisted, each serving its audience in different ways.

By the end of Late Antiquity, the spherical Earth had become a fixture of scholarly and literary tradition, firmly embedded in Western thought. But as always, evidence alone was not enough to reshape belief across the board. Rhetoric, framing, and cultural context remained just as powerful in shaping what people accepted as true.

As Christianity rose to prominence during Late Antiquity, its thinkers inherited not only the spiritual mantle of the Roman Empire but also its intellectual traditions—including the idea of a spherical Earth. Among the early Church Fathers, the question of Earth's shape was less about geometry than theology: how to reconcile inherited Greco-Roman knowledge with the revealed truths of scripture. For most, the answer was straightforward. Augustine of Hippo, one of the most influential Christian theologians of the 4th and 5th centuries, explicitly acknowledged Earth's sphericity, cautioning against overly literal readings of the Bible that conflicted with observable reality (Augustine, De Genesi ad litteram, 1.9.17). To him, reason and faith were not enemies; creation itself bore witness to God's order, and to deny what could be reasonably demonstrated was to misunderstand both science and scripture. Others, like Ambrose and Jerome, echoed this view, weaving the spherical Earth seamlessly into a Christian cosmology (Grant, 1996; Russell, 1991).

Yet not all shared this balance of faith and reason. Some Christian writers rejected the sphere, clinging instead to a literal reading of biblical language. Lactantius, writing in the early 4th century, ridiculed the idea of people walking "upside down" on the opposite side of a globe, dismissing it as pagan absurdity (Lactantius, Divine Institutes, III.24). A few centuries later, the monk Cosmas Indicopleustes offered his own flat-Earth model, likening the cosmos to the shape of the Old Testament Tabernacle, with Earth as a rectangular plane beneath a vaulted heaven (Russell, 1991). For these writers, the older, more familiar flat-Earth imagery felt more faithful to scripture, more resonant with the stories they believed God had revealed.

Their resistance illustrates how belief is rarely dictated by evidence alone. The flat Earth persisted not because it was well supported, but because it seemed more intuitively obvious and more aligned with inherited cultural meaning. For most Christian scholars, however, the spherical Earth remained the standard, a sign of the order and rationality of God's creation. Despite isolated dissenters, there was never a formal church doctrine insisting on a flat Earth, nor was such a view dominant among the intellectual and theological elite.

What this period shows, perhaps more than anything, is how rhetoric—through scripture, tradition, and sensory experience—continued to shape belief just as powerfully as evidence did. Even when reason pointed one way, the familiar story still held sway for some, reminding us that what feels true often carries more weight than what is demonstrably true.

Through the Middle Ages, the idea of a spherical Earth endured—not forgotten, not suppressed, but preserved, refined, and passed forward by scholars in both the Islamic world and Latin Christendom. Far from being lost to ignorance, the knowledge of Earth's shape became part of a shared intellectual inheritance, sustained by curiosity and faith alike. In the Islamic Golden Age, particularly from the 9th century onward, astronomers and geographers in Baghdad, Cairo, and elsewhere engaged deeply with classical Greek texts, translating, commenting on, and improving the work of figures like Ptolemy. Al-Farghānī, an influential 9th-century astronomer, refined earlier measurements of the Earth's circumference and codified them in his Elements of Astronomy—a text that would later shape European thought when translated into Latin (Russell, 1991; Vanoli, 2008).

A century later, the polymath al-Bīrūnī devised an ingenious method for calculating the Earth's radius using trigonometry and the dip of the horizon from a mountaintop. His results came remarkably close to modern measurements, demonstrating that logic and observation could transcend cultures and beliefs to uncover universal truths (Al-Bīrūnī, Canon Masudicus; Nasr, 1968). His calculation was more than scientific—it was rhetorical in its own way, framing the curvature of the Earth as something that could be seen and understood with simple, elegant reasoning.

In Christian Europe, the knowledge of Earth's sphericity was equally alive. As early as the 8th century, Bede the Venerable described the Earth as round in his Reckoning of Time, shaping monastic learning for centuries to follow (Bede, De Temporum Ratione, Chapter 34). By the 13th century, Sacrobosco's On the Sphere of the World became a standard university textbook, taught across Europe for centuries, neatly summarizing Aristotle's arguments and reinforcing the spherical model as a commonplace of medieval education (Sacrobosco, De Sphaera; Thorndike, 1949).

Still, the persistence of older, flat-Earth imagery in popular imagination reminds us that intellectual acceptance does not always erase cultural memory. For many ordinary people, the notion of a flat, stable world beneath their feet continued to feel more intuitive, more aligned with the rhythms of daily life and literal interpretations of scripture. Among educated scholars, however, the spherical Earth stood unchallenged, embraced as a testament to God's ordered creation and to humanity's ability to uncover it through reason and observation (Russell, 1991).

By the close of the 13th century, the idea of a spherical Earth was firmly entrenched in the intellectual traditions of both the Islamic and Christian worlds, a shared truth passed along through careful teaching, measurement, and rhetorical framing.

And yet, even here, it was clear that belief had never rested solely on proof. Cultural context, narrative familiarity, and the persuasiveness of tradition continued to shape what people believed, often just as powerfully as reason.

By the end of the 13th century, among scholars and theologians in both the Islamic and Christian traditions, the shape of the Earth was no longer a matter of serious debate. Centuries of observation, calculation, and teaching—from Aristotle's disappearing ships to Eratosthenes' shadows, from al-Bīrūnī's mountaintop geometry to Sacrobosco's university lectures—had woven the spherical Earth into the fabric of learned thought (Russell, 1991; Lindberg, 1992). Where flat-Earth imagery persisted, it did so not as doctrine or science, but as cultural residue: familiar stories passed down through generations, comforting in their simplicity, if increasingly irrelevant in educated circles.

This was not a triumph of evidence alone. The narrative of a spherical Earth succeeded because it resonated—because it fit within broader stories about order, reason, and divine creation. Logos provided the arguments, but ethos and pathos gave them staying power, rooting the idea in trust and identity. Even as learned consensus solidified, the history of these beliefs reminded everyone that people rarely abandon old stories merely because new facts arrive.

And yet, even as the Earth's shape was largely settled, another, deeper assumption remained unchallenged: that this spherical world sat immovably at the very center of creation. Medieval thinkers still pictured the cosmos as a grand, divinely ordered hierarchy, with Earth at its heart, steady and still, as the heavens revolved around it. This belief—so comforting in its symmetry and meaning—would itself become the focus of the next great challenge to humanity's place in the universe. Just as the flat Earth gave way to the sphere, the idea of a geocentric cosmos would soon face its own reckoning, as new observations and bold thinkers pushed the boundaries of what people were willing to see, and what they were willing to believe.

By the second century CE, a monumental synthesis of astronomical knowledge emerged from Roman Alexandria, codified by the brilliant mathematician, astronomer, and geographer Claudius Ptolemy (c. 100–c. 170 CE). In his comprehensive treatise, originally titled Hē Mathēmatikē Syntaxis (The Mathematical Treatise) but later known by its Arabic title Almagest ("The Greatest Compilation"), Ptolemy refined and systematized centuries of earlier Greek astronomical ideas, most notably those of Hipparchus (Pedersen, 1993; Toomer, 1984). His system presented a sophisticated geocentric model, placing Earth—fixed, unmoving, and central—at the heart of a vast, orderly cosmos. Transparent, nested concentric spheres carried the Sun, Moon, the five known planets, and the outermost fixed stars in perfect, predictable motion (Ptolemy, Almagest, Book I).

For people of his time, and indeed for over fourteen centuries, this vision made profound sense. It aligned beautifully with direct observation and human intuition: the ground beneath one's feet felt steady, while the heavens moved in predictable daily and annual cycles. The Sun's arc, the Moon's phases, and the stars' steady rotation all seemed to confirm Earth's centrality. Ptolemy's system, with its ingenious epicycles, deferents, and equants, could even predict eclipses and planetary positions with remarkable accuracy—making it invaluable to scholars, navigators, and astrologers alike (Grant, 1996; Gingerich, 1993). This predictive power lent the model immense logos: practical, reliable, and rhetorically persuasive.

What is often overlooked today is that this central Earth—though fixed—was universally understood as a sphere. Among the educated, the shape of the Earth had been settled since ancient Greece. Ptolemy's model addressed its position, not its shape, and it did so with immense rhetorical power: by placing humanity's home at the center of creation, it affirmed what people already felt to be true—that the cosmos itself revolved around them, both physically and spiritually (Kuhn, 1957; Russell, 1991).

This vision endured not merely because it worked, but because it resonated. For medieval minds steeped in Christian faith and classical philosophy, the idea of a fixed, spherical Earth at the center of concentric heavens was more than science—it was meaning. Theologians framed Earth's centrality as evidence of divine design, consistent with a hierarchical "Great Chain of Being," where everything had its ordained place in the cosmos (Lovejoy, 1936; Lindberg, 1992). The stable Earth anchored a universe that was moral and intelligible, offering comfort in its permanence and coherence (Koestler, 1959).

It is little wonder the model proved so rhetorically durable. Even as observation grew more precise and mathematics advanced, the story it told continued to feel true. What rhetoricians call narrative coherence—where a story aligns with expectations and lived experience—made Ptolemy's geocentric cosmos deeply persuasive, even as its predictive mechanics grew increasingly cumbersome (Fisher, 1987).

One of the most persistent myths about the Middle Ages is that people believed the Earth was flat. This misconception, still echoed in textbooks and pop culture, misrepresents the period as ignorant and superstitious, supposedly awaiting Columbus to prove otherwise. In truth, the idea of a spherical Earth remained commonplace among the educated throughout the Middle Ages, taught in monasteries and universities alike (Russell, 1991; Lindberg & Numbers, 2003). The myth of medieval flat-Earth belief was largely invented in the 19th century, popularized by romanticized biographies and polemical works that sought to dramatize the "triumph" of science over religion (Irving, 1828; White, 1896; Draper, 1874). This version of history fit a modern narrative of progress and conflict, even though it misrepresented what medieval scholars actually taught (Sacrobosco, De Sphaera Mundi; Lindberg, 1992).

The Ptolemaic model did more than shape scientific thought—it permeated art, theology, and imagination. Cosmological diagrams in manuscripts, Jerusalem-centered maps, cathedral designs pointing heavenward, and public astronomical clocks all reflected and reinforced the belief in a central, spherical Earth nested in divine order (Russell, 1991; Crosby, 1997). Medieval literature and poetry were filled with imagery of angelic choirs, celestial harmony, and the "music of the spheres," giving voice to a universe that felt purposeful and profoundly human-centered. Even as doubts began to stir, the geocentric narrative continued to frame people's understanding of their place in creation, affirming the moral and spiritual significance of Earth and humanity within a divinely structured cosmos.

By the early 16th century, however, quiet doubts began to grow. Astronomers increasingly noted that Ptolemy's elaborate layers of epicycles and deferents, designed to preserve appearances, no longer matched the most precise observations (Kuhn, 1957; Gingerich, 1993). In 1543, Nicolaus Copernicus proposed something radical: that the Sun, not the Earth, stood at the center of the cosmos, with Earth itself in motion. Though initially met with skepticism, his heliocentric model offered a profound simplification of planetary motion, even if its predictions were not immediately superior (Copernicus, 1543; Rosen, 2002).

At first, Copernicus's idea felt deeply unsettling. The geocentric model had anchored not just astronomy, but humanity's sense of meaning and place. To suggest that Earth was just another moving planet disrupted the narrative coherence people relied on: the central, stable Earth symbolized human significance; a wandering Earth seemed to deny it. The heliocentric model not only challenged scientific orthodoxy but also threatened the emotional and theological foundations of the old story (Fisher, 1987).

In the decades that followed, astronomers like Kepler and Galileo built on Copernicus's insight, offering increasingly compelling evidence for heliocentrism, culminating in Newton's grand synthesis of universal gravitation in the 17th century. By the 18th century, the heliocentric model with a spherical, orbiting Earth became the cornerstone of modern astronomy (Newton, 1687; Gingerich, 1993).

And yet, even as geocentrism fell, flat-Earth belief never fully disappeared. While dismissed by educated elites, it lingered quietly in small communities and countercultural corners, sustained by distrust of authority, literalist readings of scripture, and the comfort of familiar stories over unfamiliar truths. By the mid-19th century, profound societal shifts and mass communication gave these lingering doubts new life. Flat-Earth advocacy moved from private whispers to public defiance, setting the stage for a rhetorical confrontation with mainstream science that would echo long after the geocentric cosmos had been laid to rest.

The Zetetic Rebellion: 19th Century Doubt

By the early 1800s, the scientific understanding of the Earth's shape and its place in the cosmos was a settled matter in public and intellectual life. Two centuries of advancement—from Galileo's telescopic observations and Newton's laws of gravitation to global circumnavigations—had firmly established the spherical, heliocentric model as the foundation of modern science, education, and navigation (Sobel, 2000; Gingerich,

1993). This consensus was a triumph of logos, grounded in evidence, mathematics, and predictive power.

Yet beneath this confident consensus, seeds of doubt and defiance lingered. The Victorian era provided fertile ground for marginal ideas to resurface, fueled by profound and disorienting change. The Industrial Revolution reshaped society with new technologies, rapid urbanization, and mass media that democratized information and turned scientific debates into everyday conversation (Paradis, 2015). For many, this progress came with unease. Scientific authority seemed increasingly cold and inaccessible, clashing with religious beliefs and stripping the universe of meaning and purpose. These tensions opened a rhetorical space for voices that promised common sense over complexity, intuition over abstraction, and defiance of distant elites in favor of ordinary experience (Numbers, 2009).

This climate of skepticism fit neatly into the Victorian ideal of the "self-made man." Ordinary individuals, encouraged to trust their own observations, began to reject the need for professional expertise. For some, this spirit led to innovation; for others, it fueled rejection of even the most settled scientific knowledge in favor of what felt immediate and personally trustworthy. This appeal leaned heavily on ethos—the credibility of the "common man" over the scientist—and pathos—the comfort of familiar truths over abstract ones (Hofstadter, 1963).

Onto this stage stepped Samuel Rowbotham, a man of charisma, spectacle, and stubborn certainty. He channeled scattered doubts into the foundations of a modern flat-Earth movement, crafting a voice that resonated deeply with the disaffected. Born in 1816 at the height of industrial upheaval, Rowbotham embodied the Victorian self-made man: a showman and master of the crowd (Garwood, 2007; Schadwald, 2015). In 1865, under the pseudonym "Parallax," he published Zetetic Astronomy: Proofs of the Earth Not a Globe, codifying his views. "Zetetic," meaning "to inquire," was a shrewd rhetorical choice, presenting him as a humble truth-seeker rather than a dogmatist—a branding that appealed to audiences already suspicious of elitism (Schadwald, 2015).

Rowbotham's arguments were simple and intuitively appealing. If the Earth curved, he insisted, that curvature should be visible. He staged demonstrations, sighting down canals and claiming that distant objects remained visible rather than dipping below the horizon, "proving" flatness. He staged dramatic public events and lectures, delivering his claims with wit, confidence, and rhetorical flourish. These spectacles, often packed with eager audiences, played directly to pathos and ethos, portraying him as the heroic underdog taking on arrogant academics (Fisher, 1987; Garwood, 2007).

He positioned himself as a champion of the people, encouraging audiences to "trust their eyes" over the abstractions of experts. His vivid imagery—flat, calm canals; level horizons; motionless seas—made the flat Earth feel immediate and undeniable, appealing directly to uncritical sensory input. This style exemplified enargeia: language that makes the audience feel they are witnessing evidence directly, not merely hearing it described (Quintilian, VIII.3.61).

Even after his death in 1884, Rowbotham's movement endured. His followers carried the message forward, organizing lectures, publishing pamphlets, and forming societies like the Universal Zetetic Society in 1892. Figures like John Hampden and Lady Elizabeth Blount kept his confrontational, populist style alive, framing Zeteticism as a rebellion against elite knowledge and cultivating a self-reinforcing community (Garwood, 2007). The Bedford Level experiment became a touchstone of the movement—a flawed but dramatic "proof" repeated endlessly, a classic example of hasty generalization that ignored contradictory evidence (Walton, 1992).

What sustained Zeteticism was not new evidence but repetition, identity, and community. It became a pre-digital echo chamber, where doubts about science flourished in an environment that celebrated defiance and reinforced shared beliefs. By the dawn of the 20th century, Zeteticism had evolved into more than a claim about the Earth's shape; it had become a defiant narrative and a source of belonging.

Even as the societies dwindled in the 20th century, the seeds Rowbotham planted never truly died. His framing of science as arrogant dogma, his appeal to ordinary senses, and his rhetoric of hidden truths being kept from the masses still resonate in modern flat-Earth discourse. Slogans like "Trust your eyes," accusations of conspiracy, and the embrace of outsider status are all direct echoes of Rowbotham's Victorian rebellion. His greatest achievement was not his flawed arguments but his ability to craft a story—a narrative of defiance and self-reliance that continues to find new audiences in every age of uncertainty.

By the mid-20th century, the Flat Earth belief had largely faded from public view, relegated to the dusty shelves of historical oddities. The Zetetic societies that flourished in the late 19th and early 20th centuries were long defunct, their membership dwindling to irrelevance. Samuel Rowbotham's name lingered only as a curious footnote in the annals of Victorian eccentricity. But in the quiet suburbs of Dover, England, an engineer named Samuel Shenton began preparing to rekindle those dormant flames. Tireless, charismatic, and a natural self-promoter, Shenton envisioned a modern revival of the Flat Earth belief, giving it a new name and a distinctly mid-century sensibility (Garwood, 2007; Schadwald, 2015).

In 1956, he founded the International Flat Earth Research Society (IFERS), soon better known as the Flat Earth Society. Where Rowbotham railed against Newtonian mechanics, Shenton saw his real adversary in the emerging Space Age. The launch of Sputnik in 1957 and the rapid rise of rocketry and orbital science provided the perfect foil for his message. He framed the Society as a courageous counterbalance to the propaganda and deception of governments and scientific elites, offering his followers an identity grounded in skepticism and defiance. In newsletters and pamphlets, he cultivated what rhetoricians call an appeal to identity, casting Flat Earthers not as misled but as uniquely perceptive, brave enough to see through the great deception. This pathos-driven message gave his audience not only belonging but a sense of moral purpose (Fisher, 1987; Mercier & Sperber, 2011).

  Shenton brought a distinctly modern sense of branding and media savvy to the cause. He formalized membership structures, issued regular newsletters, and welcomed even derisive media coverage as a way to keep his message visible. He understood instinctively what would later be called the paradox of ridicule: that being mocked could reinforce the ingroup identity of his followers, strengthening their commitment to the belief by positioning them as embattled truth-tellers standing against an uncaring mainstream (Peters & Wester, 2021). In Shenton's hands, the Flat Earth movement became not just a claim about the world's shape but a rhetorical stand-in for independence, common sense, and distrust of authority. Though still dismissed by the majority, it once again had a banner to march under and a leader to follow.

  When Shenton died in 1971, the Society again teetered on the brink of irrelevance, but into the vacuum stepped Charles K. Johnson, a charismatic Californian who transformed the movement into something even more vivid and personal. Johnson embodied the fiery certainty of a preacher, the provocateur's flair for conflict, and the true believer's unshakeable conviction. Taking over leadership, he recast the Society as his own moral and spiritual crusade. Where Shenton poked at the establishment with a sly smile, Johnson openly declared it a satanic conspiracy to deceive humanity. His home in Lancaster, California—a modest trailer stacked with pamphlets and newsletters—became the unlikely headquarters of his campaign (Garwood, 2007; Schadwald, 2015).

Under Johnson's watch, the Society adopted a more militant, dogmatic tone. His newsletters dripped with moral indignation, presenting Flat Earth belief as a divine imperative and positioning himself as the lone prophet fighting to expose a vast, global lie. His confrontational style and unwavering certainty gave the Society new visibility, and for nearly three decades he became its public face. His intense, almost theatrical certainty made him irresistible to reporters, who alternately mocked and marveled at him as an oddball with a righteous streak. But Johnson understood what Rowbotham and Shenton before him had learned: ridicule could be useful. Every derisive article and mocking television segment kept the belief alive in the public imagination, even as it reinforced his followers' sense of embattled righteousness.

But his relentless, one-man crusade came at a cost. By the late 1980s, the movement began to falter under the weight of his rigid control and inability to adapt. Membership declined as younger generations, raised in the era of the moon landing and global satellite imagery, found his message outdated and his leadership style alienating. His unwillingness to embrace emerging technologies like the internet only deepened the Society's isolation, leaving it a nostalgic relic in an increasingly digital world. When Johnson died in 2001, the Society died with him—at least in its organized, formal sense. His trailer headquarters fell silent, and the movement he had carried on his shoulders for three decades seemed destined to vanish altogether.

Yet the story was far from over. The rhetorical seeds planted by Rowbotham, Shenton, and Johnson—skepticism of authority, distrust of elites, pride in resisting the "official narrative"—remained fertile. With the rise of the internet, these narratives found a vastly more powerful medium. Online forums, early social networks, and video-sharing platforms allowed believers to find one another across the globe, share arguments, and amplify their doubts free of the gatekeepers and ridicule that had constrained them for generations (O'Neill, 2017). Ideas that once took years to circulate through mimeographed newsletters could now echo virally in hours, forming self-reinforcing digital enclaves that made ridicule harder and belief more resilient. The embers Johnson left behind smoldered quietly through the early 2000s, waiting for the right conditions to ignite once again.

A Revival in the Digital Age

By the turn of the 21st century, Flat Earth belief was little more than a fading whisper—a curious relic known only to a handful of dedicated holdouts and the occasional trivia buff. Its formal societies had long since disbanded, and its most prominent proponents had passed away. Yet just as the printing press once gave Samuel Rowbotham and his Victorian followers a louder, more distributed voice, a profoundly new technology emerged to breathe unprecedented life and global reach into the ancient rhetoric of doubt: the internet.

Where earlier generations relied on pamphlets, newsletters, and localized debates, the internet leveled the playing field for fringe ideas. Suddenly, there were no editors to dismiss the topic as too absurd, no newspaper columnists to lampoon it for mass audiences, no gatekeepers to validate or suppress its claims (Benkler, 2006). For a belief system built on challenging mainstream authority, this unmediated, decentralized environment was a rhetorical paradise.

Message boards and early forums quickly became refuges where scattered believers found one another, swapping arguments and experiencing the robust validation of shared belief (Sunstein, 2001). With the rise of video-sharing platforms like YouTube, Flat Earth rhetoric found an even more powerful medium. Videos showing ships "vanishing into the horizon," shaky drone footage of endless flat expanses, and confident narration over homemade experiments tapped into what rhetoricians call enargeia—the vivid, sensory impression of evidence, no matter how misleading (Garrett, 2011).

By the mid-2010s, prominent names emerged as the movement's new public faces. Figures like Mark Sargent and Eric Dubay styled themselves as inheritors of Rowbotham's defiant tradition, armed now with webcams, professional-quality podcasts, and viral video clips (Nguyen, 2020; Garwood, 2007). Their rhetoric was not novel but familiar: appeals to what "your eyes can see," sweeping accusations of hidden truth, and unwavering faith in "common sense" over expertise. What set them apart was how skillfully they packaged these old arguments for a digital-native audience.

Mark Sargent cultivated a genial, approachable "just asking questions" persona in his YouTube videos—an ethos that drew in casual viewers who might otherwise dismiss such claims outright (Nguyen, 2020). Eric Dubay took a more aggressive tone, publishing self-styled exposés like The Flat-Earth Conspiracy and 200 Proofs Earth is Not a Spinning Ball, which lifted entire passages—often verbatim—from 19th-century Zetetic texts, underscoring the ironic fact that this supposed digital "revelation" was rooted in Victorian soil (Dubay, various; Garwood, 2007). Both men, in different ways, turned Flat Earth into a movement more about identity than evidence, offering belonging and defiance to those eager to reject mainstream narratives.

As their videos and books gained traction, a familiar dynamic resurfaced: believers reinforcing each other in tightly-knit communities, this time moving at the speed of algorithms. Slogans like "water finds its level" and "NASA lies" became digital mantras, repeated in livestreams, memes, and comment sections until they began to feel like facts. This phenomenon, known as proof by parroting—where repetition alone lends false claims an air of truth—became a hallmark of the movement (Walton, 1992).

Social media platforms amplified this echo chamber effect. Algorithms designed to maximize engagement showed users more of what they already believed, creating filter bubbles where dissenting voices were drowned out (Pariser, 2011; Sunstein, 2001). External criticism was dismissed as propaganda, and critics were branded "shills" or "sheeple," reinforcing group cohesion and insulating believers from doubt. The echo chamber became not just a side effect but a deliberate rhetorical strategy—a self-sustaining alternative reality.

By the late 2010s, Flat Earth belief had escaped its digital confines to become a media spectacle. Mainstream documentaries, major news headlines, and popular podcasts debated it, often with a tone of bemused incredulity (Garwood, 2007; Nguyen, 2020). Conferences in hotel ballrooms drew hundreds of attendees, selling books, DVDs, and T-shirts proclaiming "Research Flat Earth." Netflix's 2018 documentary Behind the Curve gave the movement even more visibility, turning its proponents into both cautionary tales and minor celebrities. Clips and memes from the documentary went viral, feeding the very narrative they sought to critique (Peters & Wester, 2021).

Far from deterring believers, ridicule only deepened their resolve. Every mocking headline, every incredulous report, was reframed as validation: proof that powerful forces were suppressing "the truth." In this way, the anti-establishment ethos that had animated the movement since Rowbotham's time found new strength, bolstered by digital virality. By the end of the decade, Flat Earth had transformed into a global performance—a blend of sincere conviction and theatrical defiance that made it one of the strangest, yet most enduring, belief phenomena of the modern age.

The long and convoluted history of Flat Earth belief reveals that it was never simply about misunderstanding evidence. Rather, it has always reflected deeper human needs for meaning, order, and belonging. In the ancient and medieval worlds, people envisioned the cosmos in ways that fit not only what they thought they saw, but also what they hoped to believe: a stable, divinely ordered creation with humanity at its center. That immense symbolic weight, reinforced by narrative coherence and repeated over centuries, shaped how generations imagined the universe—even as science slowly chipped away at the old stories.

And yet, each time science asserted its truth, the echoes of older, more comforting narratives refused to fade. Flat Earth persisted—not just as a belief, but as a rhetorical identity, rooted in appeals to "common sense," defiance of elites, and the search for certainty in an uncertain world. Those patterns, first written in scripture and myth, now reverberate in hashtags, livestreams, and crowded conference halls. The echo chamber persists. The paradox of ridicule endures.

The story of Flat Earth, then, is more than a historical curiosity. It is a cautionary tale and a mirror—reminding us that human belief is never purely about facts, but about who we are, what we trust, and where we seek meaning when certainty feels just out of reach. It shows how narrative, identity, and persuasion can make even a demonstrable falsehood feel like an undeniable truth. And it sets the stage for what lies ahead, as we turn to examine not just what Flat Earthers believe, but how they persuade—and what that persuasion reveals about all of us.

When Stories Outlast the Stars

Belief has never been just about facts on a page or shadows on a sundial. The story of a flat or round Earth was never simply a debate over maps—it was always a debate over meaning. From ancient pillars and domes to Pythagoras's perfect sphere, what endured were not measurements alone but the narratives they carried: stories of order, identity, and place in the cosmos. Each shift in the Earth's imagined shape—from myth to philosophy to mathematics—wasn't just a step in science. It was a step in persuasion, showing how language and framing can make one version of reality feel more trustworthy than another.

That is why the Flat Earth story never truly died. Even as evidence stacked up, the old, simpler narrative clung to life because it promised something science couldn't: certainty wrapped in belonging. And when Samuel Rowbotham and his successors revived that story in the Victorian era, they weren't just rejecting astronomy—they were reclaiming an older, deeper frame: that truth is what feels close, what feels right, what feels ours. In that way, the modern Flat Earth movement is less a rebellion against science and more an echo of humanity's oldest habit: choosing the story that tells us who we are.

But a story doesn't endure this long on history alone. It needs something stronger to hold it in place—a force that turns narrative into conviction, and conviction into armor. That force is certainty, and in the world of Flat Earth, certainty often wears the language of faith. Before we can understand how this belief survives in the digital age, we must understand the bonds that make it unshakable. That is where we now turn: to the gospel of certainty and the firmament it builds, not over the Earth, but over the human mind.

Chapter 2: The Gospel of Certainty — The Bonds of Belief, Faith, and Firmament

Faith isn't the enemy of truth — but it can sometimes be used as a weapon against it.

Before we dive into how Flat Earth rhetoric leans on religious literalism and borrows from cult-like language, let us make one thing clear: this chapter does not mock or dismiss sincere faith. Religion, in all its forms, has been—and still is—a deep source of meaning, moral guidance, and belonging for billions of people around the world (Smith, 1991). When it is practiced with an open heart and an open mind, it deserves respect. For many people, faith and reason do not clash—they work together. Belief gives purpose and comfort, while evidence and critical thinking help us understand the world (Polkinghorne, 1998).

Flat Earth rhetoric tells a very different story. Here, the balance between belief and reason is not just lost—it is thrown out on purpose. In this world, faith is not gentle or personal. It becomes hard-edged certainty, and that certainty is turned into a rhetorical weapon. Flat Earthers often claim that people who believe in the globe have "faith in science"—a phrase they use to dismiss real evidence, research, and critical thinking as nothing more than blind belief. They frame scientists as if they are high priests of a secular religion, treating their research like unquestionable dogma (Numbers, 2009). And yet, at the same time, Flat Earthers themselves often rely almost entirely on narrow, cherry-picked readings of religious texts—ignoring centuries of theology, interpretation, and debate (Russell, 1991).

That kind of double standard is not a slip-up. It is part of the strategy. By framing science as just another belief system, Flat Earthers create a false equivalence—a logical fallacy that tries to make two very different things seem the same. This move props up their own beliefs while tearing down the credibility of real science (Walton, 1992). In their world, faith stops being about meaning or growth. It becomes a bludgeon—used to shut down questions, silence critics, and push a version of truth that cannot be challenged.

And that is exactly what this chapter is here to explore. Not faith itself, but how it is twisted—turned into a tool for control, certainty, and superiority. This is not about belief as a source of hope or identity. It is about belief being used to build walls instead of bridges. To claim truth, not seek it. To replace thought with dogma.

Because while faith and reason can—and often do—coexist in healthy, honest ways, that is not what happens in Flat Earth circles. Here, they have been pitted against each other. And only one side is still playing by the rules of honest inquiry.

The Firmament's Echo: When Faith Shapes the Horizon

One of the more powerful — and potentially dangerous — moves in the Flat Earth playbook is known as a purity appeal. The idea is simple but loaded: trusting God's word — or rather, their interpretation of it — is a spiritual duty, while trusting fallible human knowledge is a sign of weakness, doubt, or even betrayal (Patterson & Johnson, 2022).

This kind of rhetoric often spirals into something even more intense: a purity spiral. That is when believers try to outdo one another, pushing past reasonable discussion into extremes of loyalty — rejecting evidence, questioning less, and doubling down to prove who is most faithful (Rosenberg, 2017). In these spirals, even a thoughtful question or a softer reading of scripture can be seen as a threat. Any nuance looks like backsliding.

Flat Earth influencers are well-versed in this game. They do not just say the globe is wrong — they frame it as a Satanic lie, part of a global plan to erase God and replace Him with man's pride (Sargent, 2018). Accepting science becomes more than just accepting a theory; it is portrayed as placing trust in scientists, schools, media, and governments — rather than in the Creator. In that light, rejecting mainstream science is not just skepticism. It is devotion. It is a public badge of spiritual purity (Barkun, 2003).

Moreover, the pressure to maintain that badge is real. Once the purity spiral takes hold, even small questions can feel like betrayal. The bar for "true faith" keeps moving, and those who hesitate are seen as weak or suspect. In Flat Earth circles, that leads people to reject not just science, but even centuries of rich biblical interpretation — all in favor of narrower, stricter readings that seem more "pure" (Garwood, 2007).

This tactic flatters the believer. It tells them they are standing firm while the rest of the world sleeps. It builds an identity — not just as someone who believes, but as someone who dares to believe when others will not (Hofstadter, 1963). At the same time, it pushes out doubt. Ask the wrong question, and you are seen as defiled, disloyal, or even lost.

However, here is the problem: this whole setup rests on a flawed idea — that faith and evidence must always conflict. That you cannot hold both. That you cannot trust your heart and your eyes. In the next part, we will dig into that false choice and how it is used to close doors that do not need to be shut.

One of the most persistent—and effective—rhetorical moves in the Flat Earth playbook is creating a false choice: the claim that real faith and solid evidence are natural enemies, and that you have to pick one or the other. This is a textbook example of a false dichotomy (also known as a false dilemma or either/or fallacy)—a persuasive trick that frames two ideas as being totally incompatible, when in reality they can often exist side by side or even support each other (Walton, 1992). In Flat Earth messaging, trusting evidence—especially the kind that comes from mainstream science—is treated like a betrayal of God. Followers are pushed to "choose sides" in an all-or-nothing fight: faith or science, God or man, purity or corruption. Influencers like Eric Dubay often tie modern astronomy to "Satanic deception" or call it "the biggest lie," claiming it's all designed to pull people away from the Bible (Dubay, various works).

By forcing the conversation into this rigid either/or format, Flat Earth promoters ignore centuries of deep thought and long-standing traditions where faith and evidence lived in harmony. For many believers across history, studying nature wasn't just allowed—it was a way to worship. Exploring the world was seen as a way to marvel at the design of creation, to honor the Creator by learning more about what He made (Dillenberger, 1988). People like Galileo Galilei, a devoted Catholic, saw his work in science as a form of reading "the book of nature," written by the same hand that gave us scripture (Galilei, 1615/1957). The Flat Earth approach wipes all of that away and replaces it with a forced, false standoff.

This kind of framing accomplishes two big things. First, it acts like armor. If all evidence supporting a round Earth is labeled as "anti-God" or "Satanic," then ignoring that evidence isn't dishonesty—it becomes a show of spiritual strength. Second, it puts skeptics and critics in a trap: if you accept science, you're accused of turning your back on faith. It's a powerful use of the false dichotomy—boiling a messy, complex issue down to two hardline camps and daring you to pick a side (Walton, 1992).

But here's the truth: faith and science have always asked different kinds of questions—and that's okay. Faith asks about meaning, purpose, values, and the bigger picture. Science asks how things work, how they behave, and how we can test them. They're not enemies; they're different tools for understanding the world. When seen this way, they don't cancel each other out—they fill in the gaps the other can't reach (Gould, 1999).

By pushing the idea that faith and evidence can't mix, Flat Earth rhetoric flattens that rich complexity into a black-and-white ultimatum. And in doing so, it robs believers of something beautiful: the wonder of discovery, the deep awe that can come from studying creation, and the peace of knowing that belief and understanding don't have to be at odds. As the next section will show, some of the most faithful and thoughtful minds in history—and today—have lived proof that the choice between belief and evidence isn't just false… it's unnecessary.

For all the Flat Earth rhetoric about science being a "religion of man" and genuine faith being inherently incompatible with empirical evidence, the reality observed in laboratories, observatories, and field stations around the world tells a profoundly different and far more inspiring story. Devout men and women of sincere faith routinely conduct rigorous scientific research every day, from exploring the vastness of the cosmos to unraveling the intricacies of the human genome. Their lives and work stand as a living refutation of the false dichotomy and purity spiral so often promoted within Flat Earth circles. These dedicated scientists demonstrate—quietly but powerfully—that faith and evidence are not only compatible, but can, in fact, enrich each other, offering complementary paths to understanding the universe.

It is a common tactic for Flat Earth influencers to dismiss mainstream science as a "faithless" or "godless" enterprise, populated exclusively by secular materialists intent on denying God's creation. This rhetorical framing relies heavily on straw man arguments, which deliberately misrepresent science and individual scientists, creating a simplified, distorted, and often malevolent caricature of their true goals and methods. This tactic makes them easier to attack and dismiss (Walton, 1996). They falsely claim that scientists "worship" evidence as a divine idol, while dismissing scripture entirely as irrelevant. Nevertheless, the truth is far more nuanced and, indeed, more profound. Many, if not most, scientists of faith describe their work not as an attempt to disprove God, but as a deeply spiritual endeavor—a profound way of understanding, appreciating, and even glorifying the beauty, order, and intricate design of God's universe (Barbour, 2000).

Consider historical and contemporary luminaries who embody this synthesis. The brilliant astronomer and devout Christian Johannes Kepler (1571–1630), whose laws of planetary motion laid the groundwork for Newton's theory of universal gravitation, famously described his scientific pursuits as "thinking God's thoughts after Him" (Kepler, 1619/1997). For Kepler, the elegance of celestial mechanics was a direct reflection of divine rationality, and unraveling its secrets was an act of worship. Similarly, Georges Lemaître (1894–1966), the Belgian Catholic priest and physicist, independently proposed the theory of the expanding universe, which became known as the "Big Bang" theory. He saw no contradiction between his scientific cosmology and his theological beliefs, viewing the universe's origin as consistent with, though not proving, a creator (Lemaître, 1931/1950).

More recently, Francis Collins (b. 1950), the former director of the Human Genome Project and the National

Institutes of Health, and an outspoken evangelical Christian, has written eloquently and extensively about how his rigorous study of human genetics has profoundly deepened his awe for God's creation, viewing DNA as the "language of God" (Collins, 2006). He sees scientific discovery not as an enemy of faith, but as a powerful tool for understanding the Creator's mind. Moreover, there are entire vibrant professional associations—such as the American Scientific Affiliation (ASA)—dedicated specifically to Christian scientists who actively engage in cutting-edge research across all disciplines and unequivocally see no contradiction whatsoever between their profound faith and their rigorous scientific work (ASA, n.d.).

These individuals, by simply existing and thriving in both worlds, fundamentally dismantle the Flat Earth narrative's false premise. They powerfully demonstrate that genuine faith is not diminished by engaging with empirical evidence; instead, it can be enriched and deepened by a more profound understanding of the natural world. Conversely, they show that rigorous scientific inquiry does not necessitate the erasure of faith or spiritual belief. Instead, they embody a unified mindset that sees both spiritual conviction and empirical observation as complementary lenses on the same ultimate truth—one seeking ultimate meaning and purpose, the other unraveling the mechanisms of the cosmos.

For Flat Earthers, who heavily rely on the rhetorical construct of the straw man—the oversimplified, often malevolent caricature of science as a godless religion—such prominent examples are profoundly inconvenient. They introduce a devastating level of nuance that utterly complicates the neat, binary, and easily digestible story they desperately try to sell their audiences. However, it is precisely in these inspiring examples that we find hope: irrefutable proof that the false choice between faith and evidence is utterly unnecessary, and that true, open-minded inquiry is not a betrayal of sincere belief, but rather a profound fulfillment of it. Yet, the Flat Earth movement often dismisses such nuanced understanding, instead building its case on what it presents as absolute certainty, frequently rooted in a very specific reading of sacred texts

Whose Bible? Whose Words? The Flat Earth's Scriptural Foundation

Flat Earth rhetoric often leans heavily on scripture. Influencers confidently claim that the Bible clearly describes a flat, stationary Earth sealed beneath a solid dome. Their delivery is absolute, as though the Bible speaks with one unified voice, in one perfect language, offering one obvious meaning. That kind of certainty becomes the anchor for their entire argument, especially for those seeking divine clarity.

But even a quick look at the long history of the Bible reveals a very different picture. There is no single, universal Bible. There never has been (Metzger & Coogan, 1993). The idea that scripture exists as one fixed, unchanging book is a rhetorical sleight of hand—an oversimplification that erases centuries of translation, theological debate, and scholarly effort (Burke, 1969). Flat Earth proponents skip past that complexity to present "the Bible" as one unambiguous source that just so happens to agree with their claims.

They rarely mention that there are dozens of English Bible translations in use today, each shaped by different language choices, theological goals, and historical lenses (Ehrman, 2005). The King James Version (KJV)—a favorite among Flat Earthers—was produced in 1611 in response to earlier Protestant Bibles like the Geneva Bible. It was written in poetic, authoritative English that resonated with the geocentric worldview of its time (McGrath, 2001). Words like "firmament," derived from the Latin firmamentum, reflected the idea of a solid sky. More recent translations, such as the New International Version (NIV), the New Revised Standard Version (NRSV), and the English Standard Version (ESV), aim to stay closer to the original Hebrew and Greek. They tend to replace archaic terms like "firmament" with more neutral ones like "expanse" or "sky" (Nabel, 2017).

And that is just English. The Catholic Church uses the Latin Vulgate and translations like the Douay-Rheims. The Eastern Orthodox Church relies on the Greek Septuagint. Even the list of books considered "scripture"—the biblical canon—differs between Protestant, Catholic, and Orthodox traditions (McDonald & Sanders, 2002).

By pretending there is only one "true" Bible, Flat Earth advocates create a false sense of certainty. They cherry-pick the translation or wording that best supports their case, then dismiss other versions as corrupted or part of a conspiracy. This tactic leans on the audience's deep trust in scripture, while subtly redefining what scripture even means. For many who grew up seeing the KJV as the Word of God, few stop to ask whether their certainty rests on divine truth—or on choices made by 17th-century translators and today's YouTubers.

In flattening that complexity, something sacred gets lost. The richness of biblical tradition—its layered genres, its poetry, its cultural history—is reduced to a prop for argument. A faith that erases nuance just to stay certain might not be as strong as it thinks. So the real question becomes:

Which Bible? Whose words? And why were those words chosen?

Flat Earth rhetoric depends heavily on a narrow, literal reading of the Christian Bible—usually a specific English translation—as though it were the only sacred text in human history, uniquely holding the blueprint of the cosmos. But even a brief glance beyond that narrow lens reveals a deep and diverse set of religious writings from across the world, each with its own picture of creation—and many treating the shape of the physical world as symbolic, poetic, or simply not important to the message at hand (Long, 2011).

In Judaism, the foundational texts—the Torah and the Talmud—describe the heavens and Earth with vivid imagery. These texts often use metaphor to show the dynamic relationship between God and creation, focusing more on divine power and purpose than physical details (Leibowitz, 1980). While some cosmological ideas do show up, the tradition encourages layered readings—moral, symbolic, historical—rather than demanding strict literalism (Steinsaltz, 2006).

The Islamic tradition, in its primary texts—the Qur'an and the Hadith—also includes many references to the heavens and the Earth. These passages speak to the order and balance of the world as signs of Allah's power (Nasr, 1993). Importantly, Islamic scholars throughout history have interpreted these verses as metaphorical or spiritual. Rather than trying to prove physical facts, they point to the majesty of creation and humanity's place in it (Safi, 2001). This theological approach did not stop Muslim scholars from making scientific advances. In fact, many of history's most influential astronomers were Muslim, and they worked with spherical Earth models long before the European Renaissance (Saliba, 2007).

Hinduism adds another dimension. The Vedas and Puranas describe a vast, multi-layered universe that includes multiple realms and cosmic cycles. Earth is just one part of a much larger and repeating story—one where time is measured in yugas and existence moves through endless rebirth and transformation (Klostermaier, 2007). The language is symbolic and often mythological in nature. Cosmology serves spiritual teachings about karma, duty, and the soul—not maps or physical models of the planet (Zimmer, 1946).

Buddhism, too, leans heavily into symbolic cosmology. speak of stacked worlds, different realms, and great cosmic cycles, but these are generally understood as reflections of spiritual states, not literal geography. These realms represent levels of suffering, enlightenment, and karmic progress—not measurements of physical dimensions (Gyatso, 1999).

Across all of these traditions, one theme repeats: sacred texts are meant to guide the soul and shape moral understanding—not to serve as blueprints of the physical universe. The Flat Earth approach, by focusing only on literal English-language Bible verses, leaves out this rich global conversation. It presents one narrow reading of one translation of one tradition as the only truth—while discarding centuries of reflection, scholarship, and spiritual insight.

By doing this, Flat Earth promoters erase not only science but theology. They reduce centuries of evolving spiritual wisdom into sound bites meant to win arguments. It is not just inaccurate—it is disrespectful. These traditions do not fear complexity; they embrace it. Their strength lies not in flattening the truth, but in holding space for the mystery and wonder of it all.

One of the most common moves in Flat Earth arguments is the careful picking of certain Bible verses to back up a point that's already been decided. They spotlight verses that, at first glance, seem to describe a still, unmoving Earth or a solid dome overhead. But those verses are pulled out of the bigger picture—taken without context, without attention to the style of writing, the time they were written, or what the words originally meant. At the same time, other passages that complicate or outright contradict those claims—especially ones that are clearly meant to be poetic or symbolic—are brushed aside or reinterpreted to fit the Flat Earth view (Long, 2011).

This approach is a classic example of what is called cherry-picking (or "stacking the deck")—a common tactic in arguments where someone only highlights the evidence that helps their case, while leaving out anything that does not (Walton, 2006). It makes their side seem stronger and more supported than it really is. But when this is done with sacred texts—which are deep, layered, and open to many interpretations—it can seriously twist what those texts were meant to say.

Flat Earth promoters tend to lean heavily on the King James Version (KJV) of the Bible. That is not by accident. Its 17th-century English, while beautiful, often uses old-fashioned or direct translations that, when taken out of context, can sound more literal—and more convenient—for Flat Earth ideas.

Here are a few examples they often cite:

Psalm 104:5

In the KJV: "Who laid the foundations of the earth, that it should not be removed for ever."

Flat Earthers use this to argue that the Earth is fixed in place, not spinning or orbiting.

But in the New International Version (NIV): "He set the earth on its foundations; it can never be moved."

It may seem like a small difference, but it matters. "Set" feels different from "laid," and more importantly, most Bible scholars agree this verse is poetic. It is describing God's strength and steady rule, not making a statement about the Earth's actual motion (Brueggemann & Mays, 1994). The original Hebrew word for "removed" (mot) often means to be shaken in a moral or spiritual sense—not physically moved.

Isaiah 40:22

KJV: "It is he that sitteth upon the circle of the earth..."

Flat Earthers argue that "circle" means the Earth must be flat and round like a coin.

But the English Standard Version (ESV) says: "It is he who sits above the circle of the earth..."

The original Hebrew word here is chug (חוג), and it is not so simple. It can mean "circle," "vault," "dome," or even "sphere," depending on context (Strong, 1890; Brown, Driver, & Briggs, 1907). It could describe the horizon, the sky from a high place, or a rounded shape. Interpreting it as a sphere actually lines up with many ancient views of the cosmos (Drayton, 2018).

Revelation 7:1

KJV: "And after these things I saw four angels standing on the four corners of the earth..."

This is a favorite "proof" for a flat, square Earth.

But most scholars understand this as symbolic language for the four directions: north, south, east, and west—not literal corners. It is a common Hebrew idiom. Even versions like the New Revised Standard Version (NRSV) say it the same way, but the meaning is understood as metaphorical (Mounce, 1998).

These examples show how Flat Earth arguments depend on ignoring both the variety in translations and the symbolic nature of much of the Bible's language (Kugel, 2007). Even small word changes across versions can shift the tone or meaning, depending on how the translator approached the text, what the original author meant, and what was going on at the time it was written.

By picking just the pieces that support their claim, Flat Earthers can say "God's Word is clear"—but that kind of clarity is built on ignoring context, language, and alternative readings. It is not real clarity. It's a carefully built illusion. What makes scripture powerful is not how easy it is to flatten into talking points—it is how deep and lasting it is, how it speaks to people in different ways across thousands of years. Flattening all that complexity into a few cherry-picked verses does not just weaken the text. It steals its richness and its spiritual beauty.

a set of simplistic talking points, thereby robbing the sacred text of both its inherent complexity and its profound spiritual beauty.

Among the oddest—and for many, most frustrating—citations in the Flat Earth playbook is the Book of Enoch: an ancient, mysterious text packed with cosmic visions, layers of angels, and vivid descriptions of the natural world. Flat Earthers treat this little-known book as a kind of secret weapon—undeniable, divine proof that the Earth has always been described as flat and sealed under a solid dome. To them, mainstream religion has covered up this "truth" for centuries, working hand-in-hand with science in some grand deception. The use of such a fringe text as if it were final authority is exactly the kind of move that pushes even open-minded skeptics to their limits.

But the Book of Enoch is not what they say it is. And it does not do what they want it to do. The way it is used by Flat Earth promoters says more about their need to lean on dramatic outside "proof" than it does about the book itself—or any lost cosmic truth.

Usually called 1 Enoch, the Book of Enoch is an ancient Jewish apocalyptic work, mostly written between the 3rd and 1st centuries BCE (Nickelsburg & VanderKam, 2004). It is a sprawling, layered collection of visions, parables, and cosmological ideas, all linked to Enoch—the mysterious great-grandfather of Noah. The book describes things like the fall of rebellious angels (the "Watchers"), Enoch's journeys through multiple heavens, and striking images of how the Earth is built. Yes, parts of Enoch do describe the Earth as flat and covered by something like a dome, with portals for the stars and winds (Enoch 72–82; Charlesworth, 1983).

This kind of imagery is, understandably, irresistible to Flat Earthers. They quote it eagerly, acting as though they have uncovered some hidden truth that was buried for generations. They showcase Enoch's "dome" and "four corners" as ancient confirmation of their model—even though the same language shows up in better-known Bible texts that are almost always interpreted symbolically (like Revelation 7:1).

What rarely gets mentioned, though, is one simple and unavoidable fact: the Book of Enoch is not considered part of the Bible by most Jewish or Christian groups (VanderKam, 2012). It was not included in the Hebrew Bible, and after long debate, early Christian leaders left it out of the official Christian canon (Metzger & Coogan, 1993). The only major tradition that still includes it today is the Ethiopian and Eritrean Orthodox Church. And even there, it is mostly read as symbolic and spiritual, not as a science textbook (Knibb, 2007).

Flat Earth believers also leave out a key detail about what kind of writing this is. The Book of Enoch belongs to a type of literature called apocalyptic—a genre full of dreams, symbols, visions, and cosmic journeys. These works were never meant to describe physical reality in scientific terms. They were written to stir awe, to inspire hope in times of trouble, and to show the spiritual world behind the physical one (Collins, 1998). To treat these images—like angels pushing stars or windows in the sky—as literal, physical facts is like trying to build a telescope based on the Book of Revelation.

This move—taking a rare and dramatic text and using it as secret proof—is a rhetorical strategy known as an appeal to hidden knowledge. It is the classic "They do not want you to know" argument. By pointing to a forgotten or ignored book, Flat Earthers present themselves as truth-seekers who are brave enough to follow the real evidence—while painting everyone else as either fooled or in on the cover-up (Kahane & Cavender, 2006). It is effective because it makes people feel smart, chosen, and part of a group that sees what others cannot.

The truth is, the Book of Enoch is a fascinating and valuable piece of ancient religious writing. It gives us a deep look into the imaginations, hopes, and fears of people who lived long ago. But it is not evidence of a flat Earth, and it is definitely not proof of a cover-up. Its strange and beautiful visions tell us more about spiritual meaning than physical geography. And that is what makes it powerful—not its misuse as a literal map of the world.

Few words in scripture have been stretched further by Flat Earth promoters than "firmament." To them, this single term is not just a translation choice — it is rock-solid evidence that the sky is a literal dome over a flat Earth. They quote the first chapter of Genesis with complete confidence, claiming the Bible "clearly" describes a hard, physical barrier separating the waters above from the waters below. In their view, this backs up their entire model.

The King James Version (KJV), a go-to translation for many Flat Earthers because of its older and often more literal style, puts Genesis 1:6–8 like this:

"And God said, Let there be a firmament in the midst of the waters, and let it divide the waters from the waters. And God made the firmament, and divided the waters which were under the firmament from the waters which were above the firmament: and it was so. And God called the firmament Heaven."

To modern readers, especially those unfamiliar with how ancient people saw the world, this language can sound strange—even unsettling. It may bring to mind something like a cosmic snow globe. But to the ancient Hebrews who first told and heard this story, that image made perfect sense (Walton, 2009). In their world, the sky looked like a huge, blue dome arching over the land. They imagined it as solid, holding back the waters above so life could thrive below. The Hebrew word for this dome is raqia', usually translated as "firmament." Stars moved across it, and rain came through its "windows" when God allowed it (Genesis 7:11). This was not meant to be a science lesson—it was a poetic and powerful way of saying that God brought order to chaos and made the world livable (Ramm, 1954).

Flat Earthers take that ancient image and argue it is a literal description of how the world still works. To them, even the word "firmament" itself means something hard and unbreakable—a dome above us that modern science either hides or denies. When newer Bible versions use words like "expanse," "sky," or "vault" instead of "firmament," Flat Earthers claim that is proof of deception. They argue that translators are covering up the truth, watering down God's word to fit science. In their story, the dome is still there, hidden in plain sight, and the world is just pretending it is not. That idea becomes a tool to challenge the trustworthiness of both science and modern biblical scholarship (Numbers, 2009).

But even in early Jewish and Christian traditions, not everyone took the firmament literally. Writers like Philo of Alexandria (1st century CE) saw it as symbolic—marking the line between the physical and spiritual worlds. Later thinkers, like Origen (3rd century CE), focused more on the spiritual meanings of Genesis than on its physical descriptions. By the Middle Ages, scholars like Thomas Aquinas (13th century) viewed the Genesis story as describing the world in a way people of the time could understand—not as a scientific manual (Gallagher, 2011). They believed the purpose of the creation story was to show God's power and purpose, not to offer a cosmic blueprint.

What Flat Earth arguments miss—or ignore—is that Genesis 1 was never meant to be read like a diagram or a lab report. It is a hymn. A poetic song about how God brought shape and meaning to a world that started out wild and empty. The "firmament" is part of that story—how people long ago imagined the sky and God's role in making it. It was deeply meaningful, but not meant as a literal claim about physics.

It is easy to see why a literal reading is appealing. In a world full of change and uncertainty, it gives people something solid to hang onto. But craving certainty is not the same as finding truth. And using that craving to fuel a movement does not reflect the full depth, nuance, or beauty of scripture.

To really understand what the word firmament (raqia') meant to the people who wrote and first heard the Genesis creation story, we have to step into their world—a world with no telescopes, no satellites, and no real understanding of gravity or space. To them, the sky looked exactly like it appeared: a huge blue ceiling overhead, separating the land below from mysterious waters above (Walton, 2009).

And they were not the only ones who saw it this way. All across the ancient Near East, people had similar ideas about the sky. The Babylonians pictured it as a dome made of crystal or blue stone, filled with stars like jewels and holding back the waters of chaos (Heidel, 1951). The Egyptians saw the sky as the goddess Nut, her body stretched over the Earth like a protective arch, covered in stars (Wilkinson, 1994). Early Greek thinkers imagined the heavens as a series of layered shells, with Earth sitting still in the middle, and the stars set in the outermost layer. So the Hebrew view of the sky as a dome was not unusual—it was just one version of a widely shared idea. What made it special was the way it expressed something deeper: not just what the world looked like, but what it meant (Clifford, 1994).

When Genesis talks about the firmament dividing the waters, it is not laying out a physics diagram. It is telling a powerful story: that God brought order out of chaos and created a safe, structured world where life could thrive (Sailhamer, 1992). The firmament was a symbol of that separation—a sign that even the wildest forces had been tamed and put in their place. It was not an engineering sketch. It was a message about divine control and cosmic structure (Wenham, 1987).

But Flat Earthers treat it like it was a blueprint. They read this poetic, ancient image as though it is a technical manual. They argue the writers of Genesis were being completely literal—laying out the specs of a hard, physical dome. That kind of thinking is an example of something called presentism: looking at the past through a modern lens, and expecting ancient people to speak the language of today's science (Butterfield, 1931; Numbers, 2009). It is like demanding that a folk song explain orbital mechanics.

It is also an example of what we might call literalism as authority—the idea that the more literal your reading of scripture, the more faithful and spiritually pure you are. It is a tempting approach because it seems simple and bold: "The Bible says it, I believe it, that settles it." But that mindset comes at a cost. It flattens the poetry, the symbolism, the richness of the original text. It turns something deep and layered into something rigid and shallow (Kugel, 2007).

By ignoring the history, culture, and language that shaped the idea of the firmament, Flat Earth arguments miss the heart of the story. Genesis was not trying to explain the mechanics of the universe. It was trying to show who made it, why it was made, and where we fit in that creation.

One of the most overlooked parts of Flat Earth rhetoric is how much it leans on the quirks and choices made in English Bible translations. The dramatic, old-sounding phrases they quote—like "the firmament," "the circle of the earth," and "the pillars of the earth"—are not the raw, original words of ancient Hebrew or Greek. They are the result of centuries of translators making careful (and sometimes theologically loaded) decisions, long after the texts were first written (Ryken, 2011).

Take "firmament," the cornerstone of the whole "cosmic dome" claim. In the original Hebrew of Genesis 1, the word used is raqia' (רָקִיעַ), which comes from a verb meaning "to spread out" or "to hammer thin"—like shaping metal. Most scholars agree raqia' refers to an expanse or a broad space (Walton, 2009). Ancient Hebrews likely imagined the sky as something firm or solid, based on how it looked to them, but the word itself emphasizes space and separation more than physical hardness (Sailhamer, 1992).

So where did "firmament" come from? It started when Jewish translators turned the Hebrew Bible into Greek (the Septuagint) around the 3rd or 2nd century BCE. They chose the Greek word stereoma (στερέωμα), which means something firm or solid—probably reflecting their own assumptions about the heavens and borrowing from Greek thinking about celestial spheres. Later, when Jerome translated the Bible into Latin (the Vulgate) in the 4th century CE, he went with firmamentum, a Latin word meaning solid support or structure. The 1611 King James Version picked up that same Latin word and brought it straight into English: "firmament." And that is how a poetic Hebrew word for a broad sky turned into the centerpiece of Flat Earth cosmology (McGrath, 2001).

You see this same pattern with other verses Flat Earthers use:

Isaiah 40:22 says God sits above the chug (חוּג) of the Earth. The KJV translates it as "circle," and Flat Earthers claim that proves the Earth is a flat disc. But chug can mean "circle," "vault," "sphere," "compass," or "horizon," depending on how it is used (Brown, Driver, & Briggs, 1907). Many scholars note it often refers to roundness in a poetic sense—like the curve of the horizon or the arc of the sky—not a flat pancake (Strong, 1890). Flat Earthers simply pick the one definition that fits their model and ignore the rest.

The "pillars of the earth" is another favorite. Verses like Job 9:6 and Psalm 75:3 talk about God shaking or steadying the Earth's pillars. These were never meant to describe actual stone columns under the ground. They are poetic images—ways of saying that God holds power over what seems solid and unshakable (Alter, 2007). They are about strength, not structure.

Flat Earth arguments often fall back on what you could call an appeal to archaic authority—the belief that older-sounding translations, like the KJV, are automatically more trustworthy and closer to what God "really said" (Walton, 2006). The formal, old-fashioned language feels sacred and solid, even though modern translations often reflect better scholarship, more accurate source texts, and deeper historical understanding (Fee & Stuart, 2014).

The result? Many of the Flat Earth movement's favorite verses are not just misunderstood—they are lost in translation. The arguments depend on poetic language and centuries-old translation choices while ignoring the original meanings, cultural context, and the progress we've made in biblical scholarship. Yes, words matter—but so does knowing where those words came from, why they were chosen, and how they have changed along the way.

Constructing Certainty: The Ultimate Rhetorical Barrier

For Flat Earthers, the "firmament" is not just a word from an old text—it is a symbol, and a powerful one. In their view, it is proof of a hidden truth: a cosmic secret that's been covered up by scientists, governments, and maybe even pastors. They turn the firmament into something much bigger than a dome in the sky—it becomes a rhetorical dome, a mental and emotional shield that surrounds their entire worldview. It reinforces the idea that they are the only ones who truly "see what is going on" (Barkun, 2003).

This dome fits perfectly into their broader story: a world filled with lies, and a few faithful people who still trust God's word over man's theories. In their telling, the firmament is not just something overhead—it is a divine barrier meant to keep God's truth safe from a world that's lost its way. They argue that scientists, scholars, and even church leaders are either blind to the dome or actively covering it up. This idea helps them paint themselves as the brave few, holding the line against a massive, global lie (Roberts, 2011).

But the rhetorical dome does more than just draw a line between Flat Earthers and the rest of the world. It also shuts down conversation from within. It becomes a kind of echo chamber—a closed system where only the approved "truth" is allowed in (Pariser, 2011). Questions, doubts, and alternative views are not just rejected—they are treated as proof that someone has been fooled, or worse, is working for "the other side." Anyone who challenges the dome—whether from the outside or from within the group—is often cast out, accused of being deceived, faithless, or part of the conspiracy (Dubay, various works).

In this way, the firmament becomes more than a belief—it becomes a boundary. A mental and social fence that keeps the group united and the outside world out. It is not just a model of the heavens—it is a tool that reinforces loyalty and blocks outside voices.

Here is the deep irony: the firmament, as it appears in scripture, was never meant to be used this way. As we have seen throughout this section, Genesis was not laying out a scientific structure or a rigid map. It was telling a poetic story—a way of showing that God brought order, beauty, and meaning to a chaotic world (Walton, 2009). Turning that story into a weapon, using it to prove a cover-up or create an ideological fortress, misses the entire point of the text.

In the end, Flat Earth rhetoric does not just place a dome over the Earth. It builds one over the minds of its followers. That dome—the demand for absolute certainty, the rejection of outside information, the narrowing of what is allowed to be true—becomes its own kind of trap. It shuts out the very kind of curiosity, humility, and thoughtful questioning that scripture was meant to inspire.

The Language of Belonging: Forging Unity Through a Narrowed Lens

Flat Earth rhetoric carefully builds a story where believers are cast as a brave, enlightened minority — the faithful few who know the truth and refuse to bow to the "lies" of the world. It sets up a false choice: either you are one of the righteous, "awake" people who see through the deception, or you are part of the misled masses. There is no room for honest doubt, thoughtful skepticism, or curiosity. You are either in or out — and your choice says everything about who you are (Proctor, 2020).

This kind of messaging creates a strong "us versus them" dynamic — a key feature of persuasive, tight-knit group thinking (Tajfel & Turner, 1979). People are told who they are by being told who they are not: they are not "sheeple," not "brainwashed," not asleep, and definitely not helping with the global lie. Everyone on the outside — scientists, pastors, critics, even family — is not just wrong. They are seen as morally weak, spiritually lost, or even working for dark forces, sometimes literally called "demonic" or "Satanic" (Fisher, 2018). This kind of framing strengthens group loyalty and makes it hard to even hear outside views, let alone consider them fairly.

You will hear these dividing lines everywhere in Flat Earth circles. Detractors get labeled "sheeple," "brainwashed," or "globe-tards." Believers proudly call themselves "awake," "aware," "red-pilled," or "truthers." These are not just slogans — they are ways of claiming moral high ground. Instead of offering solid evidence, the movement leans on a sense of moral and intellectual superiority. "Seeing the truth" becomes more important than proving it (Frank, 2004).

And that is a powerful draw. Being part of a special group — one that sees what others miss — feels good. It gives followers a sense of meaning, pride, and even heroism in their stand against the supposed global deception. That is no accident. Social Identity Theory shows how people build self-esteem by identifying with groups that feel righteous, misunderstood, or under attack (Tajfel & Turner, 1979). This often creates a martyr complex: the idea that being mocked, silenced, or ridiculed just proves they are on the right side. Every insult, every eye-roll from the outside world, only deepens the group's belief that they are right — and everyone else is reacting out of fear or denial (Jolley & Douglas, 2014).

But there is a cost. The more powerful the "us vs. them" story becomes, the harder it is for someone to leave. Once you have claimed your spot among the "faithful few," even a small doubt feels like a betrayal — a step backward into the "lies" you thought you escaped. The moral high ground that gave you strength can also become a trap, locking you in.

In the end, Flat Earth belief does not just offer a new way to look at the world — it offers you a role in the story: the hero, the truth-teller, the one who sees through the fog. That identity may be harder to give up than the belief itself.

For Flat Earthers, it is not enough to believe they have found the truth. Their worldview often insists that they are surrounded by enemies trying to hide it. Critics are not just mistaken—they are seen as active participants in a cover-up. Friends and family who disagree are called "brainwashed." Scientists, teachers, and journalists become "shills"—people getting paid to promote the globe. In more extreme corners of the movement, these doubters are even cast as "Satan's pawns," turning any disagreement into a kind of spiritual war (Dubay, various works; Roberts, 2011).

This is not just name-calling. It is a classic persuasive move known as a common enemy appeal—a way to unite a group by giving them a shared villain (Walton, 2006). That shared threat builds a strong sense of loyalty and purpose. If everyone on the outside is working against you, then everyone on the inside must be on the same mission. And every piece of criticism, every skeptical question, gets reinterpreted as proof that the enemy is real—and working hard to suppress the truth.

You see this everywhere in Flat Earth spaces—online groups, forums, videos. Believers swap stories of calling out "globe pushers" at school, at work, even at home. They cheer each other on for standing up to supposed agents of the lie. It creates a world where criticism is not just disagreement—it is part of the conspiracy. This is a textbook example of motivated reasoning: when people interpret any evidence in a way that confirms what they already believe (Kunda, 1990; Taber & Lodge, 2006). In this case, even arguments against Flat Earth become fuel for Flat Earth. The deeper the challenge, the deeper the belief.

Casting outsiders as enemies also strengthens the movement's sense of moral superiority. If skeptics are "working for Satan" or "spreading lies," then pushing back against them is not just brave—it is righteous. This brings together the earlier theme of moral high ground with a full-blown persecution narrative. Every insult, every rejection, becomes proof that they are on the right side of a cosmic battle (Jolley & Douglas, 2014).

But that mindset comes with a heavy cost. When everyone who disagrees is seen as a liar or a threat, there is no space left for honest conversation. No room for curiosity, for questions, or even for silent doubts. Any small crack in the story risks being labeled betrayal. And when even trusted loved ones are seen as part of the opposition, it can drive painful divisions that are hard to heal.

In the end, Flat Earth belief is not just about rejecting the globe. It is about joining a fight—and that fight demands that you pick a side. There is no middle ground. You are either with "the truth" or against it.

For many Flat Earthers, believing the Earth is flat is not just about facts or evidence—it becomes part of who they are. Their identity is shaped not just by what they believe, but by what they reject. They define themselves by being not part of the system, not fooled, not brainwashed, and definitely not one of the "sheeple." It is this strong sense of opposition that helps draw the line between "us" and "them" (Tajfel & Turner, 1979).

This pattern fits squarely with Social Identity Theory, which explains how people build a sense of self from the groups they belong to (Tajfel & Turner, 1979; Hogg & Abrams, 1988). Flat Earth rhetoric taps into that instinct by clearly spelling out who belongs: the "awake," the "truth-seekers," the ones who "see through the lies." That clear boundary makes followers feel important, united, and special—like they are part of something meaningful.

But once someone is part of that "in-group," speaking up with questions or doubts becomes risky. This is where groupthink kicks in. In tightly knit groups, there is pressure to agree, and pushing back can feel like betrayal (Janis, 1972).

Inside the Flat Earth community, even small questions about core beliefs can lead to backlash. Doubters might be accused of losing faith, being cowards, or falling for the lies again. One example is Jaren Campanella—a major Flat Earth voice who began questioning certain claims. Once he did, he was quickly shunned, mocked, and labeled a traitor by the very people who once celebrated him (Mercy, 2021).

Flat Earthers often say things like, "At least I am awake," or "I do not follow the herd." These are not just comments about belief—they are statements of identity. They say, "This is who I am—and this is who I am not." That is why it can be so hard for members to step away. Letting go of the belief does not just mean changing your mind; it also means releasing the attachment to it. It means risking your place in the group—and maybe even your sense of who you are.

The story that gives people confidence and clarity also becomes a trap. Belonging depends on total loyalty. Even quiet curiosity or open-ended questions can be perceived as a betrayal. That makes it incredibly hard for members to grow, change, or even think critically without feeling like they are abandoning their entire community.

In the end, Flat Earth rhetoric turns belief into something more than an idea—it becomes a badge of honor. And standing against the outside world becomes the glue that holds the group together. As with many insular groups, the need to belong can end up being far stronger than the belief itself. This powerful drive for belonging is often intertwined with a deeper, more coercive mechanism: the weaponization of spiritual conviction.

Belief Under Duress: Fear and Damnation

For many in the Flat Earth movement, belief is not just about facts—it becomes a spiritual test. Accepting the Flat Earth model, especially when it is framed as "biblically true," gets tied to faith itself. The story goes like this: if you believe in the Bible's version of the "firmament," then you are following God's truth. But if you doubt or reject it, you are not just wrong—you are risking your soul. You could face divine judgment, or even hell (Dawson, 2017).

This setup is a classic example of a fear appeal—a persuasion tactic that uses the threat of harm (in this case, eternal harm) to push people into line and stop them from questioning (Perloff, 2017). And when the fear is about your salvation, it is even more powerful. Once someone believes that their eternity depends on sticking to a specific cosmology, then science, evidence, and reason start to matter a whole lot less.

You see this message often in Flat Earth videos, social media posts, and forums: warnings that if you ignore the "firmament," you might be "unworthy" of heaven. This is what is called conditional salvation—the idea that getting into heaven depends on holding a very specific set of beliefs. It turns a discussion about science or history into something much more intense: a life-or-death decision about your soul (Hassan, 2015).

Fear has staying power. Once the idea takes hold—that doubting could send you to hell—it becomes very hard to shake. Psychologists call this motivated reasoning—a mental shortcut where people protect themselves from scary possibilities by doubling down on what they already believe (Kunda, 1990). Even when evidence points another way, the fear of being wrong about something this big causes them to dig in even deeper.

And it does not stop there. People who raise doubts or challenge the belief are quickly painted as dangerous. They are told they are "flirting with spiritual death" or "serving Satan." Former believers or outside critics get treated as proof that the "world hates the truth." This fits neatly into the persecuted righteousness narrative—the idea that being attacked means you must be right (Jolley & Douglas, 2014). That only reinforces the group's sense of urgency and resolve.

But fear works both ways. While it keeps people in line, it also traps them in a constant state of anxiety. They are afraid to question, afraid to explore other views, and afraid of what it might mean if they are wrong. This is what we call fear-based conformity—where staying with the group feels safer than thinking independently, even if something deep inside tells you something is not adding up.

In the end, Flat Earth rhetoric takes the language of faith and turns it into a threat. It plants a chilling idea: if you ask the wrong questions, you might burn for it. And once that fear takes root, many people stop asking questions at all.

Flat Earth rhetoric doesn't just suggest that doubters are mistaken—it warns that they are spiritually doomed. In this extreme framing, rejecting Flat Earth (presented as God's true creation) becomes more than just being wrong. It is painted as a rebellion against God, a betrayal of divine truth, with eternal consequences. Faith gets turned into a weapon against doubt.

This is where the earlier fear appeal shifts into full-blown apocalyptic rhetoric—a style that draws sharp lines between good and evil, heaven and hell, salvation and damnation (Robbins, 2017). Flat Earth promoters use this language often, describing believers in the globe model as "damned," "outside God's grace," or "on the road to hell." Disagreeing is not just a difference of opinion—it is a moral failure. And that makes it nearly impossible for believers to engage with any evidence without feeling overwhelmed by fear.

This rhetoric relies on black-and-white moral framing—a shortcut that wipes out any middle ground (Haidt, 2012). You are either with God and the truth (Flat Earth), or you are part of Satan's deception (the globe). There is no room for honest doubt or complex questions. People who do not agree are not just confused—they are condemned.

In forums, videos, and comment sections, Flat Earthers share bold warnings like "the deceived will burn" or "those who deny God's creation will be cast out." This is not just theology—it is rhetorical pressure designed to shame, control, and silence. Doubt becomes a sin. Questions become rebellion.

This dynamic depends heavily on spiritual shaming—where fear of hell gets tied to fear of being pushed out of the group (Tourish, 2019). A doubter does not just risk their soul—they risk losing their social circle, their sense of purpose, even their identity. And once that fear takes hold, it is no longer about what is true—it is about what feels safe. People hold on, not because they are sure, but because they are scared of what might happen if they let go.

What makes this even more powerful is that these hellfire warnings are not just aimed at outsiders. They are aimed at believers themselves. Flat Earth leaders often say things like "do not fall back into the lies" or "stay strong in the truth," reminding followers that even a small doubt could cost them everything. The fear turns inward. It does not just shape what people say—it shapes what they allow themselves to think.

And when critics push back or mock these beliefs, it only strengthens the group's sense of being "persecuted for the truth." As we saw earlier, this persecuted righteousness framing makes criticism feel like proof they are right. That fuels even more urgency. Warnings of doom become a sacred duty to save others from deception.

However, living in that constant state of fear comes with a cost. The threat of hell shuts down curiosity. It breeds anxiety, self-doubt, and emotional exhaustion. Flat Earth rhetoric does not just offer a version of the truth—it dictates the terrifying fate that awaits anyone who lets it go. When every private doubt feels like a step toward damnation, it is no wonder many simply stop doubting at all.

Fear can be a powerful motivator in the short term—but when it becomes the foundation for someone's belief system, the cost is steep. If a person's faith is driven by the fear of hell, the fear of being cast out by their community, or the fear of being completely wrong about something with eternal consequences, then it is not really faith anymore. It becomes a form of coercion (Hassan, 2015). That is what makes fear-based conformity so damaging: it does not just keep people in line—it wears down their ability to think clearly, ask honest questions, or trust their own instincts. Fear becomes the leash, and belief becomes a cage.

Flat Earth rhetoric is full of what is called threat-based persuasion—a way of communicating that warns people of punishment if they question the message, instead of encouraging growth or discovery (Perloff, 2017). It works because it targets our deepest anxieties: the fear of being wrong, and the fear of being condemned. But living under that constant pressure creates a quiet panic—a never-ending need to defend the belief, explain away contradictions, and shut out any creeping doubt.

Over time, that fear takes a toll. Instead of nurturing traits like curiosity, humility, or trust, it feeds shame, suspicion, and self-doubt. Doubters do not just feel confused—they feel guilty. And once that guilt takes hold, many become even more defensive and closed off, digging in deeper to avoid the discomfort of uncertainty. This is what psychologists call reactance—when people feel their freedom is being threatened, they push back by clinging even harder to the belief in question (Brehm & Brehm, 1981).

Fear also isolates. When you are told the outside world is deceived, dangerous, or even evil, you naturally start pulling away. Family members who raise questions might feel like enemies. Friends become threats. Every private moment of doubt starts to feel like a betrayal—not just of the group, but of yourself. And what began as a bold, defiant belief can slowly become a lonely one.

That sense of persecution—once empowering—can turn into something much darker. When everyone on the outside is framed as a threat, real connection becomes nearly impossible. The world feels hostile, and the group feels like the only safe place left.

Flat Earth rhetoric promises clarity and divine truth, but the price it demands is constant fear. And while fear can hold someone in place for a while, it is not sustainable. In the end, what traps people is not just the threat of hell—it is the quiet, internal pressure to belong. Those chains of conformity and fear do not feel like chains anymore. They feel like conviction. But that is the tragedy: people end up mistaking coercion for choice, and fear for faith. This deep-seated conformity, where performance often replaces belief, is further reinforced by the distinct communication patterns within the group.

Inside the Bubble: Language, Conformity, and the Self

Every distinct social group—or "tribe"—develops its own way of talking, with unspoken codes and insider language. Flat Earthers are no exception. To be accepted in this community, it is not enough to simply believe the Earth is flat. You also have to speak the language. That means calling doubters "sheeple," accusing critics of being "asleep," and declaring yourself "awake," "aware," or "walking in God's truth." These are not just throwaway terms—they are loaded declarations. They signal identity and allegiance. They say, loud and clear, whose side you are on.

This kind of shared language is what rhetoricians and linguists call loaded language—words packed with emotional weight, strong moral judgment, or clear ideological meaning (Lutz, 1989). It is designed to guide thinking, short-circuit analysis, and draw a sharp line between insiders and outsiders. Use the right terms, and you are recognized as one of the tribe. Get it wrong—or hesitate—and you risk being seen as unsure, uncommitted, or even a threat.

Spend five minutes in a Flat Earth forum, social media group, or YouTube comment thread, and this kind of linguistic control jumps out. The "globe" is not just a model of the Earth—it is "the deception." NASA is not just a space agency—it is "Not A Space Agency," or worse, a front for evil forces. Science is not a way to learn about the world—it is dismissed as "the lies of men" or "man's foolish wisdom." These kinds of phrases flatten complex ideas into moral absolutes. Moreover, that is the real power of loaded language: it tells people how to feel, what to believe, and who to trust—before they have even had a chance to think it through (Chomsky, 1988).

There is another reason this language matters: it helps police the group from the inside. Newcomers learn the jargon fast, mimicking the tone and key phrases to prove they belong. Longtime members listen closely for slip-ups—watching for hesitation or "off-brand" words that might suggest outside influence or creeping doubt. Psychologists call this linguistic in-group signaling—using language to show loyalty and build cohesion in a social group (Giles & Johnson, 1987).

This creates a lot of pressure to keep using the right words, even when doubts start to surface. Believers often keep repeating the tribe's phrases, even if they no longer fully believe them, because changing how they speak feels like confessing disloyalty—or admitting they do not belong anymore. And the more someone trains themselves to talk like the group, the harder it becomes to think independently. Over time, even private thoughts get filtered through that same borrowed language.

That is how belief can dig deeper than facts. Once someone starts speaking the language of Flat Earth, that language starts speaking for them. It reshapes how they think, and locks the worldview in from the inside.

The human need to belong is powerful. That feeling of being accepted and understood brings deep psychological comfort. Within Flat Earth circles, this sense of belonging is especially strong at first. Once someone adopts the group's language (as discussed in the previous section), embraces its core story, and feels the warmth of its welcome, they are no longer just someone with a different take on cosmology. They become "one of them"—a trusted part of a group that finally "gets it," offering powerful validation and camaraderie (Tajfel & Turner, 1979).

But that warm welcome comes with strings attached. It is not truly unconditional. You are safe and accepted only if you keep saying the "right" things, thinking the "right" way, and—most importantly—keeping any personal doubts to yourself. Step out of line, and the response is swift. Those who question too much, especially in public, are labeled "shills," "controlled opposition," "fake truthers," or worse. These labels are not just insults—they are warnings to others (Hassan, 2015).

This is how the group keeps its boundaries tight and its beliefs in check. Members learn to self-censor quickly, biting their tongues when doubts arise and staying silent about inconsistencies. Psychologists call this conditional belonging: you can stay in the group's good graces, but only by playing by its unspoken rules and embracing its shared beliefs (Tourish, 2019). The comfort of the group depends on how well you conform.

The longer someone stays in this system, the harder it gets to leave. By then, it is no longer just about rejecting a belief—it is about walking away from friends, identity, and a place in a shared story ("awake," "truth-teller," etc.). The cost of leaving is enormous. That is why many, when faced with doubts or outside criticism, choose to double down instead. At some point, holding onto Flat Earth belief is not really about proving the Earth is flat—it is about proving they still belong (Festinger, 1957).

This pressure is made worse by the quiet but constant sense of being watched. Members notice each other. Loyalty is tested often, and enthusiasm is expected. If you pause too long, use the "wrong" words, or seem less passionate, it is noticed—and possibly called out. That environment forces people to stay in line, even when part of them secretly wonders whether any of it is true.

In the end, belonging in this world becomes a kind of deal: as long as you keep playing your part, the group keeps you close. But it takes a toll. At first, it costs you your voice. Over time, it chips away at your ability to think freely, question honestly, and trust your own judgment. And that is how people get stuck—trapped in a loop where performance replaces belief, and conformity replaces conviction.

In tightly knit groups like Flat Earth communities, doubt is not just uncomfortable—it is dangerous. Not just for the individual feeling it, but for the whole group's sense of unity. To protect their fragile certainty, these circles develop clever—and often subconscious—ways of keeping doubt from ever taking root. And the most effective tools are not logical arguments or solid evidence. They are short, loaded phrases—little one-liners that get repeated so often they become automatic. Psychologists and rhetoricians call these thought-stopping clichés: emotionally charged catchphrases that shut down critical thinking and stop questions before they even get going (Lifton, 1961; Hassan, 2015).

You will hear these phrases everywhere:
- "Wake up!" (which suggests others are just "asleep")
- "Do your own research" (which usually means "go read Flat Earth-approved sources")
- "You just cannot handle the truth" (a way to paint disagreement as weakness)
- "NASA lies!" (used as a trump card, not an argument)

They sound like bold claims or rallying cries, but they are really just rhetorical noise. Their job is not to persuade—it is to signal loyalty. To the group, they show you are still on board. To yourself, they are a reminder not to ask too many questions.

These phrases carry a powerful emotional charge. They make the speaker feel brave, righteous, and "in the know." That kind of emotional boost drowns out the quieter, more uncomfortable voice inside that might whisper, "What if I am wrong?" Moreover, when everyone around you is saying the same things with the same intensity, that feeling spreads fast. Psychologists call this emotional contagion—when emotions ripple through a group and people start matching each other's energy, often without realizing it (Hatfield et al., 1993). It is far easier to ride the wave than to stand apart.

But it is not just the emotion—it is the relentless repetition. In Flat Earth spaces, the same claims, memes, slogans, and arguments show up again and again. This is not an accident. It is a powerful way to crowd out doubt (Pratkanis & Aronson, 1991). When every part of your environment echoes the same message over and over, it starts to feel safer to go along than to think for yourself or risk being the odd one out.

And that is the real trick. Over time, you do not have to fully believe every word anymore. You just have to keep saying them. The performance of belief becomes more important than belief itself. If you stay loud enough, long enough, no one—not even you—may notice the lingering doubts hiding in the background. The language becomes a kind of shield, protecting not just the group, but the speaker from their own uncertainty.

For all the anxiety, social pressure, and inner conflict that Flat Earth belief can bring, it offers something deeply appealing in return: certainty. This feeling of absolute clarity is often what keeps many followers from walking away, even when the cracks in the narrative begin to show.

Doubt, by nature, is uncomfortable. It's messy. It forces people to face the possibility that they don't know—or worse, that they've been wrong. That tension, known as cognitive dissonance, is not an easy place to live. Certainty, even if it's borrowed or fragile, feels like solid ground. It's a steady anchor in a world that otherwise feels chaotic and misleading.

That craving for stability is exactly why Flat Earth rhetoric leans so heavily on absolutes. Followers are told the Bible's descriptions of the Earth are "clear," that the "evidence" is "obvious," and that the entire mainstream world is "lying." No gray areas. No room for doubt. No nuance. And that black-and-white thinking is comforting. It lets people avoid the challenge of sorting through conflicting ideas. They don't have to question or investigate anymore—they just have to believe.

The group reinforces this feeling of certainty constantly. People are praised for being "awake" and "aware." They're told they're on the "right side" of a cosmic battle. They are reminded that "the world hates the truth," and that being mocked or challenged is proof they're correct. All of this creates a dangerous sense of calm—a kind of peace that depends on not asking too many hard questions.

And that's the real trap. Certainty feels safe. It feels good. But that comfort comes at a cost: it halts growth, blocks real learning, and clouds a person's view of the world's complexity. It trades intellectual humility for pride, and honest curiosity for the illusion of truth.

In the end, the cost of this false certainty is the same as the cost of conditional belonging: over time, a person slowly, and often without realizing it, gives up pieces of themselves just to stay inside the comforting—but confining—embrace of the Flat Earth narrative.

Certainty as Salvation

In a world that often feels chaotic, complex, and fast-moving, one of the strongest appeals of Flat Earth belief is its simplicity. For those feeling overwhelmed by information overload and existential doubt, the Flat Earth story doesn't just offer an alternative—it offers relief. It's not just another theory; for many, it feels like a kind of intellectual and spiritual rescue.

Flat Earth rhetoric frames the choice in stark, either-or terms: you can either "trust what you see" (as interpreted through their literal lens) and fully accept "what God says" (as they read it in the Bible), or you've been fooled by "the lies of men"—the grand deception of the globe model. For believers, this isn't a debate. It's already settled. They argue that the Bible spells it out "plainly" and "clearly," and anything else must be part of the lie. That conviction is often summed up in one popular line: "God said it. That settles it." (Dubay, various works). That kind of clarity offers a powerful form of faith—unshakable, comforting, and, to them, divinely backed.

But the draw isn't just theological. Flat Earth groups build on this same simplicity in social ways, too. Inside these tight-knit communities, agreement is assumed. Everyone repeats the same phrases, shares the same memes, and speaks the same coded language. In this kind of setting, questioning feels not just unnecessary—it feels risky. The unspoken rule becomes: "Why question what everyone else already knows is true?"

Psychologists refer to this desire for easy, definitive answers as need for cognitive closure—the push to resolve uncertainty quickly and avoid lingering in doubt (Kruglanski & Webster, 1996). That desire is deeply human. And Flat Earth rhetoric speaks directly to it, urging: "Don't overthink it. Just believe." It promises a fast escape from mental struggle and ambiguity.

At first, this simplicity feels like a gift. People get to stop wrestling with uncertainty. They feel confident, clear, and supported by a group that seems to finally "get it." Their identity sharpens, and they feel like they belong.

But over time, the price of that simplicity becomes harder to ignore. It discourages real learning, stifles deeper questions, and shrinks one's ability to deal with nuance or complexity. When faith becomes nothing more than clinging to easy answers, it loses its depth. And when belonging depends on keeping things simple, it stops being about connection—and starts being about control. The comfort comes at the cost of curiosity.

In the end, Flat Earth belief offers a borrowed kind of certainty. It feels good at first—like a refuge. But it comes with a steep cost. It asks you to stop thinking for yourself and calls that surrender "faith."

The Allure of Absolute Certainty

Flat Earth belief often hooks individuals by offering answers that feel final—neat, simple, and seemingly unshakable. Adherents are told the Bible is crystal clear: the Earth is fixed and unmoving, and anything that suggests otherwise is deception—"lies from men" meant to pull them away from God's truth. This clarity is presented not just as correct, but as righteous. It provides a strong sense of moral grounding and spiritual comfort.

But the appeal goes beyond faith alone. The community itself acts as a powerful social force, holding out that certainty like a lure. It's carefully packaged—slogans, memes, repeated phrases—all designed to stir a feeling of special knowledge, of being awake to something hidden from the masses. The message is clear: You see the truth. You're chosen. You're on the right side.

That sense of being uniquely enlightened and morally aligned is deeply addictive. It doesn't just shape belief—it reshapes identity. And that's where the real trap lies: once someone's sense of self, their social standing, and their place in a tight-knit group depend on holding this belief, letting go isn't just about admitting they were wrong. It feels like losing everything—identity, belonging, purpose.

Psychologists call this belief perseverance: the tendency to hold onto beliefs even when faced with clear evidence to the contrary, especially when abandoning them would challenge one's self-image or social bonds (Ross & Lepper, 1980).

Flat Earth rhetoric feeds this tendency. Doubt is cast as weakness. Questions are treated as betrayal. Those who waver risk being labeled "shills," "deceivers," or even "tools of Satan." But those who stand firm are praised as "awake," "faithful," and "worthy." The group rewards certainty—and punishes anything less.

This is why many double down on the belief, even when evidence piles up against it. It's not about logic anymore. It's about survival—psychological, emotional, social. The words, the memes, the affirmations aren't always spoken with conviction. They're spoken because stopping feels like pulling down the entire structure that props up one's identity.

In the end, Flat Earth belief lures people in with the promise of clarity and conviction. But over time, that very certainty becomes a cage—not built from facts, but from fear, belonging, and a carefully constructed identity. The longer someone stays, the harder it becomes to find their way back to independent thought and a broader, more nuanced view of the world.

Simplicity's Hidden Costs

Simplicity feels good — but it comes with a cost.

Flat Earth belief promises you a world where everything makes sense. The Bible says it, the group confirms it, and all the so-called "evidence" of the globe is just lies and deception. It's neat. Clean. No messy questions or uncomfortable doubts. And at first, that kind of certainty feels like freedom.

But that simplicity comes at a price you don't always see at first. To keep it intact, you have to ignore what doesn't fit. Evidence that contradicts the story gets dismissed as fake. Doubts that creep in get silenced — not just by the group, but by yourself. In Flat Earth spaces, nuance isn't a virtue. It's weakness. Admitting that something might be more complicated than it looks is treated like betrayal.

That's the rhetorical trap — and it's a clever one. The more you buy into the simple story, the more it trains you to see every question as disloyalty and every doubt as weakness. It's a belief system designed to protect itself by punishing you for thinking too hard.

The longer you stay in it, the more you stop noticing what you're giving up: your curiosity, your ability to weigh evidence, your willingness to consider another perspective.

Simplicity feels safe, but it narrows your world. Over time, it stops being faith or conviction — and starts being fear of what might happen if you let yourself think too hard.

Courage in Complexity

Certainty often feels like refuge—a safe harbor from the relentless storms of doubt and ambiguity. But the truth—the real truth of the universe and the human experience—has never been that simple.

Flat Earth belief, by design, offers a clarity that feels immensely comforting at first. It paints the world in stark black-and-white: good versus evil, faithful versus deceived, righteous versus damned. This rigid framework erases nuance, creating a reality that's easy to grasp—but ultimately constricting. The longer one lives within that binary worldview, the smaller that world becomes. The room for independent thought shrinks. The freedom to question fades.

It takes real courage to step into the gray—to admit you don't have all the answers, and maybe never will. That's not weakness. That's strength. Because intellectual and spiritual humility creates space for growth, for deeper understanding, and for a view of reality that expands rather than contracts.

Authentic faith doesn't demand you shut your mind down to protect it. The strongest faith is the kind that can face hard questions head-on—and still stand. It's not afraid of scrutiny, because it values truth over dogma.

The same goes for belonging. You don't need to trade your voice for acceptance. True community doesn't require conformity; it thrives on shared values, mutual respect, and the freedom to think, speak, and question without fear.

And that's what makes walking away from simplistic answers so hard—and so vital. The world is complex, layered, and deeply mysterious. But once you stop running from that complexity—once you lean into it—you begin to see more. Understand more. Become more.

Yes, it's easier to cling to manufactured certainty. But it's braver—and infinitely more rewarding—to live with questions, to stay open, and to let your understanding evolve.

Faith or Fracture?

What begins as a seemingly harmless exploration of biblical cosmology often evolves into something far more complex and psychologically consuming. Flat Earth belief doesn't just offer an alternate map of the world—it offers a map for identity, belonging, and perceived righteousness. From the first moment someone is told that the "truth has been hidden," they're not simply invited into a new belief system—they're recruited into a tightly regulated community, one where the price of entry is certainty and the cost of exit is personal unraveling.

This chapter has traced the subtle but powerful rhetorical and psychological machinery at work behind Flat Earth evangelism: the appeals to divine authority, the emotional leverage of fear, the manipulation of language to signal loyalty, and the intense social pressure that enforces conformity while masquerading as fellowship. At its core, the Flat Earth movement operates not as a free exchange of ideas, but as a closed loop of emotional reinforcement and thought control. It promises clarity and freedom, yet demands silence, suppression, and surrender. Faith, when weaponized this way, becomes something unrecognizable—not a search for deeper understanding, but a script to be recited in exchange for conditional belonging.

Yet in peeling back these layers, the deeper story isn't just about Flat Earth—it's about how belief itself can be captured, packaged, and sold. The real question isn't whether the Earth is flat. It's whether the language of certainty, fear, and isolation is being used to replace the harder, braver work of genuine inquiry, spiritual humility, and intellectual freedom. And if that's the case—then the true vanishing point may not be on the map at all, but within the boundaries of belief itself.

When belief is bound this tightly to identity, and certainty is shaped into armor, it becomes more than a personal conviction—it becomes a tool. Flat Earth rhetoric doesn't just build that tool; it sharpens it for use, turning faith into a rallying cry and doubt into an enemy. But in the modern movement, that tool doesn't stay confined to personal belief. It is amplified, echoed, and packaged for a digital age where certainty itself can be cultivated, marketed, and sold. To understand how this ancient story has found new life, we must step into those echo chambers and watch how unshakable belief becomes a network, a brand, and, for some, a livelihood.

Chapter 3: Narrative by Design: Crafting a Flat World

Belief doesn't just happen. It's built—layer by layer, story by story—until it stops feeling like persuasion and starts feeling like reality itself.

In the modern Flat Earth movement, that construction isn't accidental. It's intentional. Every villain named, every hero crafted, every simple phrase repeated until it echoes in your head works like a brick in a wall, shaping a world where doubt can't find a foothold and certainty feels like truth.

Step back far enough and a pattern emerges. A shadowy enemy gives the story weight. A chosen hero gives it a heartbeat. Simple words smooth out complexity until they sound like common sense. And a sharp line between "us" and "them" seals the edges, building an echo chamber where the story doesn't just survive—it thrives (Douglas et al., 2017)..

These aren't isolated tricks. Together, they form the architecture of a belief system designed to endure. Language and identity weave themselves into a narrative so tight it stops being a claim and starts being the air around you. Once that world is built, breaking through it takes more than facts—it takes dismantling the story itself.

Every Story Needs a Villain: The Power of a Clear Enemy

In a constructed world, the first brick is always the enemy. Naming a villain lays down the boundary lines of the story, making everything outside dangerous and everything inside safe.

Every good story needs a challenge, something to push against. In the Flat Earth narrative, that "something" almost always turns into a "someone." Giving the story a clear enemy makes it feel urgent and important. Think about it: without a villain, that dramatic tale of "waking up" loses all its punch — and drama, let us be honest, is what keeps people hooked.

This is a classic move called contrast framing. It is a way of making sense of things by setting one idea or group against another, creating meaning through opposition (Chong & Druckman, 2007). By drawing a hard line between "us" (the brave truth-seekers) and "them" (the bad guys), the story hands believers a clear role and a mission. In Flat Earth circles, the enemy is not just wrong; they are actively hiding the truth from everyone (Douglas et al., 2017). That one twist turns the whole thing from a debate into a crusade: if "they" are tricking the entire world, then "we" have to stand up and expose them.

You can hear this enemy story loud and clear in the language believers use. They will say things like, "NASA is not in the business of exploration; they are in the business of deception." Alternatively, they will ask, "Why is every picture you have ever seen of Earth computer-generated?" Another favorite line: "Science stopped being about discovery a long time ago — now it is about keeping you asleep." These are not just random accusations. They are deliberate moves to chip away at the ethos, or credibility, of the so-called enemy (Aristotle, trans. 2007). If NASA and mainstream scientists cannot be trusted, then everything they produce crumbles by association. The story does not actually have to disprove the data; it just has to make you doubt the source.

There is also a heavy dose of pathos here — that is the rhetorical term for appealing to emotions. This villain story taps straight into fear (of being duped) and betrayal (when trust is broken). Those emotions give the story urgency and make it feel deeply personal.

From a psychological angle, having a villain can actually make the world feel more stable. Instead of wrestling with a messy, complicated reality, the story offers a neat solution: the world is not complex, it is just corrupted. Pinning all the blame on one group is a classic move called scapegoating (Girard, 1986).

The enemy narrative also leans on what is known as a binary frame, or false dichotomy (Walton, 1989). It forces a simple, all-or-nothing choice: either you see "the truth," or you are automatically siding with the deceivers. That sharp dividing line is convincing because it wipes away all the gray areas — and with them, any room for doubt.

Moreover, when the very existence of this villain becomes "proof" that the conspiracy is real ("They are hiding the truth, so it must be true"), that is a textbook self-sealing argument (Kitcher, 1993). It is a rhetorical loop, where the claim uses its own assumption as evidence, making it almost impossible to challenge once you are inside the belief system.

The real power of having a villain is what it hands the audience: a simple dividing line, a heroic role to play, and a powerful reason to keep believing. Flat Earth rhetoric cannot survive without that bad guy. The villain is not just part of the story; they are its anchor, tied together with a web of rhetorical techniques that make the narrative sharper, stronger, and harder to question. And that need for a villain rarely stays abstract. The story almost always gives the enemy a name, a face, and even a logo.

Casting NASA and Science as the Deceivers

Nowhere is the need for a clear bad guy more evident than in how Flat Earth rhetoric locks onto NASA—and science itself—as the perfect deceivers. The very agencies and institutions that stand for exploration and discovery are flipped into symbols of control and secrecy, making them ideal targets for the story's opposition.

In the Flat Earth narrative, no villain looms larger than NASA. For believers, NASA is not just a space agency; it is the ultimate embodiment of "the lie." Putting NASA at the center of the conspiracy gives the story both a face and a name. It turns a vague distrust into a clear narrative with a specific antagonist. This is textbook symbolic villainy, where one figure or institution comes to stand for an entire opposing worldview, becoming the scapegoat for every perceived societal wrong (Douglas et al., 2017; Girard, 1986). NASA stops being an agency and turns into the ultimate symbol of deception itself.

Rhetorically, NASA is a perfect target because it naturally carries ethos—that mix of authority, expertise, and public trust (Aristotle, trans. 2007). Furthermore, that is precisely why the Flat Earth story goes after it so hard. By flipping NASA's credibility into "proof" of its corruption, the narrative pulls off a move known as ethos inversion. It is the rhetorical equivalent of using someone's own strength against them. The reasoning goes: "If they are that powerful and that trusted, they must be hiding something huge." You hear it in familiar accusations: "NASA's budget is not for exploration; it is for maintaining the lie," or "All their photos of Earth are composites—why can't they show us just one real image?" And, of course, "The same agency that faked the moon landing wants you to believe the globe."

All of this leans heavily on an appeal to suspicion—a rhetorical strategy that does not need solid proof, just doubt. By making the evidence look manufactured and the motives sound corrupt, the burden of proof flips completely. The Flat Earther does not have to prove the Earth is flat; they just have to make you question the source of the globe model (Lewandowsky et al., 2012).

Science as a whole gets pulled into the frame. Scientists are often recast as "high priests of scientism," portrayed as demanding blind faith instead of earning trust through discovery. This is framing through analogy, comparing scientific consensus to religious dogma (Chong & Druckman, 2007). It is a clever way of weaponizing faith itself: "If you trust science, you are just practicing a different religion—and you are just as blind as any other believer."

There is also a strong layer of visual rhetoric here (Foss, 2017). The constant attacks on images—calling them "CGI" or "fake composites"—play on the sheer power of what we see. In a world where pictures are treated as proof, casting every photo as a lie undercuts one of the most persuasive kinds of evidence we have.

Psychologically, NASA makes such an effective villain because it takes a massive, abstract idea like "the corrupt system" or "the global elite" and compresses it into something concrete, nameable, and easy to hit. That is a classic move called personification of the opposition—turning a sprawling, faceless idea into a single name or logo makes it easier to fight, easier to fear, and easier to rally against.

Flat Earth rhetoric does not just accuse NASA and science of lying; it turns them into the story's engine. They become the perfect deceivers: trusted, authoritative, and therefore the most shocking to expose. That sense of betrayal is not just an emotional byproduct of the story—it is the fuel that drives it. Furthermore, in this elaborate narrative, NASA is never acting alone. A lie this big, they argue, always needs an even greater hand pulling the strings behind the curtain.

Government as the Puppet Master

If NASA is the visible face of the lie, then in the Flat Earth story, the hand pulling the strings belongs to an even bigger, more shadowy power: the government. In this version of the narrative, the government is not just another player; it is the ultimate orchestrator. That framing makes the conspiracy feel not just massive, but total—inescapable.

Flat Earth rhetoric almost always widens its scope beyond space agencies to include a vast, secret network of authorities. Governments, militaries, powerful global organizations—all allegedly working together in a single, coordinated effort to keep the truth buried. This is a textbook example of conspiratorial framing, a rhetorical technique where separate institutions and unrelated events are woven into one highly organized, sinister plot (Douglas et al., 2017). By tying NASA's supposed deception to the reach of government power, the story immediately raises the stakes: the lie is not just one agency's secret; it is the entire system's.

Flat Earth content drives this point home with familiar lines: "NASA is just the storefront. The real owners are the governments of the world." Or, "Every space agency answers to the same masters." Another staple: "All governments are working together to keep the lie alive," often followed by the sarcastic jab, "Funny how they cannot agree on anything—except hiding the truth." This is an excellent example of amplification through scale. By expanding the villain from one institution (NASA) to many (all governments, militaries, global organizations), the conspiracy suddenly feels enormous and unstoppable. And here is the rhetorical payoff: the bigger and more powerful the enemy, the more heroic the believer feels in standing against it.

Another subtle device here is ethos transfer (Pfau & Wan, 2006). Any distrust or skepticism people already carry toward governments gets quietly redirected onto specific targets like NASA and mainstream science. The hidden message is simple: if you cannot trust the government on anything, then anything linked to it—like scientific consensus on the shape of the Earth—must also be corrupt.

Emotionally, this story taps hard into pathos, especially the fear of being controlled and the universal human drive for autonomy. Believing in a flat world is not framed as just a matter of evidence; it's pitched as an act of rebellion, a way to reclaim personal freedom from a hidden authority bent on controlling your reality.

The language also leans heavily on monolithic framing, painting dozens of different governments and countless individuals as one single, unified, evil force (Entman, 1993). That extreme simplification feeds directly into the binary frame—the false dichotomy we have already seen (Walton, 1989). The choice becomes stark: either you accept the official story and submit to this oppressive control, or you courageously reject it and "wake up" to the truth. No middle ground, no shades of gray.

Psychologically, casting the government as the "puppet master" adds both danger and purpose to the Flat Earth story. Rhetorically, it is a deliberate escalation: the villain is not just lying; they are actively shaping your entire perception of reality. And once the story pins down a villain that powerful, it sets the stage for the next persuasive move—the strange comfort that comes from finally naming the source of everything that feels wrong in the world.

The Comfort of Blame

That pivotal moment when vague suspicion hardens into clear-cut blame is what gives this narrative its real weight. It shifts the story from being just a theory into a direct accusation—and for many, accusation feels a lot like certainty. The enemy stops being a fuzzy "them" and becomes someone you can actually point to. That simple act of pointing is itself a powerful piece of persuasion.

Every compelling story needs resolution, and in Flat Earth rhetoric, that resolution often comes in the form of blame. This belief system does not just imply a deception exists; it confidently names the deceivers. That move turns nagging doubt into rock-solid certainty, delivering an emotional gut punch to the believer.

This is scapegoating in its purest form—a rhetorical device where one group or entity is blamed for a massive, often overwhelming problem (Girard, 1986). Scapegoating does something remarkable: it takes chaos and distills it into a single, simple cause-and-effect story. Suddenly, the world is not messy or confusing; it has been corrupted on purpose. The chosen villain becomes the clean, easy answer to every unsettling question.

Flat Earth content frames this blame as both a shocking revelation and undeniable proof. You will hear claims like, "They have been hiding God's creation for centuries, and we are finally exposing them," which pushes the conspiracy to a cosmic scale. Alternatively, "The globe lie is the greatest crime ever committed against humanity," framing it as an unforgivable betrayal. And then there is the chilling line, "We have been enslaved by their deception since birth—and they know it," which drives the accusation straight into personal territory.

All of these lines lean hard on pathos, tapping into emotions like anger, betrayal, and righteous outrage (Aristotle, trans. 2007). But they also pull in an appeal to justice, a rhetorical strategy that casts belief as a moral duty—not just about uncovering hidden truth, but about correcting a profound wrong (Perelman & Olbrechts-Tyteca, 1969).

Blame also creates a shortcut through motivational framing. If "they" are wholly responsible for this massive lie, then "we" are morally bound to fight back. The story stops being just a theory; it becomes a call to action, demanding loyalty and engagement from every believer.

Another layer here is moral framing. Casting the deceivers as inherently evil and Flat Earth believers as undeniably righteous does not just simplify the narrative—it elevates it into an epic struggle. The debate no longer sits on the level of evidence; it becomes a battle between good and evil. And that is a frame that's incredibly hard to argue against (Chong & Druckman, 2007; Entman, 1993).

Rhetorically, naming the villain provides narrative closure. It gives the story a clear beginning (the original lie), a dramatic middle (the process of exposure and "awakening"), and a satisfying sense of an impending showdown. Even when the evidence is thin or contradictory, the complete arc—especially with a villain included—makes the story feel whole and internally consistent. That sense of completeness powerfully reinforces belief (Bruner, 1990; Polkinghorne, 1988).

Psychologically, blame offers emotional relief from cognitive dissonance. Rhetorically, it locks the story in place by giving the audience both a concrete enemy to fight and a moral reason to keep fighting. And once the villain is named, the narrative takes one more step: the enemy stops being just a character in the story and becomes the "proof" that the story itself must be true.

When the Villain Becomes the Proof

Beyond simply naming and blaming the enemy, this narrative takes an even more insidious step: it turns the opposition itself into the proof the conspiracy needs. Every denial from NASA, every eye-roll from a scientist, gets instantly reframed as confirmation: "Of course they are lying—that is what liars do." In this logic loop, the enemy's very existence—and their predictable reactions—become the most substantial evidence of all.

Flat Earth rhetoric does not just use the villain as part of the story; it often turns the villain into the evidence. The accusation becomes a perfectly sealed circle: "They are hiding the truth, which proves the truth exists." This is a classic self-sealing argument, where a claim cleverly uses its own assumption as evidence (Kitcher, 1993). The story no longer depends on outside, verifiable proof. Instead, the supposed act of hiding or denying becomes the ultimate validation. That is why this belief system can survive even in the face of overwhelming scientific data—because every rebuttal slides neatly into the story as confirmation.

You can see this logic play out in familiar lines: "They do not censor lies—they censor the truth," turning content removal into proof. Or, "All the censorship just proves we are right," treating suppression as a badge of honor. And then there is the chilling, "The fact they laugh at us tells you everything—we are over the target," recasting ridicule as a sign of victory.

Each of these uses what we can call confirmation framing—a technique that reinterprets any opposition as validation. Instead of weakening the argument, ridicule, censorship, or pushback becomes rhetorical fuel, making believers feel even more certain.

This also taps straight into an appeal to persecution, a persuasive strategy where being attacked, mocked, or silenced is spun as clear evidence of righteousness (Douglas & Sutton, 2011). The more resistance the narrative meets, the "truer" it paradoxically becomes.

Layered on top of that is a subtle argument from silence (Walton, 1996). The absence of what believers consider "real evidence" (for example, a single unedited photo of Earth from space taken by a layman) is reframed as proof of a cover-up. If the villain is not showing the "truth," it must be because it is too damning to reveal.

Flat Earth rhetoric often combines this with a full inversion of evidence, where what would normally disprove a claim becomes its strongest support (Cook & Lewandowsky, 2011). Every debunking, every scientific explanation, is flipped on its head: "If they have to explain it that hard, they must be hiding something." The more effort mainstream science puts into refuting the belief, the more it seems to confirm the conspiracy to those inside it.

Psychologically, this creates an almost impenetrable safety net. Any contradiction, any fact that should unravel the story, is easily absorbed and turned into more proof. Rhetorically, it locks the entire narrative into a closed system. The villain stops being just a character in the story and becomes the keystone holding the entire structure in place—using their very opposition as the ultimate evidence.

The Hero's Journey: Framing the Believer as the Protagonist

A wall can hold a story, but only a heartbeat can make it live. The hero turns a claim into an identity, building a belief that feels like your own reflection.

Every great story needs a hero, and in this belief system, that hero is always the believer. The narrative doesn't just describe a world or reveal a hidden truth—it casts the audience right into the starring role. This is classic narrative framing, where the story isn't simply told to the listener but carefully built around them as the central character (Bruner, 1990; Polkinghorne, 1988).

Instead of leaning on hard evidence, the language focuses on elevating the listener's identity. This dynamic also leans on ethos construction—the deliberate building of credibility to make a claim feel authoritative before the evidence even arrives (Aristotle, trans. 2007). When the rhetoric says, "Only a few are brave enough to see past the lie," it isn't offering proof—it's offering a prestigious role.

That role runs on pathos, drawing from pride and courage. The believer isn't just curious; they're framed as the lone, insightful seeker standing against impossible odds. The story stops being a model of the world and turns into a personal journey of transformation. This structure borrows heavily from mythic framing, echoing the archetypal hero's journey found in legends, folklore, and epic tales across cultures (Campbell, 2008).

A key device working here is direct address—the language that speaks right to the audience with "you" and "your," making them feel chosen, unique, and special. That subtle move blurs the line between the larger story and the individual self until the two are woven tightly together.

Rhetorically, this does more than make the story engaging. It binds the belief to personal identity. When the narrative casts you as the undeniable protagonist, walking away from the Flat Earth isn't just changing your mind about a scientific fact; it feels like erasing yourself from the heart of a heroic story. That's not just persuasion—it's narrative entrapment, making it incredibly hard to step away.

This powerful framing of the believer as hero sets up the next crucial move in the story: pitting that newly minted hero against the entire world.

Standing Against the World: Contrast as Persuasion

One of the strongest currents running through this narrative builds directly on that heroic role we just explored: the powerful feeling of standing alone against overwhelming opposition. The story isn't just about a different model of the Earth—it's about courage in the face of a world that's been completely deceived. This is a sharp use of contrast framing, the rhetorical move of defining something by setting it hard against its opposite (Chong & Druckman, 2007; Entman, 1993).

The tension between "us," the awakened few, and "them," the sleeping masses, gives the story its charge. Even when the language doesn't use those exact words, the frame is impossible to miss. Lines like, "Most people are too scared to question what they've been taught," don't just make a claim—they draw a deliberate line in the sand, building the believer's identity in direct opposition to the majority.

This dynamic also leans on ethos construction. Inside the story, the courage to stand apart from the crowd is treated as proof of unique insight. If everyone else is fooled, then the one who resists must be closer to the truth (Aristotle, trans. 2007).

There's a heavy dose of pathos here, too, especially in the emotional weight of isolation. But the narrative flips that isolation on its head, turning it into a badge of honor and a deep source of pride (Aristotle, trans. 2007). It taps into a universal, mythic theme: the lone voice speaking truth to entrenched power. That archetype—the solitary rebel—has echoed through countless legends and epic tales (Campbell, 2008), and here it's given new life.

Rhetorically, this is also a clean example of inversion framing. The majority, which normally signals social proof and validation, is recast as evidence of mass deception (Douglas & Sutton, 2011; Kahneman & Tversky, 1979). The few are right precisely because they are few. It's a persuasive twist that flips the usual rules of consensus upside down.

Psychologically, this approach locks identity to opposition. Rhetorically, it creates a self-sustaining loop: the more people reject the Flat Earth, the more it confirms the believer's role as the brave, insightful outsider. Resistance doesn't weaken the story—it's what keeps it alive and burning.

And once the believer is cast as both hero and rebel, the narrative needs a voice—or many voices—to carry that conviction out into the world.

The Confident Truth-Teller: Performing Ethos

Enter the confident truth-teller: the voice of absolute certainty in this narrative. This isn't just someone who talks about the belief—they embody it. Every compelling story needs a clear voice of authority, someone who doesn't just deliver the message but becomes the message. In the Flat Earth world, that person is the confident truth-teller: calm, unshakable, and utterly sure of themselves. They don't just argue; they perform their conviction. And that performance is what makes the message land so effectively. This entire act is a deliberate play on ethos, the rhetorical foundation of credibility and trustworthiness (Aristotle, trans. 2007).

At the center of this technique is what we can call a credibility illusion. It's that powerful sense that someone is knowledgeable and trustworthy even when they have no actual evidence or expertise to back it up. This illusion is built through subtle, almost invisible cues: a steady tone of voice, confident posture, direct eye contact, and an unhurried way of speaking (Burgoon et al., 1996; Mehrabian & Ferris, 1967). Before they've said anything concrete, the confident truth-teller has already signaled authority. The trust they create isn't grounded in the content of their message but in the way they deliver it. This taps into what psychologists call the fluency heuristic—the mental shortcut where smooth, easy-to-process information feels more true simply because it's delivered cleanly and confidently (Reber & Schwarz, 1999).

Performative certainty is their strongest weapon. Here, confidence itself becomes evidence. A claim with shaky logic or no support at all, when stated with absolute conviction, can feel more solid than a carefully reasoned argument delivered with any hesitation. In this belief system, certainty isn't just a byproduct of conviction—it's engineered to function as the proof itself. This is amplified by the illusory truth effect, which shows that a statement repeated often enough—and especially with unwavering confidence—starts to feel true regardless of its actual validity (Hasher et al., 1977).

These influencers know how to layer visual and verbal signals to strengthen that authority. Props like globes they can dismiss, charts dramatically revealed, or even a simple backdrop arranged to look like a professional studio or lecture hall all feed into the performance. Visual rhetoric of this kind signals legitimacy before a word is spoken (Messaris & Abraham, 2001). Language plays its part too: short, punchy phrases like "water finds its level" or "they don't teach you that in school" act as sticky, common-sense sound bites. When spoken with absolute certainty, they bypass critical thought and lodge themselves in memory.

The confident truth-teller doesn't just narrate the Flat Earth story—they are the story. Persuasively, that mix of persona, performance, and manufactured credibility can overpower even the strongest scientific data or logical counterarguments. The voice isn't just part of the narrative; it's the narrative's core.

With the believer now positioned as a hero and guided by a voice that radiates authority, this belief system turns to its most subtle, but most dangerous, test: the handling of doubt.

Doubt as the Villain, Certainty as the Weapon

Against the bold conviction of the confident truth-teller, this narrative introduces a quieter but incredibly powerful antagonist: doubt itself.

In the Flat Earth story, you have your obvious enemies—NASA, the government, "the system"—but lurking underneath is a more insidious one: hesitation. Inside this belief system, even the smallest sliver of doubt isn't treated as healthy curiosity; it's cast as betrayal. If you start to waver, you're not just questioning—you're seen as sliding back into the deception you supposedly "woke up" from. That's how the story demands all-or-nothing commitment: total buy-in or nothing at all.

This is where binary framing hits full force (Walton, 1989). It's the rhetorical move that crushes everything into two sides: you're either completely awake and "in the know," or you're entirely fooled and still "asleep." No middle ground. No shades of gray. In this setup, doubt isn't just a crack in the story—it becomes the villain you're told to fight, both inside yourself and when talking to others.

To keep that internal villain at bay, certainty is elevated to something almost sacred. This is performative certainty in its purest form, the same force the confident truth-teller embodies: the act of delivering absolute conviction as if that conviction itself were evidence (Hasher et al., 1977; Reber & Schwarz, 1999). It's a variation of assertion-as-evidence, where the sheer strength of the statement is designed to stand in for proof. When someone declares, "We know the Earth is flat, no question about it," that unwavering tone is meant to make the debate feel over before it even starts.

The emotional weight here leans heavily on pathos, drawing on ideas of inner strength and courage (Aristotle, trans. 2007). In this frame, doubt isn't a question; it's weakness. Certainty, on the other hand, is framed as bravery—the mark of someone willing to stand firm in their newfound "truth" even as everyone else supposedly gives in to the "lie."

There's also a clever inversion at work. In genuine science, doubt is a tool. It's how progress happens and theories get refined. Flat Earth rhetoric flips that on its head with inversion framing (Cook & Lewandowsky, 2011; Douglas & Sutton, 2011). The very thing that makes a claim stronger in real inquiry—open questioning—is recast as a flaw, a weakness, even a trap set by the "system." In this belief system, questioning isn't critical thinking; it's a step back into deception.

That's why this part of the story hits so hard. Psychologically, it builds an almost impenetrable shield around the belief. Rhetorically, it forges certainty into both weapon and armor—the thing used to assert the "truth" and the thing protecting the believer's mind. Once doubt itself is cast as the enemy, the language doesn't just defend the story; it locks the door from the inside, sealing the believer in.

And once certainty is framed as both weapon and shield, the story makes its final, crucial move: tying belief directly to identity.

The Ego Hook

At the heart of the Flat Earth story's lasting grip is something much deeper than evidence: it's the way the belief latches onto a person's sense of self.

Every persuasive story has that point where it stops being just a story and grabs you so hard it won't let go. In this narrative, that grip isn't on facts or data—it's on identity. That's why the ego hook—a tactic that ties belief directly to a person's sense of self—isn't about persuasion in the usual sense (Bruner, 1990; Polkinghorne, 1988).

Rhetorically, the ego hook blends pathos (emotional appeal) with ethos construction (building credibility around the audience's own self-image). Instead of saying, "Here's the evidence for a flat Earth," the language reframes it as, "You're the kind of sharp, brave person who can see the truth when others are still blind to it." That one shift moves the focus away from facts and straight onto how you see yourself, offering a flattering reflection back at you (Aristotle, trans. 2007).

Psychologically, it works because we're wired to protect our identity. If believing the Earth is flat becomes part of who you are—the smart one, the brave one, the "awakened" one who sees through the grand deception—then questioning that belief doesn't feel like changing your mind about a model of the Earth. It feels like betraying yourself, like erasing a core part of who you've become.

Flat Earth rhetoric reinforces that tie between belief and self with lines like, "You broke free from the greatest deception humanity has ever known," or "Most people can't handle the truth, but you can, because you're strong enough." These aren't just arguments; they're invitations to step into a heroic role that feels uniquely validating. That's why the ego hook isn't about persuasion in the usual sense. It's about creating a deep, personal connection that makes the belief feel inseparable from you.

There's also a layer of motivational framing here, where the story casts the believer as a key part of a critical mission (Chong & Druckman, 2007). Once the ego hook is in place, the narrative doesn't just offer a worldview; it hands you a purpose:

spread the truth, "wake others up," and fight the deception. That sense of mission makes the bond between belief and identity even tighter.

Rhetorically, the ego hook is one of the hardest techniques to break. It doesn't just anchor the Flat Earth idea in your mind; it anchors you inside it. Once belief and identity are fused this closely, letting go of the idea doesn't feel like dropping a theory. It feels like losing a piece of yourself.

Mystery and Forbidden Knowledge: The Rhetoric of the Hidden Truth

Nothing feels more valuable than what's been hidden. The promise of forbidden knowledge builds doors where none existed and makes the lock itself feel like proof of the treasure inside.

Few things are more persuasive—or more tempting—than the promise of a secret. Flat Earth rhetoric thrives on this, framing its story not just as an alternative view of the world but as the ultimate truth that "they" desperately don't want you to know. That sense of something hidden hits a deep emotional chord: a mix of raw curiosity and rebellious defiance.

At its core, this is a textbook appeal to secrecy, a rhetorical move that gives information immense power just by making it feel forbidden or suppressed (Simons, 1971). The harder this "truth" seems to reach, the more valuable and urgent it feels to the believer. When the narrative claims, "They've been hiding this for centuries," it isn't just tossing out a line—it's wrapping the Flat Earth idea in an instant aura of weight and importance.

This also leans heavily on pathos, tapping into the emotional pull of exclusivity. Being told you've uncovered something hidden—or grasped a truth others can't see—creates an instant sense of privilege, validation, and even intellectual superiority (Aristotle, trans. 2007). It's also a clever use of ethos construction, making the audience feel uniquely qualified and insightful enough to see through the grand deception.

Rhetorically, the "hidden truth" frame supercharges the story's stakes. If this knowledge is really being suppressed by powerful forces, it must be dangerous to them—and therefore, it must be true. That's confirmation framing at work (Chong & Druckman, 2007; Entman, 1993). The secrecy itself becomes the evidence.

There's also a layer of narrative suspense carefully built into this approach. Phrases like "What they don't want you to see..." or "The truth they've kept from you all your life..." aren't just hooks; they act like pacing devices in a thriller, making the story feel like a live discovery and pulling the listener deeper into the "revelation."

Psychologically, this taps straight into our hardwired curiosity and our desire to feel empowered with rare, privileged knowledge. Rhetorically, it flips that universal need into a tool: the more hidden and forbidden the "truth" feels, the more persuasive the Flat Earth story becomes—often regardless of evidence.

And this seductive promise of a concealed truth sets up the next powerful layer of persuasion: the addictive sense of belonging to an exclusive inner circle.

Being 'In the Know': Exclusive Ethos

Part of what makes the Flat Earth story so magnetic isn't just the claim itself—it's the feeling that you've stepped into a reality most people will never see. In this narrative, believing isn't just about understanding a different model of the Earth; it's about entering an exclusive circle of insiders who "get it." That intoxicating sense of belonging and rarity is what gives this piece of the story so much pull.

The language here builds credibility through belonging. It's a form of ethos construction, but instead of leaning on outside evidence or authority, it draws power from your identity and your place inside this special group (Aristotle, trans. 2007; Tajfel & Turner, 1979). When the story says that only a select few can truly see the truth, it's not offering proof in the usual sense. It's handing you a coveted role and, with it, the satisfaction of feeling inherently credible just because you can perceive what others can't.

That pull runs on emotion as much as logic—maybe more. It's a textbook appeal to pathos, tapping into the deep human need to belong and the pride of being one of the rare, enlightened few (Aristotle, trans. 2007). This isn't an argument you pick apart with your head; it's one you feel in your gut. It's the rush of believing you're part of something special, set apart, and intellectually superior.

The narrative pushes that even further by tying it tightly to who you are at your core. This is identity framing in action, linking the belief directly to your self-image (Bruner, 1990). If you can "see the truth," then you must be the kind of person who can't be fooled—someone insightful, discerning, and sharp. That subtle shift makes questioning the belief feel less like challenging an idea and more like doubting your own intelligence and worth.

Underneath it all, the story draws a hard dividing line: those who understand and those who don't, the "awake" and the "asleep." That kind of rigid split is a potent use of othering, a rhetorical move that strengthens the in-group by clearly defining itself against a lesser out-group (Tajfel & Turner, 1979).

Ultimately, the promise of being "in the know" has less to do with the information itself and everything to do with what holding that information says about you. It's not persuasion through facts; it's persuasion through identity.

And that deep sense of exclusivity—the feeling of being part of a hidden inner circle—feeds seamlessly into one of the narrative's most enduring and seductive tools: using unanswered questions as irresistible bait.

The Hook of the Unknown

Flat Earth rhetoric doesn't really run on answers or proofs—it runs on questions. Compelling, lingering questions. These questions are dangled just far enough out of reach to create a constant sense of mystery: "Why are there no real photos of Earth?" "What are they hiding beyond Antarctica?" The real power isn't in the claim itself but in the space between what's asked and what's left unsaid.

That space is where human curiosity takes over. This is persuasion built on what's often called the hook of the unknown: using unanswered questions as irresistible bait to keep the audience leaning in and searching for answers (Loewenstein, 1994). In this setup, the lack of explanation from "official" sources becomes the point. That silence sets the stage for the Flat Earth story to step in with its "truth" as the only thing that can fill the gap.

This is also where question framing does its work. The language is crafted so the question itself quietly suggests the answer. "Have you ever wondered why they never show you the edge?" doesn't just stir curiosity; it slips in the idea that the edge exists and is being hidden. The question isn't really an open invitation—it's a guide rail, nudging you exactly where the narrative wants you to go (Lakoff, 2004).

There's a strong emotional charge behind this technique, too. Curiosity mixed with suspicion creates a subtle but potent form of pathos (Aristotle, trans. 2007). This isn't simple wonder; it's wonder sharpened into defiance, fueled by the thrill of believing you're about to uncover something profound that "they" tried to bury.

The hook of the unknown works so well because it rarely feels like persuasion. It feels like discovery—a personal awakening to hidden knowledge. Rhetorically, it's a soft trap that doesn't look like one: the carefully crafted question becomes the answer, and the mystery itself turns into proof.

And that pull of the unknown, that thrill of unraveling secrets, leads straight to the next move in the story: making the very act of secrecy itself the ultimate evidence.

Forbidden Knowledge as Proof

One of the most powerful twists in Flat Earth rhetoric is how it turns secrecy itself into proof. The story doesn't just claim the truth is being hidden—it argues that the act of hiding it is the evidence that makes the claim real. In this frame, the cover-up isn't a side detail; it's the centerpiece, the linchpin holding the entire argument together.

This is confirmation framing at its most effective (Chong & Druckman, 2007; Entman, 1993). Instead of relying on outside validation or tangible evidence, the logic flips: if they're working this hard to suppress it, that must mean it's true. The lack of proof isn't treated as a weakness. It's spun into the strongest proof of all.

That move leans heavily on an appeal to persecution (Douglas & Sutton, 2011). Any censorship, ridicule, or pushback against the Flat Earth idea is instantly reframed as validation. "If they're attacking it," the story tells you, "it must be because it's a threat to those in power." In this inverted logic, the enemy's reaction—their denial, their attempts to discredit—becomes the believer's ultimate confirmation.

Layered on top is another key device: inversion of evidence (Cook & Lewandowsky, 2011). Anything that would normally disprove the claim gets flipped to support it. When mainstream science explains why we see curvature from an airplane, the story doesn't really challenge the explanation point by point. Instead, it reframes the explanation itself as evidence of deception: if they have to work that hard to justify it, they must be hiding something. The more effort goes into debunking Flat Earth, the more convincing the conspiracy feels to those inside it.

There's also a strong emotional pull here. The idea of holding something forbidden taps directly into pathos, especially the appeal of defiance and rebellion (Aristotle, trans. 2007). Believing isn't framed as just knowing a hidden truth; it's framed as courage—actively protecting that truth from those conspiring to bury it.

Psychologically, this technique sticks because it seals the argument into a closed loop. Rhetorically, it's even more powerful: it creates a self-reinforcing frame that doesn't just survive without evidence but feeds on that absence, making the story remarkably resistant to challenge.

All of this carefully sets the stage for the narrative's emotional peak: the exhilarating rush of discovery.

The Thrill of Discovery

Every carefully crafted part of the Flat Earth story leads to one crucial moment: the exhilarating rush of feeling like you've uncovered something monumental. The exact model of the world often matters less than that electrifying spark when the pieces seem to click into place. The narrative isn't just designed to deliver this revelation—it's designed to make the feeling of revelation itself serve as proof.

The persuasive force behind that revelation comes from how strongly it leans on pathos, persuasion through emotion (Aristotle, trans. 2007). The story wraps the initial "aha" experience—whether it's questioning a NASA photo or rethinking the horizon—in a wave of wonder, defiance, and intellectual triumph. When a realization carries that kind of emotional weight, our minds are wired to tag it as truth, creating a potent cognitive shortcut (Kahneman, 2011).

Flat Earth rhetoric makes this spark of discovery feel deeply personal. Instead of saying, "Here is the evidence," the story whispers, "Look what you found. Look what you saw for yourself." That framing creates a powerful sense of personal ownership over the moment of realization. It's narrative immersion at its strongest, pulling the listener so far into the story that they don't just hear it—they live it (Polkinghorne, 1988). The belief doesn't feel handed down from an outside authority; it feels earned through their own insight.

That sense of owning the discovery is exactly what empowerment framing amplifies. By casting the believer as an independent thinker who broke free on their own, the language reinforces the idea that this breakthrough wasn't given to them—it was claimed by them (Chong & Druckman, 2007). Even when influencers are guiding the path, the narrative sells the journey as self-driven, which makes the belief far harder to release later. At that point, letting go of the Flat Earth story doesn't feel like abandoning an argument—it feels like undoing a personal victory.

The emotional charge tied to that breakthrough becomes part of the argument itself. This is confirmation framing turned inward (Entman, 1993). If the discovery feels this profound and this real, the story suggests, then the truth behind it must be real as well. The intensity of the experience becomes the evidence, locking in conviction without the need for external validation.

The thrill of discovery isn't just a byproduct of the Flat Earth narrative; it's one of its most carefully engineered tools. By turning that surge of revelation into self-validating proof, the story doesn't simply tell people what to believe—it makes them feel the belief so powerfully that walking away becomes almost unthinkable.

Presentism: Framing the Past to Serve the Present

Rewrite the past, and you reshape the foundation. In a constructed belief, history isn't a record—it's a tool for shoring up the walls of the present.

Flat Earth rhetoric often looks backward, twisting history to legitimize what it claims in the present. In this narrative, history isn't treated as a factual record; it becomes a pliable tool. Old maps, ancient texts, and selective stories are pulled into the tale, then reshaped to say exactly what the modern Flat Earth claim needs them to say. This isn't simply referencing the past—it's actively reframing it.

At the center of this move is historical framing, the technique of interpreting past events and artifacts entirely through the biased lens of a current belief (Chong & Druckman, 2007; Entman, 1993). Instead of asking what a piece of history meant in its own time, the Flat Earth story bends it to serve today's agenda. A centuries-old map, for example, isn't treated as a reflection of its era but as "evidence" of what the modern believer insists is true now.

This strategy leans heavily on anachronism—the rhetorical habit of imposing modern ideas or contexts on historical sources where they don't belong (Kelly, 1978). A passage from an ancient text is read as if it were written for today's scientific debates, ignoring its original meaning. The real historical context fades, and the Flat Earth narrative fills the gap with its own pre-set conclusion.

Layered on top is a heavy dose of cherry-picking. Quotes, drawings, and fragments of history that can be made to fit the story are amplified as "proof," while anything that contradicts the claim is dismissed as irrelevant, corrupted, or part of the cover-up (Walton, 2008). What's left isn't history; it's a carefully curated version of the past, selectively built to support the belief.

Rhetorically, bending history does more than offer "evidence." It creates a sense of continuity and legacy. It paints the Flat Earth idea as an ancient thread woven through time, supposedly understood by sages and civilizations long before. That manufactured lineage lends the modern narrative a false weight and credibility, even when the history itself has been distorted to fit.

And once the story casts this long, selective shadow over the past, it sets up the next tactic: choosing only the pieces of history that can be molded into support, and discarding everything else.

Cherry-Picking and Anachronisms

When Flat Earth rhetoric dips into history, it almost never takes the full, complicated picture. Instead, it carefully carves out the bits that can be made to fit the story. This selective use of evidence is classic cherry-picking (Walton, 2008). By spotlighting only what appears to support the claim and conveniently ignoring the rest, the narrative constructs a version of the past that feels solid—while leaving out the pieces that would challenge or completely contradict it.

One of the favorite tools for this tactic is the obscure phrase in an ancient text or a single line from a historical figure. These fragments, ripped from their original context, are spun into what sounds like early warnings of a massive global cover-up. This is where anachronism slides in. Modern scientific ideas or even contemporary conspiracy language get projected onto centuries-old words, as if those writers were secretly debating the exact same issues Flat Earth influencers raise today (Kelly, 1978).

The real persuasive weight comes from what's missing. Stripping away the context—the beliefs of the era, the author's intent, the limits of knowledge at the time—creates a powerful illusion of agreement across centuries. A map drawn long before accurate measurements or satellites can be held up as "undeniable proof" of a flat Earth, while the obvious reality—the severe limitations of early cartography and cosmology—is pushed to the side and forgotten.

There's also an emotional layer at work. These fragments are often framed as if they've miraculously survived despite a massive effort to erase them. That framing adds a subtle pathos-driven pull. The pieces feel like treasures, sacred clues that "the truth" could never fully be buried (Aristotle, trans. 2007). Even scraps of history gain enormous weight when they're presented as relics of a suppressed reality.

Together, cherry-picking and anachronism create what looks like a sturdy bridge back through time. It doesn't matter if that bridge is made of mismatched, misread planks. What matters is the illusion—that it connects the modern Flat Earth claim to the authority and weight of the past.

And once the story lays that false bridge, it takes the next step: reaching even further back to draw on the perceived wisdom and authority of antiquity itself.

The Authority of the Ancients

Flat Earth rhetoric often doesn't just borrow pieces of history; it reaches deep into antiquity to borrow weight and authority. When the story invokes ancient maps, revered scriptures, or whispers of "forgotten knowledge," it isn't just pointing to evidence in the modern sense. It's reaching for a form of credibility that feels almost beyond question. Old ideas are framed as inherently pure, untouched by modern corruption, and therefore presented as more trustworthy than anything contemporary science can offer.

This strategy plugs directly into ethos, the appeal to credibility (Aristotle, trans. 2007). But here, the credibility isn't drawn from the speaker's expertise or character—it comes almost entirely from the age of the source itself. A phrase like "the ancients knew…" isn't really about the specifics of what they knew. It's a rhetorical shortcut, borrowing the perceived wisdom and unquestioned legitimacy of the past to lend enormous weight to the modern Flat Earth claim. The argument shifts away from what is true and centers on who across the centuries has the perceived authority to declare it.

There's also a strong psychological undertone. Ancient knowledge carries an air of mystery, of something profound lost to time and now miraculously rediscovered. The rhetoric plays this expertly through pathos, evoking nostalgia for a simpler, "purer" era when humanity, the story suggests, was closer to "real truth" before modern institutions corrupted it (Aristotle, trans. 2007). That emotional pull turns the appeal to antiquity into more than a historical argument—it becomes a call back to humanity's unspoiled origins.

Rhetorically, this is a classic appeal to tradition (Walton, 2008). It rests on the assumption that if an idea has deep roots in the past, it must carry authenticity or truth. Flat Earth narratives amplify this by casting modern science as manipulative and deceitful, while elevating ancient voices as pristine and trustworthy. The contrast isn't just informational—it's moral, pitting supposed ancient wisdom against modern corruption.

Layered on top is a subtle use of mythic framing. The ancients aren't just historical figures; they're cast as keepers of a profound secret, a sacred lineage of truth-seekers that the modern believer is now stepping into (Campbell, 2008). This shifts the argument away from evidence entirely and into a story of inherited wisdom and cosmic purpose, which is far more persuasive on an emotional and identity-driven level.

By leaning on the perceived authority of the ancients, the rhetoric builds a bridge so strong it bypasses the need for modern scrutiny or scientific validation altogether. This isn't just a claim about the shape of the world—it's a claim about who truly has the right to speak about it. And the further back that voice is made to sound, the louder and more compelling it becomes.

That carefully built bridge into antiquity sets the stage for the next move: reshaping the past itself until the present Flat Earth belief doesn't just look plausible—it feels inevitable.

Rewriting as Legitimizing

Flat Earth rhetoric doesn't just borrow bits of history or cherry-pick what fits. It goes a step further: it reshapes history itself, crafting a version of the past that makes the present belief feel not just possible, but inevitable. This isn't a casual retelling. It's a deliberate act of rewriting historical narratives so that the Flat Earth story appears to have always been there—a timeless truth waiting for the "awakened" to uncover it.

This technique leans heavily on narrative framing—the way a story shapes how facts are seen by controlling their context (Chong & Druckman, 2007; Entman, 1993). Here, the context being manipulated isn't just a single event but entire stretches of human history. When the rhetoric claims, "People always knew the Earth was flat until modern science corrupted the truth," it isn't presenting evidence. It's reframing centuries of intellectual progress into a neat, continuous line that points straight to the modern Flat Earth belief.

Running alongside this is continuity framing. By carefully stitching together selective moments and anecdotes while ignoring contradictions, the story creates the illusion of an unbroken thread of belief stretching back through time. The gaps, the messy debates, the evolving cosmologies—they all get smoothed over until the fabricated past appears to flow naturally into the present.

On an emotional level, this rewriting of history taps into pathos through a powerful appeal to restoration. The story suggests the believer isn't embracing a fringe theory but reclaiming something authentic and pure—a lost truth obscured for too long (Aristotle, trans. 2007). That sense of restoration adds a moral charge, making belief feel not just correct, but righteous and courageous.

The rhetorical power here doesn't come from historical accuracy (which is often absent) but from the instant legitimacy this fabricated past creates. Once history is bent to perfectly mirror the modern claim, the belief stops feeling like a challenge to authority and starts feeling like the authority itself—a voice echoing across millennia, now finally restored.

And once this carefully constructed version of history is in place, the story adds its final layer: making that entire arc simple, clean, and easy for the believer to hold onto.

The Comfort of a Simple Storyline

Flat Earth rhetoric isn't just about arguing "facts" or debating historical accuracy. At a deeper level, it delivers a story that feels clean, direct, and incredibly easy to grasp. In a world overflowing with complex scientific models, nuanced data, and shifting information, that simplicity isn't just a feature of the narrative—it's one of its most powerful tools of persuasion.

At the core of this approach is cognitive ease, the psychological effect where information feels more true when it's easy for the mind to process (Kahneman, 2011; Reber & Schwarz, 1999). A simple phrase like "water always finds its level" bypasses equations and data entirely, offering a conclusion wrapped in an image anyone can instantly picture. The Flat Earth story trims away ambiguity and inconvenient details until it becomes a straight, unbroken line that feels naturally right.

That same simplicity taps into narrative coherence, the way a story's internal consistency can make it feel true even without strong external evidence (Bruner, 1990; Polkinghorne, 1988). When the Flat Earth narrative stitches together its arc—ancient wisdom, suppression by powerful forces, and a glorious rediscovery—the sheer tidiness of the storyline becomes persuasive. A clean, simple arc satisfies the human craving for order and clear cause-and-effect.

Emotionally, this simplicity leans hard on pathos by offering something subtle but profound: relief (Aristotle, trans. 2007). For many, adopting the Flat Earth belief isn't just gaining a new idea—it's shedding the weight of confusion and uncertainty. The messy reality of scientific inquiry, with its constant revisions and probabilities, is swapped for something intuitive, whole, and easy to understand. That sense of clarity doesn't just persuade; it soothes, making the narrative deeply "sticky" because it doesn't just convince the mind—it comforts it.

Rhetorically, that comfort is what locks the entire Flat Earth frame in place. It isn't the individual "proofs" that do the heavy lifting, but the overall shape of the story. Once the narrative feels intuitively right and emotionally satisfying, everything inside it—every distortion, every leap in logic, every appeal to mystery—feels right too.

The Seductive Power of Simplicity

Complex stories leave cracks; simple ones seal them. The easiest answer doesn't just explain the world—it cements it.

Flat Earth rhetoric doesn't try to compete with the abstract, intricate layers of scientific models. Instead, it uses a different strategy: replacing that scientific complexity with a story so clean and straightforward that it instantly feels like common sense. A simple line like "water always finds its level" doesn't read like a technical argument—it lands as a self-evident truth, something you feel like you've always known. That sense of familiarity and intuitive obviousness is where much of its persuasive power comes from.

The strength of this entire approach rests on cognitive ease—the psychological effect where our brains equate simplicity and fluency with truth (Kahneman, 2011; Reber & Schwarz, 1999). When an idea is easy to grasp, process, and repeat, it immediately feels more valid than one wrapped in dense equations or abstract concepts. The mind, craving efficiency, tags the "easy" version as more reliable, even when it lacks depth or evidence. Rhetorically, this isn't an accident; it's a deliberate strategy that turns a mental shortcut into a tool of persuasion.

To make this work, Flat Earth influencers use what can be called reduction framing. Instead of wrestling with the full complexity of physics or astronomy, they cut the story down to a single, seemingly undeniable image: a still, flat body of water. No equations, no variables—just a concrete visual anyone can picture. By stripping away everything except the most basic element, they create the illusion of absolute certainty and undeniable truth (Entman, 1993; Chong & Druckman, 2007).

That simplicity is reinforced through loaded language (Perelman & Olbrechts-Tyteca, 1969). Phrases like "plain truth" and "obvious reality" aren't neutral—they're linguistic cues designed to frame the Flat Earth story as honest and straightforward while casting scientific explanations as intentionally complex or deceptive. The language itself subtly pushes the audience to see simplicity as authenticity and complexity as evidence of a cover-up.

On an emotional level, this taps into pathos through the comfort of clarity (Aristotle, trans. 2007). A simple, unambiguous story doesn't just persuade the mind—it soothes it. In a world full of contradictions, overwhelming data, and shifting information, that sense of intuitive stability feels like relief. For many believers, embracing the Flat Earth model isn't about weighing data—it's about feeling anchored to something simple and unchanging.

There's also contrast framing at work here. Complexity is positioned as confusion, obfuscation, even dishonesty; simplicity is presented as honesty and truth. The narrative doesn't have to win the scientific debate point by point. It only has to make complexity look suspect and simplicity look self-evidently pure.

The reason these simple stories hit so hard isn't because they align with reality, but because they feel true. Rhetorically, simplicity isn't just a style choice—it's a core tool that turns cognitive ease into "evidence" and perceived clarity into conviction.

And once the story builds on that foundation of simplicity, it can take the next step: transforming the gap between "simple" and "complex" into a sharp moral divide.

Clarity vs. Complexity

Flat Earth rhetoric doesn't just make its story simple and intuitive. It takes a bigger step, casting simplicity itself as proof of honesty and truth while painting complexity as a sure sign of deceit, obfuscation, or elitist arrogance. In this frame, the clean explanation isn't just easier to believe—it's presented as the morally superior one.

This is where contrast framing becomes one of the narrative's most effective tools (Entman, 1993; Chong &

Druckman, 2007). The story sets up a hard dichotomy: Flat Earth offers "plain truth," "common sense," and "what anyone can see," while mainstream science allegedly hides reality behind jargon, equations, and convoluted theories. The divide isn't just intellectual—it's moral. Simplicity stands in for purity and honesty; complexity is cast as deliberate obfuscation or even malicious deception.

Language drives this divide even deeper through loaded language (Perelman & Olbrechts-Tyteca, 1969). Words like "clear," "obvious," and "simple" are consistently attached to the Flat Earth story, giving it a quiet moral weight. Meanwhile, terms such as "complicated," "abstract," and "mathematical" are used to describe the scientific model, carrying a subtle, suspicious undertone. The framing plants a powerful idea: the nature of an explanation—whether it feels simple or complex—signals whether it's telling the truth or hiding it.

Cognitive ease resurfaces here, but now it's amplified through direct comparison (Kahneman, 2011; Reber & Schwarz, 1999). The Flat Earth narrative doesn't just make its version simple; it deliberately makes the alternative feel mentally heavy and exhausting to even consider. That contrast does the persuasive work. The story that's easiest to process begins to feel like the truest one—not because of its content, but because it demands so much less effort to understand and defend.

There's also ethos construction woven into this frame (Aristotle, trans. 2007). By portraying the believer as someone who sees through "unnecessary complexity" and "elite obfuscation," the narrative grants them intellectual and moral credibility. Rejecting the "complicated lie" of mainstream science becomes evidence of their clarity, courage, and discernment, reinforcing both personal identity and the belief itself.

On an emotional level, this taps into pathos by offering empowerment. Choosing the Flat Earth story isn't just picking a model of the world—it's framed as a defiant stand for clarity over deception, for honesty over manipulation. That sense of making a righteous choice gives the believer the feeling of taking back control in a world full of noise and hidden agendas.

Rhetorically, this "clarity versus complexity" frame does more than make the Flat Earth narrative appealing. It flips the burden of proof (Walton, 2008). Once simplicity itself is treated as evidence of truth, any detailed or nuanced explanation automatically looks suspect. The simplest claim in the room begins to feel like the most honest—and therefore, the most true.

That weaponization of simplicity sets up the next tactic: cutting away every remaining trace of complication until the story stands on a single, stark, and seemingly unassailable claim.

Stripping Away Nuance

One of the quiet but aggressive strengths of Flat Earth rhetoric is how systematically it pares everything down. Any element that introduces complexity—context, variables, inconvenient exceptions—gets trimmed away until only a single, solid-sounding, seemingly undeniable claim remains. This isn't just simplification; it's a deliberate rhetorical move designed to create the illusion of absolute certainty.

This is reduction framing in its sharpest form (Entman, 1993; Chong & Druckman, 2007). Instead of presenting a balanced picture that accounts for all factors, the story cuts off anything that could spark doubt or require deeper thought. A line like "You never see curvature" wipes out critical details such as altitude, atmospheric effects, optical illusions, and the massive scale needed to perceive Earth's curve. By removing all those moving parts, the claim feels absolute and intuitively true.

That aggressive cutting down taps directly into cognitive ease (Kahneman, 2011; Reber & Schwarz, 1999). A message with fewer elements, caveats, and conditions is easier to remember, repeat, and internalize, which in turn makes it feel more reliable. The smoother the claim runs in the mind, the more convincing it becomes—even if what was trimmed away contained the actual explanation.

Layered into this is framing by omission. This technique shapes a story as much by what's left out as by what's included. Flat Earth rhetoric doesn't need to invent elaborate lies; it simply decides which inconvenient details never make it into the picture. What's left is a clean, persuasive version of reality that feels certain and comforting compared to the messy, nuanced truth of scientific understanding.

On an emotional level, this approach hits pathos by tapping into the deep human desire for stability (Aristotle, trans. 2007). Certainty feels safe; nuance and ambiguity often feel like instability. By cutting away gray areas and delivering black-and-white answers, the story satisfies the craving for something fixed and unchanging in a complicated world.

Rhetorically, stripping away nuance doesn't just make the claim easier to accept—it changes what "truth" feels like. When a story removes the "it depends" and the "under these conditions," it doesn't just present an argument; it offers certainty as an experience. And that experience itself becomes powerfully persuasive.

That manufactured feeling of seamless certainty sets the stage for the final layer: crafting a story so smooth, so internally consistent, that its very structure feels like undeniable proof.

The Comfort of Clean Lines

Flat Earth rhetoric doesn't just simplify the story—it shapes it into something that feels perfectly straight, with no rough edges, no dangling threads, and no unanswered questions. That level of smoothness isn't accidental. A narrative presented with such clean, unambiguous lines creates the powerful sense of a world that simply "makes sense." For many, that feeling of order and completeness can be more persuasive than any piece of factual evidence.

This effect draws heavily on narrative coherence—the way a story's internal consistency can make it feel true even without external proof (Bruner, 1990; Polkinghorne, 1988). When every piece of the Flat Earth story—from supposed ancient wisdom to a modern cover-up to the believer's personal "discovery"—locks neatly into place, the seamlessness becomes the argument itself. The audience isn't just accepting individual claims; they're buying into the satisfying way those claims interlock.

It also taps into cognitive ease in a subtler way (Kahneman, 2011; Reber & Schwarz, 1999). It's not only that the story is simple to process—it's that the lack of loose ends and contradictions makes it feel safe and intellectually secure. Our brains are wired to associate smooth, ordered patterns with stability, and stability with truth. The absence of friction in the story feels like validation.

There's a strong emotional current here as well. That meticulous neatness offers pathos through comfort (Aristotle, trans. 2007). It quietly promises a world where everything lines up, where ambiguity falls away, and where the answers aren't buried in complexity. For someone overwhelmed by the messy, shifting nature of scientific reality, that sense of perfect clarity is almost irresistible.

Rhetorically, those clean lines give the Flat Earth story a self-reinforcing power. Once the narrative feels seamless and complete, any outside challenge that tries to add nuance or complexity doesn't just question a claim—it threatens the sense of order the entire story provides. That's why, in this narrative, simplicity isn't just a stylistic choice. It's both a shield against scrutiny and a refuge for the believer.

With the story now smoothed into those perfect, undeniable lines, the final persuasive move comes into focus: turning simplicity itself into the ultimate evidence.

When Simplicity Becomes the Proof

In the Flat Earth narrative, simplicity isn't just a persuasive tool—it becomes the argument itself. The story doesn't merely say, "this is true." It declares, "this is true because it is simple." The clean lines, plain language, and lack of intellectual friction stop being just a delivery method and start functioning as the evidence itself.

This is where the appeal to simplicity comes into full focus as a core rhetorical strategy. By framing the absence of complexity or nuance as an undeniable sign of honesty and authenticity, the story flips the burden of proof (Walton, 2008). The more straightforward and intuitively obvious a claim sounds, the more it's treated as self-validating, needing no outside support. In this frame, the presentation of the argument is the justification.

That effect is reinforced over and over through confirmation framing. Each time the narrative calls the truth "obvious," "plain," or "easy to see," it trains the audience to equate simplicity with proof. Any explanation that requires nuance or detailed reasoning is immediately framed as deception or deliberate complication. The loop sustains itself: the less intellectual depth the claim has, the more "real" and authentic it feels.

Emotionally, this use of simplicity leans heavily on pathos by tapping into the craving for certainty (Aristotle, trans. 2007). A simple, unambiguous explanation offers a sense of safety and control in a world that often feels overwhelming and chaotic. That emotional comfort does more than make the story appealing; it makes it feel immovable, a solid anchor against confusion.

Rhetorically, once simplicity itself is treated as proof, the Flat Earth story becomes almost immune to challenge. It doesn't invite complexity or deeper examination because anything that adds nuance threatens the very foundation of its appeal. In the end, the narrative doesn't just argue for a simple model of the Earth. It constructs an entire worldview where simplicity is the ultimate, non-negotiable sign of truth—one that makes the belief remarkably resistant to being debunked.

Us vs. Them: The Narrative Need for Sides

A story becomes a fortress when the walls are drawn sharp enough. Inside is belonging; outside is betrayal. The line between "us" and "them" is what keeps the world intact.

Every compelling story draws lines. Whether it's an ancient myth, a gripping novel, or a modern conspiracy theory, narratives instinctively divide the world into distinct roles: heroes and villains, insiders and outsiders, "us" and "them." Flat Earth rhetoric leans hard into that instinct. In this story, the actual shape of the Earth often takes a back seat to the more powerful narrative of who believes and who doesn't.

This is contrast framing at work—the rhetorical move where meaning is built by setting two opposing sides against each other (Entman, 1993; Chong & Druckman, 2007). The "truth-seekers," those who reject the mainstream narrative, are defined in direct opposition to "the deceived" or "the complicit" who accept the globe model without question. Without a clear "them," the story can't create a meaningful "us." The Flat Earth believer's identity is forged in the act of drawing that line.

The emotional weight behind this move comes straight from pathos, especially the powerful appeal to belonging

(Aristotle, trans. 2007). Being part of the exclusive group that "sees the truth" offers security, validation, and a shared purpose. That division doesn't just shield the Flat Earth belief from outside challenges—it reinforces the believer's sense of self and strengthens their new social identity.

Identity framing drives this even deeper (Tajfel & Turner, 1979). The story isn't only telling people what's true; it's telling them who they are if they embrace that truth: awakened, brave, discerning, intellectually uncorrupted. That identity only holds meaning in contrast to the outsiders, who are cast as blind, ignorant, or complicit in the grand deception.

Psychologically, this "us versus them" framing scratches a deep human itch for order, boundaries, and belonging. Rhetorically, it's a shortcut that bypasses the need to win a dense scientific argument. The story doesn't have to prove its claims with data; it only has to define the teams and offer the audience a choice of sides.

And once the lines are drawn, the narrative is ready for its next move: turning belief itself into the very essence of belonging.

Turning Belief Into Belonging

Flat Earth rhetoric doesn't stop at persuading someone of an idea; it transforms that conviction into something much larger—a shared identity. The moment of "awakening" isn't presented as the end of discovery but as the doorway into a tight-knit, exclusive community. The language deliberately shifts the story from "I discovered the truth" to "we are the truth-seekers."

That shift is built on identity framing, the rhetorical move that ties belief directly to self-image (Tajfel & Turner, 1979). The narrative doesn't just describe a different world—it defines a different you. Seeing the "truth" isn't framed as simply learning a fact; it's framed as becoming a particular kind of person: awake, courageous, uncorrupted, discerning. Once belief fuses with identity like that, Flat Earth isn't just an idea anymore—it's woven into the believer's sense of self.

The rhetoric strengthens this bond through a unique form of ethos construction. Here, credibility doesn't come from credentials or scientific evidence—it comes from belonging. Being part of the Flat Earth group itself is cast as proof that you are trustworthy, informed, and enlightened. Phrases like "Only the awake can see" or "We are the few who stand against the lie" aren't just motivational—they signal that credibility is earned through shared identity and collective mission rather than external validation.

This move leans hard on pathos by tapping into a universal human need: connection and affiliation (Aristotle, trans. 2007). Belief, especially when it runs against the mainstream, can be isolating. But shared belief instantly turns that isolation into comfort, creating a sense of belonging and mutual support. Flat Earth rhetoric doesn't just offer arguments; it offers a movement—something bigger than oneself to step into.

There's also a protective layer built into this strategy. When belief becomes belonging—when identity is bound to the group—walking away stops being about changing your mind. It becomes the emotional pain of leaving a family, abandoning people who "see" what you see. That bond makes the rhetoric self-reinforcing: the stronger the sense of community, the harder it is to challenge the belief, whether from within or outside.

Rhetorically, this shift from belief to belonging isn't accidental—it's a calculated, sophisticated move. It creates a self-sustaining loop: the community sustains the belief, and the belief sustains the community. This isn't just persuasion; it's the construction of a social infrastructure designed to fortify the core message.

And from that strong base of shared identity, the narrative adds its next layer: using language itself to draw and reinforce the boundaries of the group.

Language as a Boundary Line

Inside the Flat Earth story, words do far more than convey ideas—they draw borders. Phrases like "water finds its level" or "the globe lie" aren't just catchy slogans; they're markers of identity. Speaking this language signals, loudly and clearly, who's inside the circle of believers and who's not.

This is language framing at work, where the choice of words doesn't just describe reality but actively shapes it (Lakoff, 2004; Entman, 1993). Repeating insider terms and specific rhetorical constructions creates a shared vocabulary that reinforces the group's unique version of the world. Once that vocabulary takes root, stepping outside it can feel like betraying the group itself.

That shared lexicon builds a distinct form of ethos construction through language (Aristotle, trans. 2007). In this community, credibility isn't just about what you say but how you say it. Using the "right" phrases becomes proof of alignment with the truth and loyalty to the movement. This is why simple, loaded terms like "heliocentric deception" or "indoctrinated globe thinkers" carry more weight inside the group than any complex scientific data. The words aren't just conveying meaning—they're signaling belonging.

There's also a strong emotional pull here. Shared language taps directly into pathos by creating a sense of instant connection every time those phrases are spoken and echoed back (Tajfel & Turner, 1979). Saying the words isn't just affirming the belief—it's affirming the shared identity of the group itself.

Rhetorically, this insider language acts as a boundary defense. Once the vocabulary defines the group, anyone who questions the narrative without using it automatically sounds like an outsider, or even an enemy. Their arguments become easy to dismiss simply because they don't "speak the language." The words themselves turn into a gate, and using them correctly becomes the price of entry.

In the Flat Earth narrative, language isn't neutral—it's a sophisticated tool for shaping identity, reinforcing persuasion, and protecting the group. Every phrase draws that invisible line between "us" and "them," and every time the words are spoken, the boundary grows stronger.

As that distinctive language hardens, the story and the community carrying it start to fuse into one inseparable thing.

When the Story Becomes the Community

In the Flat Earth movement, the story isn't just something the community tells—it gradually becomes the community. The shared narrative turns into the glue holding individuals together, and every retelling—whether it's a conversation, a meme, or a video—functions like a ritual, reinforcing both the core belief and the social group built around it.

This is narrative reinforcement in action. Constant repetition doesn't just strengthen individual claims; it solidifies the entire social structure wrapped around the story. Each interaction is a collective affirmation, reminding members not only what they believe but, more importantly, who they belong to.

At the heart of this is identity anchoring, the rhetorical move that fuses personal identity to a dominant narrative. Once that bond forms, questioning the story stops being an intellectual exercise and starts feeling like questioning yourself—or worse, betraying a part of who you are. In Flat Earth circles, that anchoring expands to include the group itself, tightly welding individual identity to the collective. Belief and community become inseparable, creating a psychological and social wall that's hard to penetrate.

The emotional layer here is just as strong. Through pathos, the story offers comfort, validation, and collective strength (Aristotle, trans. 2007). Sharing and reaffirming the narrative becomes a communal declaration: "We are still here. We still see the truth. We are not alone." That emotional echo keeps the group resilient and distinct, even under intense outside pressure.

Rhetorically, once the story and the community merge, the argument stops relying on external evidence. The very existence of a passionate, unified group becomes the proof. Being surrounded by people who all share the same story makes it feel inherently true, while the story's endurance feeds the group's sense of purpose. It's a self-sustaining loop: the community reinforces the story, and the story reinforces the community.

That merging of story and group sets the stage for the final step: building the echo chamber's walls around both.

Foreshadowing the Chamber

The "us versus them" divide at the heart of the Flat Earth story does more than create a sense of belonging—it quietly lays the groundwork for the echo chamber that will soon surround the belief. Every insider phrase, every ritualized retelling, every line drawn between believers and outsiders works together to build those invisible walls, often long before anyone realizes they're being constructed.

This is pre-framing at work, a subtle but potent rhetorical device (Entman, 1993; Lakoff, 2004). By defining early on who can be trusted and who can't, the narrative sets up powerful cognitive filters that shape how all future information is received. When critics are labeled "agents of deception" or "system shills" and fellow believers are framed as "truth-seekers" and "the awakened," the echo chamber doesn't need to silence outside voices. It teaches the audience to automatically dismiss them before they're even heard.

The emotional weight behind this setup leans heavily on pathos, particularly the appeal to security (Aristotle, trans. 2007). The Flat Earth community is cast as a safe harbor, a sanctuary where every unsettling question has already been answered and where outsiders are portrayed as threats to that newfound peace. That emotional safety net makes the forming echo chamber feel comforting and protective rather than restrictive or limiting.

Layered into this is inoculation rhetoric (McGuire, 1964). The story often exposes listeners to watered-down versions of opposing arguments and dismisses them in advance, building psychological resistance to genuine challenges later. By the time the echo chamber fully closes, the mental and emotional defenses are already strong, making outside persuasion almost impossible to penetrate.

Rhetorically, this stage isn't about proving the Flat Earth claim itself—it's about preparing the audience for the environment in which that claim can thrive unchallenged. By the time the walls are fully built, the "us versus them" frame has trained the listener to see the echo chamber not as a trap but as a logical, even comforting, home.

The Frame as Proof

Every deeply held belief needs more than a strong argument to survive—it needs a durable frame to live inside. As this chapter has shown, Flat Earth rhetoric carefully constructs that frame piece by piece, not with scientific data or empirical proof, but with deliberate rhetorical design. A perceived villain like NASA or "the elites" injects urgency and moral weight. A relatable hero—the "awakened truth-seeker"—gives the story a human face and a sense of personal triumph. Simplicity trims away complexity until the claim feels like undeniable common sense. And the stark line between "us" and "them" transforms what could be just a claim about the Earth's shape into a living, breathing community.

These aren't random tricks thrown together—they're interconnected parts of a larger, meticulously built structure. Each rhetorical element locks into the next until the story stops feeling like a debate and starts feeling like a fully realized world you can step into. That's why the belief holds so tightly, even when stacked against overwhelming empirical evidence. The frame itself becomes the proof.

What makes this framework so powerful isn't the specific content of the Flat Earth claim—it's how expertly it taps into needs far deeper than facts. It offers certainty when the world feels uncertain. It wraps belief in identity, making it part of who you are. It delivers the comfort of belonging to a chosen group. When those deep psychological needs are bound together in a story that feels simple, clean, and full of purpose, it doesn't just ask to be believed. It creates the visceral sense that it has always been true, simply waiting for someone to uncover it.

And once a story reaches that point, it doesn't just shape ideas. It shapes people. It becomes a place to stand, a banner to rally under, and a shield against anything that threatens it from outside. The question of the Earth's shape may be the hook, but the real persuasion—the part that lasts—lives entirely in the intricate world built around that claim.

Chapter 4: The Stage of Echoes - The Theater of Belief

Every performance needs an audience, but the best ones make you forget you are watching a play

When you step into an echo chamber, you're not just joining a conversation—you're walking into a stage production. What you hear isn't casual debate; it's a performance. In the Flat Earth world, language doesn't just share belief; it puts that belief on display. Every phrase feels scripted, every repetition a cue, every voice an actor delivering their lines with practiced conviction.

Those slogans and catchphrases? They're not just words. They're the chorus—the familiar refrains that tell you you're in the right theater and part of the cast. Saying them isn't small talk; it's ritual. Each mantra earns you applause and belonging, and every echo adds another piece to the set until the world it builds starts to feel solid under your feet.

In this kind of performance, doubt gets treated like a heckler in the back row. It's silenced quickly because the show only works if the script runs perfectly. Certainty, on the other hand, is the star. It gets the spotlight, the cheers, and the validation until confidence itself starts to feel like proof.

This chapter isn't just about the words themselves. It's about the production behind them—the way an echo chamber turns language into a living script that holds the whole belief system together. Because here, words aren't just tools; they're the stage, the set, and the performance keeping the Flat Earth world alive.

Inside the Chamber

An echo chamber isn't just a casual conversation; it's a meticulously constructed space designed to make one voice sound like the only voice.

Step into almost any Flat Earth community online—whether it is a busy Facebook group, an active Discord server, or a YouTube livestream—and it does not take long to notice something unusual: the conversation does not really move forward. It loops. The same core claims circle back again and again. Familiar phrases get repeated almost word for word. The same "evidence" shows up, repackaged or presented by a different voice. It feels less like a debate and more like stepping into a padded room where only certain echoes are allowed to bounce.

That is the real mark of an echo chamber. It is not just people agreeing with each other; it is a space deliberately shaped so that only one kind of voice can survive and thrive. Rhetorically, that is framing in action. Framing is the way language and presentation quietly set the boundaries for what a conversation can include—and just as importantly, what gets pushed out entirely (Entman, 1993; Lakoff, 2004). Inside a Flat Earth echo chamber, the frame is drawn so tightly that anything outside it either gets twisted to fit the story or tossed aside as irrelevant, misleading, or deliberately false. There is no flashing sign saying "Other perspectives not allowed." Instead, it is built in layers: moderators who quietly delete questioning comments, loyal members who pile onto skeptics, and a shared insider language that makes outsiders sound clueless before they even finish a sentence.

One of the most powerful forces holding those walls in place is confirmation bias—the human habit of seeking out and favoring information that supports what we already believe, while downplaying or ignoring anything that challenges it (Wason, 1960; Nickerson, 1998). In an echo chamber, that bias is not just a quirk of individual thinking; it is woven into the design. The entire structure funnels conversation in a way that rewards agreement and quietly punishes doubt. Every meme shared, every slogan repeated, every story told to affirm the Flat Earth view becomes another brick in the wall reinforcing the narrative.

And here is the paradox: for people inside, this does not feel restrictive. It feels liberating. There is a deep comfort in being surrounded by voices that echo your own, easing cognitive dissonance and making you more certain. There is rhetorical power in hearing your own thoughts reflected back to you by a chorus of like-minded people. That is why these spaces do not just keep believers—they create new ones. The more often you hear the same story told the same way, the more "true" it starts to feel. Psychologists call this the illusory truth effect: the simple act of repetition makes statements feel more credible, even when the facts do not back them up (Begg, Anas, & Farinacci, 1992).

So when we talk about the Flat Earth echo chamber, we are not just talking about a group agreeing on a fringe belief. We are talking about a deliberate rhetorical construction—a carefully built stage where one story is told over and over until every other voice fades. And once you are inside, the walls do not just keep other voices out. They make the one inside sound like the only one worth hearing.

Ritual and Repetition

If the echo chamber is the structure, repetition is the force that keeps its walls upright and makes them stronger. Spend even ten minutes in a Flat Earth discussion and you'll notice the language does not just get spoken—it loops, over and over, like a mantra. Lines such as "Water finds its level," "Do your own research," and "NASA lies" are not just statements; they are rituals. Every time they are said or typed, they don't merely make a claim—they shore up the frame of the conversation and the worldview holding it together.

Rhetorically, this constant recycling is where pathos (emotional appeal) and ethos (credibility) intersect (Aristotle, trans. 2007). There is comfort in that familiar rhythm, especially when dozens or even thousands of voices are echoing it back. It is more than information sharing; it is belonging in action. Each repeated line carries an unspoken message: "You are not alone. You are part of something bigger. You have seen the truth." That kind of resonance does not just build a group—it builds identity.

It also plugs directly into the illusory truth effect: the more often you hear something, the more fluent it feels, and the more your brain tags it as true—even if there is zero supporting evidence (Begg, Anas, & Farinacci, 1992). In a Flat Earth echo chamber, that is not a side effect. It is the engine. The same claims, questions, and slogans show up across livestreams, memes, comment threads, and forum posts until they stop sounding like opinions and start feeling like undeniable facts. Familiarity itself becomes the proof.

What makes this so effective is how natural it feels to the people saying it. It does not feel like reciting a script; it feels like speaking plain truth. That is the subtle magic of ritual in rhetoric: when a phrase is used so often that it slips into everyday conversation, it stops being "just words" and becomes culture. Inside the chamber, that shared culture is what keeps the belief not just alive but reinforced every single day.

You can see it clearly through phatic communication—a kind of language that is not about exchanging new information, but about maintaining connection and affirming shared understanding (Malinowski, 1923). When someone posts "Research Flat Earth" and another immediately answers "NASA lies," no one is offering new data. They are performing a ritual handshake in words, reaffirming the bond that holds the group together.

Ultimately, the looping phrases are not designed to convince outsiders. They are built to sustain insiders. Every echo strengthens the walls. Every repetition makes the whole structure feel less like persuasion and more like truth—an unchanging certainty revealed and affirmed, again and again, by the collective voice.

Identity Inside the Walls

Spend even a short time inside a Flat Earth space—whether scrolling through an online forum or sitting quietly in a meetup—and you will notice something almost immediately: the language is not just about the shape of the Earth. It is about the shape of the people speaking. The words and phrases you choose mark you before your evidence ever does. Call someone a "globetard" or "asleep" and you have drawn a hard line. Call someone "awake" or a "truth seeker" and you have handed them a badge of belonging. These are not throwaway insults or compliments; they are signals. They define who is in, who is out, and who has just stepped over the threshold. In these spaces, language does not just communicate belief—it weaves the fabric of identity itself.

Rhetorically, this is ethos operating at its most personal level (Aristotle, trans. 2007). Ethos is not just about credentials; it is about character—the person you appear to be when you speak. In Flat Earth communities, certain words instantly frame that character. Calling yourself "awake" does not just say you believe something different; it claims moral and intellectual high ground. Rejecting the "globe" is not simply a scientific disagreement—it is a rejection of an identity that the chamber has cast as deceived, corrupted, and complicit with the so-called powers that be.

This is in-group/out-group framing at full strength: a rhetorical and psychological mechanism that defines identity by contrast (Tajfel & Turner, 1979). Every "they are asleep" and "NASA lies" is not just aimed at the outside world; it is a social border post, a way of saying "us" and "them" in the same breath. That line in the sand does not just create solidarity; it reinforces the sense that the in-group is enlightened, righteous, and alone in holding the truth.

For newcomers, this language acts like a quiet initiation rite. No one hands them a glossary, yet within days they are picking up the cues—learning the affirming words, the dismissive ones, and the ones that draw applause. This is linguistic accommodation in action: the subtle, often unconscious shift of speech to match the surrounding group (Giles, Coupland, & Coupland, 1991). Moreover, as new members echo the language back, something deeper kicks in, that repeated performance starts to shape self-perception itself (Bem, 1972). The more they speak the language of "truth seekers," the more they begin to feel like one.

Inside the chamber, words are more than tools of persuasion. They are mirrors. They reflect the group's values back to itself and, in doing so, reshape the people using them. When someone proudly declares they are "awake," they are not just making a claim about the Earth. They are making a claim about themselves. That is the real power of identity language: it does not just shift what you believe. It slowly, insistently rewrites who you think you are.

Language as a Barrier

Before a skeptic ever types a word in a Flat Earth space, the language has usually already done its work. In these communities, words do not just describe reality—they draw the boundary line before the conversation even starts. Labels like "indoctrinated," "sheep," or "globetard" are not random insults. They are preemptive strikes, carefully shaped to turn any opposing voice into a caricature that's easy to dismiss. By the time an outsider speaks, the chamber has already framed them as someone whose argument is not worth hearing.

This is rhetorical framing at its sharpest edge. Framing is not only about what you say—it is about what you make it possible for the audience to believe, and what you quietly make impossible for them to accept (Entman, 1993; Lakoff, 2004). Flat Earth rhetoric leans on this heavily. By labeling mainstream science as "indoctrination" or the product of "the system," it does not have to refute specific evidence. It defines the entire opposing worldview as tainted. The debate stops being about data or physics and turns into a battle over moral and intellectual "purity." If you can convince your audience that the other side is corrupted or ill-intentioned, you do not need to engage with their facts at all. The argument is over before it begins.

That effect is amplified by loaded language: words chosen less for what they mean objectively and more for the emotional weight they carry (Perelman & Olbrechts-Tyteca, 1969). Calling someone a "sheep" does not just say they follow—it mocks and diminishes them, casting their thinking as weak or inferior. Calling someone "awake" does the opposite. It instantly elevates their status, granting moral high ground in a single word. These labels are not built to win on evidence; they are built to win on feeling. They turn disagreement into something that does not just sound wrong—it feels shameful, even morally suspect, inside the chamber's walls.

This is also where the us-versus-them divide becomes a core rhetorical engine. This language forces a binary choice: you are either firmly inside the circle of "truth" or hopelessly outside in "deception" (Tajfel & Turner, 1979). There is no middle, no room for nuance or partial agreement. That is by design. The stronger and more rigid the linguistic barrier, the less room there is for uncertainty to sneak in.

And there is another layer to this boundary-setting language: it does not just keep outsiders out; it keeps insiders in. When you have called yourself "awake" and dismissed everyone else as "sheep," even a flicker of doubt feels less like questioning a belief and more like betraying your own identity. That subtle shift turns language into a social and psychological lock. Those same words that keep skeptics at arm's length also make it far harder for believers to reach for the door.

The Chamber as a Constructed Reality

Step back from the day-to-day chatter and the looping conversations in a Flat Earth space, and the bigger picture starts to come into focus. None of it—the repeated slogans, the boundary-setting language, the carefully curated conversations, the instant dismissal of outsiders—happens by accident. The echo chamber is not just a side effect of shared belief; it is a deliberately crafted environment, designed to make that belief feel not just plausible, but inevitable. Inside, Flat Earth is not up for debate. It is staged to feel like the only reality that could ever make sense.

This is the payoff of the rhetorical construction we have been tracking. Every repeated phrase adds another layer of framing. Every banned skeptic or derided "globetard" is another patch in the wall. Every meme, slogan, and piece of "evidence" is not just arguing—it is laying bricks. The result is a space where the Flat Earth story is not just told, it is lived. Moreover, much like a well-built stage or an immersive film set, the design is so seamless that you stop noticing the craft and start believing the world it is meant to represent (Berger & Luckmann, 1966).

Psychologically, this creates what can only be called a sense of enclosure: the feeling of being inside a complete, self-contained reality. Every thread of conversation, every "data point," every shared experience all lead to the same conclusion—that the Earth is flat and everyone outside is misled. This closed loop does not just guard the belief; it makes it feel like the only rational, even moral, choice. When every voice you hear echoes the same story, the claim stops sounding like an argument and starts feeling like a fact of life.

And here is the clever part: the people inside are not just passive audience members. They are the builders and the caretakers of the chamber itself. Every repeated slogan, every confirming meme, every phatic "NASA lies" exchanged between members helps reinforce the walls. This collective maintenance, performed constantly and often unconsciously, is what makes the chamber so durable—and so hard to walk away from (Tajfel & Turner, 1979).

Spend enough time inside and the walls do not just hold the belief. They hold you. The chamber stops feeling like a space you can leave and starts feeling like the world itself, making doubt feel less like a question and more like betraying reality.

Voices in Unison

"The first voices aren't there to tell the story—they're there to make you feel it."

Step into almost any Flat Earth digital space—a busy Facebook group, an active Discord channel, or a live YouTube stream—and the first thing that hits you is not complex "evidence" or intricate arguments. It is the sound. Short, sharp, almost musical slogans ripple through the conversation: "If the Earth were spinning, we would feel it." "If the Earth were curved, pilots would have to keep dipping the nose." "Antarctica is the ice wall." These are not just statements thrown into the air.

They are signals. They are the verbal handshake of the community. Say them yourself, and you are instantly marked as "inside." Hear them echoed back, and it is as if the chamber itself answers, wrapping you in belonging.

Rhetorically, these simple lines are doing several jobs at once. First, they are classic examples of phatic communication (Malinowski, 1923). This kind of language is not meant to deliver new facts or move a debate forward. It exists to build connection—to say, "We are in this together." When one member declares, "If the Earth were spinning, we would feel it," and another responds with "Exactly!" the exchange is less about evidence and more about affirmation. It is a ritual call-and-response, a performance of shared truth.

These slogans are also heuristics—mental shortcuts that make complex ideas feel simple and instantly graspable (Kahneman, 2011; Tversky & Kahneman, 1974). A quick, repeatable phrase skips the heavy lifting of deep analysis. Because it is easy to remember and effortless to repeat, it slides neatly into the brain. That ease of processing feeds directly into the illusory truth effect: the more often you hear a statement—especially one this concise—the more "true" it feels, regardless of whether there is any real evidence behind it (Begg, Anas, & Farinacci, 1992).

Framing adds another layer. A slogan does not just state an opinion; it quietly sets the rules of the conversation (Entman, 1993; Lakoff, 2004). "Pilots would have to keep dipping the nose" does not just raise a question about aviation—it reframes all of flight as supposed evidence against Earth's curvature, shifting the burden of proof to the "globe" model. "Antarctica is the ice wall" does not describe geography; it frames the entire world map as part of a conspiracy. These lines do not just enter the debate. They shape it.

What makes these slogans so powerful is not just what they claim. It is what they signal about identity. Saying the right words in the right space is not simply about sharing a belief—it is a declaration of who you are and who you stand with. Inside the echo chamber, these phrases stop sounding like arguments and start functioning as credentials. They are badges of belonging, affirmations of being "awake." Moreover, the more they are echoed by others, the less they feel like claims at all. They start to sound like the opening notes of a story that has always been true—just waiting for you to join the chorus.

Memes as Mini-Arguments

Before anyone in a Flat Earth community says a word, the images often start talking first. A distant horizon photo with the caption "Where is the curve?" A diagram of an airplane over a globe stamped with "Pilots would have to keep dipping the nose." A glass of water sitting perfectly still on a table, labeled "Still flat." In these digital spaces, memes are not just decoration or throwaway jokes—they are arguments compressed into a single, potent frame.

Rhetorically, these memes work as visual enthymemes. An enthymeme, going back to Aristotle, is an argument where one part—sometimes even the conclusion—is left unsaid so the audience fills it in themselves (Aristotle, trans. 2007). When a meme pairs a perfectly calm horizon with the text "If the Earth were spinning, we would feel it," it does not explain rotational physics or gravity. It does not have to. The image plus the line nudges you toward the missing piece: "If it looks this flat and I do not feel movement, the Earth must be flat." That subtle mental leap is exactly what makes memes hit so hard. The audience finishes the argument in their own heads, which makes the conclusion feel like their own discovery rather than someone else's claim.

Memes also double as visual framing devices (Messaris & Abraham, 2001). The picture is not just there to catch your eye; it is part of the persuasion. A perfectly flat horizon frames Earth as inherently stable. A meme of a wide-eyed kid pointing at the sky frames the argument as so simple even a child "gets it." A crude cartoon mocking scientists frames mainstream science as ridiculous without ever touching actual evidence. In a handful of pixels and a few words, a meme quietly defines who is credible (the "awake"), who is not (the "indoctrinated"), and what the debate is "really" about (the conspiracy).

Psychologically, memes have a built-in advantage: they slip past the mental defenses that heavier, text-based arguments run into. They are fast to process, ridiculously easy to share, and they hit both the visual and verbal parts of your brain at once. That combo is the dual coding effect in action—when words and images work together, the message sticks harder and feels more convincing because it is encoded in multiple ways in memory (Paivio, 1986). Layer that with the echo chamber's constant repetition, and memes stop being casual content. They become cultural currency, shorthand language, and shared understanding all rolled into one.

Inside Flat Earth spaces, memes are not just arguments; they are recruitment tools. They affirm. They teach the chamber's language. They make the narrative feel easy, playful, and obvious—which is exactly why they slip under critical thinking so smoothly. One glance, one quick share, and the "argument" has already landed, taken root, and added another brick to the chamber's carefully constructed reality.

The Power of Short Phrases

In the Flat Earth world, entire arguments often get packed into just a handful of words. Lines like "If the Earth were spinning, we would feel it," "Boats do not disappear over a curve—it is just perspective," or the definitive-sounding "Gravity? Just density and buoyancy" are not casual throwaways. They are highly compressed claims, deliberately engineered to sound like obvious truths or self-evident common sense. Their brevity is not a quirk; it is a deliberate rhetorical strategy.

Rhetorically, these short, punchy phrases work as topoi, also called commonplaces—stock lines that feel like shared, universal wisdom even when they are not. (Aristotle, trans. 2007). It does not need a stack of data or elaborate explanation because the audience supplies the missing reasoning themselves. When someone hears "Water finds its level," the implied premise pops into their mind automatically: if water always levels itself, then vast bodies like oceans must be flat. That leap feels personal, like you connected the dots on your own, which makes it far harder to challenge. You're not just arguing against a statement—you are arguing against what feels like common sense.

These phrases also lean heavily on cognitive fluency, the psychological principle that we are more likely to believe ideas that are easy to process, repeat, and remember (Reber & Schwarz, 1998). A simple line, repeated enough inside the chamber, starts to feel truer than a complex scientific explanation—even one backed by overwhelming evidence. That is why slogans like "Pilots would have to keep dipping the nose" or "No curvature seen from planes" stick. They are effortless to recall and require no mental heavy lifting, which makes them extraordinarily hard to shake once they have settled in.

There's another layer at play here: rhetorical condensation. These short phrases act like compressed files, packing an entire worldview or conspiracy into a single line. Say "Antarctica is the ice wall," and you do not have to unpack hidden cartography, secret treaties, or a suppressed cosmology—

the phrase carries all that weight in four words. Inside the chamber, they become instant shortcuts and identity markers.

The power of this brevity is not just efficiency; it's durability. These phrases can be dropped into any conversation, turned into memes, or chanted during a livestream without losing their punch. Because they are so compact, they survive endless repetition without breaking down. Each time they are spoken, they do not just reinforce a claim—they reinforce who is speaking and who is listening as "awake" or "truth-seekers." That is why these short lines are not just rhetorical convenience. They are a strategic weapon, designed to make the argument feel not only right, but undeniable—a truth stitched directly into how the world itself is perceived.

Chorus and Refrain

In the contained world of a Flat Earth space, it is not only the slogans or the memes that linger—it is the deliberate way they are repeated. Again and again, the same core lines cycle through livestreams, chats, and comment threads until they stop sounding like arguments and start to resemble the lyrics of a familiar song. "If the Earth were spinning, we would feel it." "Boats do not disappear; it is just perspective." "Gravity is just density and buoyancy." Through sheer repetition, these phrases shift from attempts at proof to collective, affirming performances.

This is where the rhetoric begins to take on a musical quality. Repetition here works like a chorus—the part of a song everyone knows and can join without hesitation. In rhetorical terms, this deliberate echoing of words and phrases, especially at the beginning of sentences, is known as anaphora (Perelman & Olbrechts-Tyteca, 1969). Traditionally, it is used to build rhythm and emphasis, making a message more memorable. Inside the echo chamber, it does something more profound: it builds community. Speaking the same refrains in unison reinforces both the belief and the shared identity of the group (Tajfel & Turner, 1979).

This constant looping also engages the illusory truth effect—the psychological tendency to mistake familiarity for truth (Begg, Anas, & Farinacci, 1992). The more often a statement is heard, the easier it becomes for the brain to process, and that very ease is subconsciously taken as a sign of validity (Reber & Schwarz, 1998). This is why these refrains do not merely survive; they thrive. Each repetition is more than an echo; it is another layer of psychological reinforcement, making the belief feel not only familiar but self-evident.

This repeated chorus also creates what might be called ritual certainty. Saying and hearing the same lines over and over generates a sense of stability and conviction that comes not from evidence but from the shared act itself. It is less about proving something with data and more about feeling convinced through collective affirmation. Like a hymn sung together, the persuasive power is not in the individual voices or the complexity of the lyrics but in the overwhelming sense of unity created by the performance.

Inside the chamber, these refrains are never just background chatter—they are the score against which the entire Flat Earth story is performed. The more fervently they are "sung," the more they shape the scene and blur the line between argument and identity. At that point, repeating the claim is no longer just about belief; it is about sustaining the entire performance, keeping the constructed reality alive and beyond question.

Repetition as Construction

Every time a phrase, slogan, or core claim bounces around the echo chamber, it does not just repeat what was said before—it adds weight. Take the familiar lines: "If the Earth were spinning, we would feel it." "Boats do not disappear; it is just perspective." "Antarctica is the ice wall." Each echo does not just keep the idea alive; it lays down another layer, like stacking brick after brick into the same wall. Over time, the argument stops feeling like something up for debate and starts feeling like part of the very architecture of reality itself.

Rhetorically, this is constructive repetition at work—the deliberate use of recurring language not just to emphasize, but to build an entire framework around a claim (Perelman & Olbrechts-Tyteca, 1969). In this setting, a statement does not rely on outside evidence to gain weight. It gains weight simply by existing everywhere, over and over again. Inside the Flat Earth chamber, the act of repeating something is what makes it "true." The language becomes the evidence.

This is also where psychology kicks in, specifically schema building—the way our minds create mental blueprints to interpret the world (Bartlett, 1932). Each slogan or meme reinforces the same mental model until it stops feeling like a theory and starts feeling like the natural lens through which everything else is seen. A line like "Gravity is just density and buoyancy" does not need a physics lesson or experiment to back it up inside the chamber. After enough echoes, it settles into place as a "given," a core piece of the belief system.

Repetition also builds rhetorical inertia. Once a phrase becomes part of that mental scaffolding, it is not just hard to challenge—it is like trying to knock out a load-bearing wall in a building. Everything else is resting on it. That is part of why Flat Earth rhetoric can feel so impossible to penetrate from the outside. The language is not just conversation anymore. Its structure. And that structure naturally resists anything that tries to dismantle it.

Inside the chamber, every echo of a slogan is not background noise—it is construction work. Each repetition does not just make the belief louder; it makes it heavier, more ingrained, more permanent. The walls of this world are not built of stone or steel. They are built of words. And the relentless use of constructive repetition is the mortar that locks those words together into a fortress that feels unshakable from the inside.

Weaponized Mockery

Flat Earth spaces may echo with certainty, but just as often they ring with laughter—and that laughter has teeth. Memes mocking "globeheads," cartoons of blindfolded scientists, captions like "Still believe in spinning water balls?" or a ship vanishing over the horizon labeled "Perspective, dummy"—these are not throwaway jokes. They are deliberate, sharpened tools of persuasion.

Inside the echo chamber, mockery functions as pathos turned on its head. Instead of appealing to empathy, it binds the group through shared derision and a collective sense of intellectual superiority. That communal laugh, the knowing eye-roll at the "unawakened," often bonds members more strongly than any elaborate argument about physics or astronomy ever could (Perelman & Olbrechts-Tyteca, 1969). And it does something even more strategic: it frames outsiders as ridiculous long before they have spoken a word. When the other side is consistently treated as a punchline, their evidence does not need to be refuted. It has already been disarmed by laughter.

That is where the irony cuts deep. The same Flat Earth believers who weaponize ridicule as "proof" of their insight are often the first to cry persecution when mockery comes from the outside. A skeptical video calling Flat Earth claims absurd does not register as criticism; it is instantly reframed as, "See? They are trying to silence us. They are afraid of the truth." Inside the chamber, internal mockery strengthens the walls of belief; outside, external mockery becomes fuel for the narrative of victimhood. The hypocrisy is not just rhetorical—it is a core part of how the belief sustains itself.

Psychologically, this dynamic leans heavily on social identity theory (Tajfel & Turner, 1979). Every shared laugh at a "globehead" meme is not just humor—it is a pledge of allegiance. It loudly signals loyalty to the in-group and reinforces the line between "us" and "them." It also draws on the superiority theory of humor, a centuries-old idea that we laugh to affirm our own status by ridiculing the perceived weakness or folly of others (Plato, Aristotle, Hobbes). That quick hit of superiority is not just entertainment; it is identity rehearsal. Each joke becomes a ritual affirmation: we are awake, they are blind.

And here is the double edge that makes it so effective. The ridicule that keeps outside arguments at bay also keeps outside influence from ever reaching in. Yet the more Flat Earth communities lean on mockery, the more they inevitably invite it back. That external derision then feeds right back into the narrative: "We are over the target. That is why they are laughing at us." The cycle completes itself. In this loop, laughter is not just noise; it is armor, reinforcement, and justification all at once.

But behind every meme and every sneer, there is always a voice delivering it with complete conviction. The chorus may carry the tune and provide the comfort of unison, but the performance hinges on the figures willing to step into the light, set the tone, and lead the story forward.

Center Stage

In the echo chamber, conviction doesn't just deliver the message—it is the message.

When the chorus of slogans and memes finally fades and the digital room quiets, a single voice steps into the spotlight. In the Flat Earth story, that voice is the Confident Truth Teller. You might remember him from Chapter 3, where he stood as the "hero" figure in the larger narrative. But here, he is not just part of the story; in many ways, he is the story. His unwavering certainty does not just support the Flat Earth claim. Through the force of his delivery, that certainty becomes the claim.

This is ethos turned into a performance. Ethos—the appeal to credibility—usually comes from a speaker's character, their perceived goodwill, and the strength of their evidence (Aristotle, trans. 2007). In the Confident Truth Teller's hands, credibility is built almost entirely through delivery. The calm, steady voice. The direct eye contact, even through a webcam. The absolute, unshakeable conviction. Together they create what can only be called a credibility illusion: the sense of authority does not come from the facts themselves, but from how those "facts" are performed. It is persuasion through the peripheral route, where audiences are swayed less by the message and more by cues surrounding the messenger (Petty & Cacioppo, 1986).

This is where the fluency heuristic kicks in. Our brains are wired to trust information that feels smooth and easy to process. A claim delivered with calm confidence often feels true, even when the logic underneath it is weak (Reber & Schwarz, 1998; Kahneman, 2011). Flat Earth influencers lean on that shortcut. A shaky argument, spoken with absolute certainty, can land far harder than a fact-filled explanation delivered with the slightest hint of doubt.

That is also why so many of their lines sound almost identical across videos and debates. The same points, the same phrases, over and over, until the delivery becomes second nature. You can even catch it slipping into autopilot. In one livestream, a prominent influencer started with his usual opening line—only to realize moments later that he had mentioned the wrong location entirely. The line was so ingrained from endless repetition that it surfaced automatically, proof of how deeply rehearsed the performance really was.

What makes that single voice so powerful is not just what it says, but what it signals: absolute certainty, without compromise. Inside the echo chamber, where outside doubt is already filtered away, that conviction becomes the proof. The Confident Truth Teller does not just make the case for Flat Earth; he embodies it. And when the spotlight hits and the audience holds its collective breath, the performance does not just tell the story. For those immersed in the chamber's carefully built reality, that performance is the story itself.

The Language of Absolutes

Flat Earth talk leaves no room for "maybe," "possibly," or "it seems to indicate." The language lands like a verdict: "That's a fact." "There is no debate." "The evidence makes it clear." These aren't just emphatic lines; they are classic examples of what rhetoricians call dogmatic assertions—claims delivered with such absolute conviction that they signal they cannot, and should not, be questioned.

This is where an appeal to certainty does nearly all the rhetorical heavy lifting. The calm, unwavering delivery of the Confident Truth Teller, paired with the uncompromising language itself, is presented as if it were direct proof. A statement like "There is no debate" does not actually engage with a counterargument or offer supporting evidence—it slams the door on the conversation entirely. The effect is immediate: it creates the feeling that the matter is already settled, the "truth" already revealed, long before any real discussion can take place.

What makes this strategy stand out is how completely it inverts the way real science speaks. Scientific language is full of qualifiers: "based on current evidence," "our findings suggest," "according to the latest data." That cautious tone isn't a sign of weakness—it's the strength of a system that expects to be tested, retested, and refined with new information. Flat Earth rhetoric flips that on its head. Inside the chamber, absolutism signals strength and truth, while any hint of provisional language reads as hesitation or ignorance. This is not just two sides disagreeing on facts; it is two completely different rhetorical languages clashing over what "truth" even looks like and how it's established.

There is also a deep psychological hook buried in this preference for absolutes. Human beings are drawn to certainty. In a world that feels messy and overloaded with shifting information, a clear, unambiguous line like "That is a fact" feels solid and reassuring. It does not just present an argument; it provides comfort. That reassurance works in two directions: it calms the audience's doubts and reinforces the speaker's own conviction. Repeat an absolute enough times, and it stops functioning like a claim at all. It becomes a self-affirming mantra, strengthening the group's shared belief with every echo. This taps directly into the need for cognitive closure, the psychological drive to land on a definite conclusion and avoid ambiguity (Kruglanski & Webster, 1996).

The irony, of course, is that the lines delivered with the most confidence are often the ones built on the weakest evidence. But inside the echo chamber, that does not matter. When a statement is framed as beyond question and performed with unwavering certainty, it does not have to stand up to outside scrutiny. In this rhetorical world, it is not the data that makes something a "fact"—it's the sheer, unshakeable conviction with which it's said.

Rehearsed Monologue

In the Flat Earth world, very little of what you hear is truly "off the cuff." Listen long enough to a handful of videos, podcasts, or debates, and you start to notice the same precise lines surfacing again and again. "If the Earth were spinning, we would feel it." "Boats do not disappear; it's just perspective." "Pilots would have to keep dipping the nose if the earth was curved." The delivery is so consistent, so polished, that it stops sounding like conversation at all and starts sounding like dialogue from a well-rehearsed play. And in a very real sense, that is exactly what it is.

This is rhetorical rehearsal in action: the deliberate polishing of a line until it lands with flawless precision every single time. When those words finally reach the audience, they carry more than just the claim itself—they carry the weight of repetition, the authority of something that has been spoken so often it now feels etched into reality. And it is not just the audience who is affected. For the speaker, each repeat hardens the belief a little more, shifting it from a talking point into a reflex. Over time, it stops feeling like a claim and starts feeling like muscle memory, making it extraordinarily difficult for the speaker to step back and question it.

Psychologically, this relentless rehearsal plugs straight into the illusory truth effect: the more we hear something, the more "true" it feels, regardless of its actual evidence (Begg, Anas, & Farinacci, 1992). Inside the echo chamber, this is not just present—it's amplified. The influencer repeats a line; the audience echoes it back; the algorithms send it ricocheting around the network until it comes back sounding inevitable, almost self-proving.

There is also a performance layer here that's impossible to miss. A perfectly smooth, automatic delivery signals authority all on its own. It sounds like the voice of someone who has said this so many times because it is simply and obviously right. This is where appeal to certainty and rehearsal fuse together: the polish becomes part of the proof. The delivery itself is the argument.

Every now and then, though, the script slips. A familiar line pops out in the wrong context, or a standard greeting gets dropped in a setting where it does not fit—a telling moment where the performance runs ahead of the situation. Far from being a minor mistake, those slips expose the machinery at work. They reveal just how deeply these words are programmed and how little of this rhetoric is truly spontaneous. And inside the chamber, that's not a flaw. For the Confident Truth Teller and his audience, the performance is not just a vehicle for truth. It is the truth, built one carefully rehearsed line at a time.

Charisma vs. Content

When the Confident Truth Teller steps into the spotlight, the words themselves are only half of what makes the moment persuasive. The other half—the part that often carries even more weight—lives entirely in the delivery: the measured, steady voice, the calm cadence, the unflinching gaze, the absolute certainty radiating from every syllable. In rhetorical terms, this is the classic balance between ethos (credibility and character) and logos (the content and logic of the argument). Inside the Flat Earth echo chamber, that balance tilts hard toward ethos. More specifically, it tilts toward charisma—and charisma often outweighs content entirely.

This is where the credibility illusion (as explored in The Performance of Certainty) reaches its peak. A statement that might seem flimsy or even absurd when written down takes on a surprising weight when delivered with quiet confidence and unshakable calm. That is part of why these spaces value "the voice" so highly. It is not just about what is said—it is about the performance of being someone who sounds inherently worth believing. This plays directly into the peripheral route to persuasion, where the appeal of the messenger bypasses critical engagement with the message itself (Petty & Cacioppo, 1986).

What is striking is that the most persuasive figures are not always the loudest or most aggressive. Often, the voices that land hardest are the ones wrapped in an almost meditative calm. That deliberate serenity, maintained across countless videos, streams, and interviews, becomes a kind of evidence all its own. Even the weakest claim can feel grounded when delivered without a hint of doubt. It does not sound true because of the content. It sounds true because the speaker never wavers.

Psychologically, this taps into the halo effect (Thorndike, 1920). One positive impression—calmness, confidence, apparent rationality—bleeds into everything else the person says. A smooth, unhesitating delivery makes the statement itself sound smooth and unassailable. A relaxed tone makes the argument feel level-headed and rational. The content does not have to work as hard; the performance does the heavy lifting.

This is not accidental. Many prominent Flat Earth influencers lean into this dynamic intentionally. They frame themselves as calm, rational truth-seekers in contrast to "angry," "emotional," or "dismissive" mainstream scientists and critics. The performance becomes the proof. The equation is simple: a calm voice equals a rational mind. An unflinching tone equals undeniable truth. The audience does not just hear claims; they see a reflection of what they want to believe—a steady hand in a chaotic world, a voice of certainty when everything else feels uncertain.

But here is the tension, and the danger: when charisma consistently outweighs content, the argument stops being about facts at all. It becomes a feeling—the experience of being convinced. And inside the echo chamber, where emotional resonance often eclipses logical reasoning, that feeling can carry far more weight than any data ever could. The words, the claims, the so-called proofs all become secondary. The real "evidence" becomes the person saying them, and the unwavering performance itself becomes the story.

Confidence as Contagion

Inside the echo chamber, conviction is not just something the Confident Truth Teller projects—it is something the entire room picks up, amplifies, and feeds back. A single line, delivered with absolute certainty, does not stay confined to the digital stage for long. It ripples outward, spreading through comments, live chats, and casual conversations until that one voice starts to feel like many. Soon, it is no longer one person speaking with authority—it is the entire community speaking in unison.

This is the moment where a single performance fuses with collective psychology. Persuasion stops looking like a one-way exchange between speaker and audience and becomes something much more powerful: a shared event. Certainty moves through these groups the same way laughter can sweep through a crowded theater. One person sparks it, but within moments, everyone feels it as if it were their own.

Psychologists call this phenomenon emotional contagion (Hatfield, Cacioppo, & Rapson, 1994). It is the subtle, often subconscious way emotions spread through a group until they feel like a shared truth. Rhetorically, that effect multiplies the message. A confident line is not just heard—it is absorbed, repeated, and echoed back so many times that it gains weight every time it passes through another voice. Layered on top of that is social proof, the powerful tendency to see a belief as "correct" when it is clearly embraced by the group around you (Cialdini, 1984).

This is also where the appeal to certainty (Kruglanski & Webster, 1996) hits its highest gear. A single voice declaring, "If the Earth were spinning, we would feel it," can be dismissed. A thousand voices repeating it in the same calm, matter-of-fact tone transforms it into something that sounds less like an argument and more like an axiom. The repetition does not just trigger the illusory truth effect (Begg, Anas, & Farinacci, 1992)—it supercharges it, making the statement feel less like a claim and more like a cornerstone of reality.

And once that certainty stops belonging to a single person and becomes shared property of the group, it does more than persuade. It builds belonging. The chamber does not just echo the message—it takes that confidence and turns it into a collective shield, a wall so solid that doubt is not just silenced; it is systematically erased. At that point, alternative perspectives do not even have space to enter. The belief does not just sound true. Surrounded by that chorus, it feels inevitable.

The Actor's Mask

Every compelling performance leans on a carefully built role, and every role, sooner or later, calls for a mask. In Flat Earth rhetoric, that mask is not just hiding something—it is actively creating someone new. The Confident Truth Teller who appears on screen or commands a debate is not necessarily the whole person behind the camera. He is a carefully constructed character, designed specifically for the demands of the echo chamber: a persona built to project unshakable certainty and unquestionable authority in every word, every gesture, every steady look into the lens.

Rhetorically, this is constructed ethos at its sharpest. Ethos is not only about credibility you "have"; it is also about the credibility you project (Aristotle, trans. 2007; Perelman & Olbrechts-Tyteca, 1969). Inside the chamber, that projection is no accident. A calm tone, controlled expression, and a voice that never wavers—these are not incidental traits, they are part of the costume. The audience is not just listening to an argument; they are watching a role so consistently and convincingly performed that it merges with their sense of the "truth" itself. This is classic impression management: carefully curating how others see you (Leary & Kowalski, 1990).

Over time, though, something interesting happens. Perform the same certainty long enough, and the mask starts to fuse with the skin beneath. Spend hours rehearsing and inhabiting a role built on absolute conviction, and eventually that conviction begins to feel authentic, even off-camera. Goffman (1959) called this the blurring of self and performance; Bem's self-perception theory (1972) explains it as learning what you believe by watching what you do. Add Festinger's (1957) insight on cognitive dissonance, and the picture sharpens: if you are publicly playing certainty day after day, the discomfort of private doubt often pushes you to internalize the role fully. The act becomes identity.

This is where the theatrical metaphor hits hardest. In traditional theater, the mask serves the story. Inside the echo chamber, the mask is the story. The persona itself becomes the ultimate "evidence." The unspoken logic is simple and powerful: if someone can stand so calm, so steady, so absolutely sure, then surely the truth behind that mask must be just as solid.

But masks always work both ways. They do not just project an image outward; they shield inward. Behind the unflinching face and the steady tone often sits the same uncertainties, the same need for belonging, the same human anxieties that first drew the audience into the chamber. The mask does not just protect the story from outside criticism—it protects the storyteller from their own cracks of doubt.

And that is why the chamber itself becomes essential. A performance this dependent on absolute certainty can't survive long in open air. It needs those walls. It needs the closed system to keep the mask from slipping, to keep the illusion of unshakable truth intact, to maintain the safe stage where character and narrative can feed each other without interruption. What comes next is not just persuasion anymore. It is defense. The mask may sell the story, but it is the fortified walls of the echo chamber that keep both the story—and the performer wearing that mask—from breaking apart under the weight of reality.

Holding the Walls

A story built on conviction rather than hard evidence can often weather direct challenges. What it can't survive is neglect.

Every echo chamber, much like a carefully constructed building, depends on strong walls to define its boundaries and hold its reality together. But walls do not hold themselves up. What truly keeps the structure intact is constant, quiet upkeep—the deliberate, often unseen work of guarding the narrative.

Inside Flat Earth spaces, this is not passive moderation or casual content filtering. It is a strategic, ongoing performance of control. Every choice—what gets pinned and amplified, what slips quietly into the background, and what gets silenced entirely—is a rhetorical move. Those decisions do not just shape what the audience hears. They shape what the audience is allowed to believe.

At the center of that defense is framing at its most sophisticated (Entman, 1993; Lakoff, 2004; Chong & Druckman, 2007). Outside challenges are not always deleted outright. More often, they're reframed into something that strengthens the story. A skeptic's question or a scientist's rebuttal is not just dismissed; it is spun into "proof" that the chamber is under attack by "globe trolls" or "agents of the system." Even a clip of mainstream science that leaks in does not just get erased—it gets recast as deliberate "disinformation," wrapped in urgent language about threats and deception. Here, timing—kairos—becomes everything (Aristotle, trans. 2007). The guardians move fast, sealing the crack before doubt can seep in.

Selective amplification is just as critical. Not every piece of internal content gets the same treatment. Stories and "evidence" that reinforce the group's identity or feed the sense of shared conspiracy rise to the top, pinned, shared, and echoed everywhere. Content that hints at cracks in the narrative? That gets buried—subtly muted or allowed to vanish in the churn. This is not simple censorship. It is a precise form of narrative maintenance and gatekeeping, curating what thrives to keep the story seamless and the belief unblemished (Lewin, 1947; White, 1950).

Over time, this constant guarding does more than filter content. It trains the audience to filter themselves. The lines of acceptable belief and permissible questions are not written in a rulebook; they are performed in plain view. Every deleted post, every pinned video, every "safe" question that gets applause becomes a lesson in what belongs and what does not. In rhetorical terms, this is active enactment: the wall is not just defended—it is rebuilt, brick by brick, in every visible act of defense.

There is nothing flashy about this process. It is not the booming voice on center stage. It is the stagehands moving props in the dark, adjusting lights, sweeping away anything that might break the illusion. In the Flat Earth chamber, these quiet, constant adjustments are the invisible scaffolding. They are what keep the story coherent, the performance seamless, and the belief system alive.

Language of Exclusion

Inside the tight weave of a Flat Earth echo chamber, language is not just a tool for conversation—it is the fence line.

The words people reach for, the phrases they repeat, even the tone they use all serve as subtle, often unconscious markers of who is "in" and who is definitely "out." You do not need a membership card to tell where someone stands; you only have to listen.

This is where Kenneth Burke's idea of terministic screens comes sharply into play. Burke (1966) argued that language does not neutrally describe reality; it acts like a filter. Every word we use highlights some parts of reality while deflecting or hiding others, all while reflecting back a particular worldview to the speaker. In Flat Earth spaces, that screen is drawn razor-thin: "truth-seekers" versus the "asleep masses," "globe believers" versus "real observers," "the lie" versus "the flat truth." These are not just labels; they're lenses. And the moment someone drops a phrase like "gravity" without the customary air quotes, or calls NASA a "reputable" source, the shift is immediate. The language itself gives away whether they belong inside the walls—or outside looking in.

These linguistic choices also double as powerful in-group signals (Tajfel & Turner, 1979). When someone says "water finds its level" or "Antarctica is the wall holding the oceans in," they are not just tossing out evidence; they are declaring, "I am one of you. I speak our language. I live in our reality." It is ritual as much as rhetoric. And for newcomers, these repeated phrases act like training wheels, teaching them—quietly, subconsciously—the exact words and rhythms they need to blend in. This is accommodation theory in action: people naturally shape their speech to match the group in order to gain approval and acceptance (Giles, Coupland, & Coupland, 1991).

What makes this system so effective is how invisible it feels to the people inside. There is no formal glossary, no list of banned words pinned to the top of the forum. The boundaries of acceptable speech are enforced in real time, in the everyday churn of conversation, inside the soothing repetition of shared words. That is what keeps this squarely in the realm of maintenance rather than active defense: the chamber does not need to react to outside threats here. It simply speaks its walls into existence every time someone opens their mouth.

Eventually, this language of exclusion becomes second nature. Members do not just know what phrases to use—they know what not to say, which words will instantly brand someone a "shill," and how to frame every thought in the safe, familiar cadence of the group. The walls of the echo chamber aren't just holding the belief; they are speaking it. And every word, every repeated phrase, is another coat of paint, keeping those walls smooth, unbroken, and perfectly intact.

Fear of Contamination

If the "Language of Exclusion" keeps the walls of the echo chamber quietly standing through the careful choice of words, then "Fear of Contamination" is where those walls brace themselves for impact. In Flat Earth spaces, outside information—especially anything that challenges the core belief—is not treated as neutral or even just wrong. It is framed as toxic. A NASA photo, a peer-reviewed study, even a curious newcomer asking "What if?" is not seen as honest inquiry. It is seen as a direct threat to the truth and to the group itself.

This is inoculation theory in its purest form. William J. McGuire (1964) likened persuasion resistance to a vaccine: expose someone to a weakened version of a counter-argument, and they become resistant to the full dose later. Inside the echo chamber, before an outside idea can even be heard on its own terms, it's pre-labeled as "globe propaganda," "mainstream indoctrination," or deliberate manipulation. By the time the unfiltered argument shows up—if it ever does—the group is already psychologically primed to reject it instantly, no debate required. What starts as quiet maintenance of the narrative quickly shifts into active, aggressive defense.

The rhetoric here leans heavily on purity framing and group isolation tactics. Inside the chamber, belief isn't just about what's embraced; it is just as much about what is rejected. Loyalty is not measured only in how often someone repeats the slogans or defends the "truth," but in how fast they denounce "contaminated" information. Even a moment of curiosity about mainstream explanations can mark someone as suspect—a potential "shill" or "unwoke" infiltrator. It is a hard-edged application of in-group/out-group boundaries (Tajfel & Turner, 1979).

What makes this strategy so effective is how protective it feels to those inside. Statements like "We are just guarding the truth" or "We cannot let lies confuse new members" sound responsible, even caring. But rhetorically, they work like a firewall: filtering what gets in and, more importantly, teaching everyone to do the filtering themselves.

Given enough time, that fear of contamination moves from external policing to internal instinct. Moderators don't have to delete as much because members have learned to self-censor, to flinch away from anything that might "break the frame." The wall stops being just a set of digital rules and becomes a mental boundary everyone carries inside their own head. That is when the belief stops just being defended from the outside and starts being locked in from within, making the chamber's reality feel not just convincing but untouchable.

The Sound of Silence

Sometimes, the most potent and unambiguous statement an echo chamber makes is not spoken at all; it exists in the stark absence of sound. In that unsettling quiet, there is a familiar darkness that greets you like an old friend as uncomfortable questions, inconvenient facts, and dissenting voices simply vanish into silence.

In Flat Earth spaces, silence is far more than the absence of noise. It is a deliberate, calculated rhetorical move. When skeptical questions or conflicting evidence disappear without explanation, the vacuum left behind sends a message louder than any words could: This does not belong here. This will not be tolerated.

This is where defensive maintenance—the quiet, constant act of guarding the narrative—becomes unmistakably visible. After defining "inside" language through terministic screens and framing outside ideas as dangerous through inoculation theory, the next step is to make sure no trace of that "contamination" survives. Posts with the wrong questions are quietly deleted. Comments introducing doubt vanish mid-thread. Entire accounts can disappear overnight without a word. The silence that follows is not empty. It is performative. It tells everyone still inside that the walls are alive, constantly patrolling, and utterly unforgiving.

Rhetorically, this is erasure framing at its sharpest. The absence of argument becomes its own argument. When no counterpoint is visible, the chamber frames that void as proof the counterpoint never had merit. If there is nothing to see, then nothing worth seeing was ever there. This pairs perfectly with inoculation theory (McGuire, 1964): if any opposing view slips past the pre-framing, its swift removal and the vacuum left behind reinforce the purity of the narrative.

For the people inside, that silence works on two levels. Outwardly, it keeps the Flat Earth "performance" seamless. There are no visible cracks, no evidence of dissent for outsiders or wavering insiders to notice. Inwardly, it teaches everyone to police themselves. After you have seen enough threads vanish into nothing, you do not need a moderator to tell you what is off-limits. You feel the invisible edges of the walls before you ever reach them. You start editing your own thoughts to stay safely within the frame. That is the spiral of silence in action (Noelle-Neumann, 1974): the fear of being cast out becomes so strong that people stop voicing, and even stop forming, dissenting ideas.

That is why silence in the chamber is never passive. It is a tool, a message, and a weapon all at once. It says, without ever saying it: This is reality. Everything else is just noise, and we will erase it.

Ritual Defense

Once fear has hardened the chamber's walls and deliberate silence has swept away any lingering "noise," the next phase kicks in: ritual defense. This is not just reacting to threats. It is a highly visible, almost ceremonial performance of protecting the story so thoroughly and so consistently that the act itself becomes part of the chamber's identity.

Flat Earth spaces—whether a Facebook group, a Discord server, or a real-world meetup—develop predictable routines for this. Picture it: a new member posts a question that hints, subtly or blatantly, at a "globe" perspective. What follows isn't a slow trickle of thoughtful debate. It is a flood. Familiar slogans cascade in rapid-fire: "Water finds its level." "NASA lies." Links to the same "debunk" videos. Screenshots of iconic Flat Earth maps that have been shared a thousand times before. It is less a conversation than a ceremony, a collective recitation designed not to persuade a skeptic, but to reinforce the story for everyone watching—especially the insiders.

This is performative rhetoric in its purest form. The point is not to win over the outsider; the point is the ritual itself. The repeated lines, the predictable arguments, the reflexive deployment of "evidence" all signal strength and unity. A challenge, no matter how small, is not treated as a threat to be debated—it's a cue. And the chamber answers with a synchronized, well-rehearsed script. That call-and-response is not about the content of the question; it is about the performance of certainty.

Psychologically, these rituals do double work. Outwardly, they project a formidable wall of unity, making the belief look unshakable to any observer. Inwardly, they deeply reassure the group. The act of defending the narrative together does not just protect the story; it reinforces belonging. Taking part in the ritual itself becomes as meaningful as the belief it protects (Tajfel & Turner, 1979). Every shared meme, every copied link, every slogan posted on cue quietly says, we are in this together, and what we're guarding matters.

With time, these rituals stop feeling like conscious acts at all. The same memes, the same images, the same lines come out on autopilot, deployed like muscle memory. At that point, the ritual doesn't need the outsider. It doesn't matter if the person who asked the question stays, leaves, or even listens. The defense was never really for them. It was for the chamber itself—a communal act of self-preservation that says, over and over, in perfect unison: the story is safe, and by protecting it, so are we.

The Walls as Comfort

After every defense has been mounted—the guarding, the shaping of language, the silencing, the rehearsed rituals—what settles inside the echo chamber is not just quiet. It is a profound sense of safety. Once the narrative has been shielded from outside "contamination," the walls that once felt like barriers begin to transform. They do not feel restrictive anymore; they feel like a shelter. What began as constant, deliberate acts of maintenance gradually shifts into something deeper: the comforting sense of belonging.

This is the emotional payoff of the echo chamber. At its core, it is not just about sealing out dissent or protecting a particular claim; it is about making the inside feel like home. The familiar slogans, the endless stream of shared memes, the well-worn "debunking" videos, even the collective act of silencing dissent all merge into a single, powerful effect: the creation of a shared sanctuary. The rhetoric here softens. Fear and defense give way to the language of comfort, identity, and belonging.

At this point, pathos—the appeal to emotion—becomes the glue holding everything together (Aristotle, trans. 2007). The belief in a flat Earth is still present, but it is no longer the only thing being protected. What the members are really defending is the feeling: the certainty, the purpose, and the deep sense of being part of something that matters in a confusing, shifting world. The walls do not just keep threats out—they hold in warmth, affirmation, and the quiet reassurance of community.

You can hear this shift in the language. "Fellow truth-seekers." "The few who truly see." "Our community." These are not just labels. They are emotional touchstones, wrapping the members in the story and, more importantly, in each other. The chamber stops being about an abstract argument over the planet's shape. It becomes a collective selfhood, a shared identity forged through mutual protection and belief. That identity is what holds the group together (Tajfel & Turner, 1979) and what makes the appeal to certainty so powerful (Kruglanski & Webster, 1996).

This is where narrative transportation and identity fusion meet. Members are pulled so deeply into the story that it starts to feel like their own lived reality (Green & Brock, 2000). Their personal sense of self begins to blend with the group's collective identity until the two are nearly indistinguishable (Swann et al., 2012). Walking away at that point does not just feel like abandoning a belief—it feels like leaving a family, like stepping outside a warm, sheltering house into a cold, uncertain night. That is why the walls do not just stand. They hold. And for those inside, that embrace can feel impossible to ever let go.

Carrying the Echo

Every captivating performance, no matter how tightly contained, eventually spills beyond the theater.

The applause, the whispered reactions, the quotable lines—they do not stay within the walls. They leak into the street, gathering momentum and shaping the conversation outside. Flat Earth rhetoric works the same way. The echo chamber is not designed just to reinforce belief internally; it is built to project it. What is forged inside those insulated walls rarely stays put. Instead, the core messages, carrying the tone and absolute certainty honed within the chamber, push out through platforms, algorithms, and conversations, echoing far beyond their original space.

You can watch it happen in real time across the digital landscape. A 30-second clip of a Flat Earth proponent "debating" a mainstream scientist gets sliced for TikTok, then stitched, remixed, and shared until it racks up millions of views. A meme about "pilots dipping their noses" to fly over a curve, or the iconic "Antarctica is the ice wall" image, jumps from Facebook to Instagram to X (formerly Twitter) in hours. The claim itself does not change, but the scale and reach do. That is rhetorical amplification in action—not just repeating a message, but boosting it until it starts to shape the larger public conversation.

Social media architecture supercharges this process. Platforms reward certainty, emotion, and repetition because they generate engagement. A calm voice stating, "If the Earth were spinning, we would feel it," hits all three. The confidence sparks agreement, outrage, and sharing, and the algorithm does the rest.

This is where classical rhetorical kairos—the perfect timing of a message (Aristotle, trans. 2007)—meets platform code. Drop that clip during a moment of public skepticism about authority or a trending science story, and the Flat Earth message lands with disproportionate impact.

There is another layer here that makes the effect even more potent: ethos transfer. Inside the chamber, the Confident Truth Teller's credibility is carefully built and reinforced. When their clips and sound bites leave that space, that constructed ethos travels with them. The calm tone, the steady delivery, the polished confidence—all of it signals authority to an outside viewer who has no idea how carefully that persona was manufactured. The performance itself makes the message feel trustworthy, even when the claim behind it is paper-thin (Messaris & Abraham, 2001).

This is rhetorical circulation at its most deliberate. The chamber does not just produce messages to echo internally; it engineers them to move, to survive, and to resonate outside. The repetition, the certainty, the sharp us-versus-them framing, the simple narratives—none of that is accidental. It is baked in so the message can carry the chamber's acoustics wherever it lands. When those clips and memes hit the wider digital world, they do not just carry a claim. They carry the performance itself, confidence and all, largely intact.

Amplified by Design

Viral moments in the digital world do not simply "happen." Inside the Flat Earth echo chamber, the language and content are built—sometimes consciously, sometimes just by instinct—with one eye fixed on the immediate audience and the other aimed squarely at the vast digital platforms outside. It is not accidental resonance or random virality; it is rhetorical engineering. Phrases are sharpened for shareability. Memes are boiled down to one striking punchline or a single visual designed to survive endless screenshots, reposts, and remixes. Even the Confident Truth Teller's calm, unwavering delivery is not just meant to reassure insiders—it is crafted to travel, carrying that same aura of authority into every new feed it lands in.

Take a line like, "If the Earth were curved, pilots would have to keep dipping the nose." That is not just an argument—it is a soundbite built to move. It fits neatly into a meme caption, a 15-second clip, or a comment thread and still keeps its punch. That kind of compact, portable phrasing is rhetorical amplification at work: crafting a message so it does not just land once, but is designed to echo effortlessly, to be repeated, shared, and eventually absorbed into wider conversations.

There is also an intuitive grasp of what makes a message "sticky." The chamber favors phrases with simple rhythms and vivid imagery because those are the ones that lodge in memory and roll off the tongue (Heath & Heath, 2007). "Water finds its level" spreads not because it is scientifically valid, but because it is short, paints a clear mental picture, and sounds like common sense. That simplicity taps into cognitive fluency: when a statement is easy to process, the brain is more likely to accept it as true (Reber & Schwarz, 1998).

This rhetorical design syncs perfectly with the way social media platforms work. Algorithms reward short, repeatable content—especially when it carries emotional weight, whether that is agreement, outrage, or curiosity. Over time, the Flat Earth chamber, through repetition and feedback, has learned to create language and visuals that plug directly into that system. A punchy meme, a confident clip, a slogan-sized claim—these are not just arguments; they are built to trigger the machine of virality.

What you get is a feedback loop. Messages are crafted to move. The platforms reward the ones that move best. Each successful viral echo teaches the chamber how to refine the next one, shaping language and visuals ever closer to what the algorithms love. In that sense, the Flat Earth narrative is not just being carried by digital megaphones—it is being written with them in mind from the very beginning, designed to ride the wave of amplification the moment it leaves the chamber.

Echoes Beyond Believers

Not every echo that leaves the Flat Earth chamber is meant to win someone over completely—or even to speak directly to the already faithful. Some of the most quietly effective rhetoric is not designed for full conversion at all. Its job is subtler and, in some ways, more potent: to linger. A short clip, a pithy slogan, or a striking meme does not have to change someone's mind outright. All it has to do is plant a question, create a little bit of informational "noise," and make the official, mainstream story feel just a touch less steady, a little less certain, and a lot less trustworthy.

This is where rhetorical inoculation extends beyond the chamber to a wider, unsuspecting audience. A line like "If the Earth were spinning, we would feel it" or "Antarctica is the wall holding the oceans in" is built to stick—not necessarily to persuade instantly, but to wedge itself into the back of someone's mind. Even a skeptic who would normally laugh off Flat Earth ideas might find the line resurfacing later as a splinter of doubt: a thought they cannot quite shake when they glance at a globe or hear a scientific explanation they once took for granted. The chamber's architects, whether consciously or through learned practice, understand that sometimes the goal is not conversion. It is corrosion. The mission is to subtly weaken confidence in the mainstream narrative so that the "alternative truth" starts to feel less far-fetched in comparison.

That corrosive power works because it borrows a page straight from pervasive advertising: repeated exposure. When the same phrase, meme, or visual pops up over and over across TikTok, YouTube shorts, Facebook groups, and Twitter threads, it does not just feel familiar—it starts to feel culturally present. It becomes "that thing people are talking about," even if most of the conversation is mockery or outrage. At that point, rhetorical circulation slips into cultural saturation. The claim's presence becomes the message. This effect is underpinned by the mere exposure effect: the simple act of repeatedly encountering a stimulus, even without agreeing with it, increases its familiarity and, with it, a subtle sense of validity (Zajonc, 1968).

Layered on top of this is the quiet, often invisible work of ethos transfer. When a clip of a calm, unflinching speaker makes its way outside the chamber, the audience encountering it for the first time has no context for the persona's construction. They do not see the constant internal rehearsal or the echo chamber's self-reinforcing scaffolding; they just see authority. The speaker's cultivated credibility seeps into the claim itself, lending weight to the words even when the content is immediately rejected. The confident delivery leaves a mark long after the details of the argument are forgotten (Petty & Cacioppo, 1986).

Whether this spread is the result of careful strategy or a natural byproduct of digital dynamics, the result is the same: presence. The echo chamber is not just reinforcing belief inside its own walls; it is leaking out, quietly and persistently, into the larger cultural conversation. The slogans, memes, and confident tone do not have to convince anyone outright to succeed. They just have to be heard often enough that the performance of certainty—and the doubt it is designed to seed—lingers in the air far beyond the chamber's carefully constructed stage.

The Feedback Loop

Every echo that makes it past the chamber's walls—a viral meme, a trending TikTok clip, a slogan that suddenly starts showing up in outside comment threads—does not just vanish into the wider digital noise. Almost immediately, it finds its way back home. Screenshots of trending posts are shared in internal forums. Metrics like views, likes, and shares are celebrated as proof, not just of reach, but of righteousness. For the chamber, this is not just content leaving the walls; it is reconnaissance. Each echo that returns carries vital intelligence about how their message is performing in the outside world.

That returning echo does more than fuel celebration. It acts as a calibration tool, a real-time tuning fork for the entire rhetorical system. Any phrase that demonstrates stickiness (Heath & Heath, 2007) gets repeated with renewed fervor. Any meme or clip that travels far is instantly treated as a model, replicated and remixed until it becomes a template for the next wave of content. This is not random iteration; it is a textbook rhetorical feedback loop. The chamber's messages shape external perception, and the external reaction—measured in engagement and reach—quietly shapes the chamber's next moves in return.

This is where the "Amplified by Design" dynamic becomes truly self-reinforcing. Every successful viral moment is not just proof that the rhetoric works—it becomes a blueprint for how to make it sharper, louder, and more shareable next time. The language and imagery of Flat Earth belief evolve in real-time, refined by the very audiences the chamber seeks to influence. A short, confident line like "If the Earth were curved, pilots would have to keep dipping the nose" spikes engagement? It gets folded into dozens of new videos and posts almost overnight. A meme about the Antarctic "ice wall" goes viral?

Variants bloom across platforms, each one iterating on the last until the image feels iconic and unavoidable.

Modern platforms supercharge this process by handing the chamber instant, granular analytics. No focus groups, no expensive research studies—just raw, immediate data. Likes, shares, comments, watch time, and reach become the chamber's constant pulse check. The numbers do not just measure success; they silently instruct the community on what to make next, turning every external echo into both validation and direction.

That external validation does something deeper than shaping content strategy. Psychologically, it hits the core identity of the group. When members see their message resonating, when they see "proof" that the outside world is listening—even if it is mocking or arguing—they do not just feel vindicated in their belief. They feel vindicated in who they are. That returning echo becomes applause, a powerful affirmation of both the narrative and the identity tied to it (Swann et al., 2012). And applause is addictive. It keeps the performance alive, driving the chamber to create more, share more, amplify more.

In this iterative loop, the echo chamber is not just a sealed container bouncing sound back and forth. It becomes a living, adaptive system—a creator and curator all at once, tuning its voice for maximum reach. The walls do not just hold the echo inside; they sharpen it, shaping the sound to carry farther, louder, and with more precision every single time it makes the trip back.

Voices Made Viral

Every echo, every resonant message, needs something to carry it. Inside the echo chamber, the Flat Earth story feels like a collective chorus—a wall of agreement built from countless voices. But once that carefully crafted sound slips beyond the chamber's walls, it changes form. Out in the wild, the message rarely travels as a full conversation or a long argument. It most often appears as something far more compact: a 30-second TikTok, a clipped line from a livestream, a screen-captured meme, or a perfectly timed soundbite. Here, the focus is not just on the person speaking—it is on the package. The digital artifact itself becomes the message.

When a single clip goes viral, it is not just the words that move. The whole performance—the certainty, the authority, the insider tone—is distilled into a portable format built to thrive in the digital ecosystem. This is rhetorical embodiment in a different sense than the "Confident Truth Teller" of Section 3. There, the person was the argument. Here, it is the content itself. The human face and voice give it texture and authenticity, but it is the snippet—the small, self-contained artifact—that does the real persuasive work as it races across platforms.

That is why certain lines—"If the Earth were spinning, we would feel it" or "Antarctica is the wall holding the oceans in"—are repeated endlessly inside the chamber. They are designed to survive outside it. Each one functions as a miniature performance, engineered to be clipped, reposted, and recognized even when stripped of its original context. When those snippets move, they carry the chamber's tone of absolute certainty with them. This is where rhetorical amplification (Heath & Heath, 2007) intersects perfectly with platform design: short, emotionally charged, easy-to-process content is exactly what algorithms love to boost, and the chamber has learned, consciously or not, to craft its rhetoric to fit that mold, leveraging cognitive fluency to make the message stick (Reber & Schwarz, 1998).

Layered over all this is a subtle kind of ethos transfer. When someone outside the community encounters one of these viral clips, they do not see the scaffolding that built the speaker's credibility inside the chamber. They just see the calm tone, the steady delivery, the absolute conviction. That confident performance wraps itself around the clip, making the content itself feel inherently trustworthy (Messaris & Abraham, 2001). The "how" often matters more than the "what."

This is why virality in the Flat Earth narrative is not really about creating breakout stars. It is about creating breakout content. The snippet, the soundbite, the bite-sized performance becomes the vessel. It is no longer the Truth Teller stepping outside the walls; it is the carefully engineered artifact of the performance carrying the echo into the wider world.

But there is a trade-off baked into this process. Once those echoes leave the chamber, they do not always return in the same shape. Some come back louder, sharper, amplifying the story's core tenets exactly as intended. Others return warped or diluted, stripped of context in ways that subtly change the message. This risk—the possibility that the echo comes back sounding slightly off—is the unavoidable cost of building rhetoric to move so far and so fast. It raises an uncomfortable question for the chamber: how much control can you really keep over the sound once it escapes the walls?

Resonance vs. Noise

Every echo carries a built-in risk: the moment it leaves the chamber's walls, the community loses control over how it will land—or how it will be reshaped. Digital platforms do not just amplify messages; they actively reframe them. A line like, "If the Earth were spinning, we would feel it," delivered inside the echo chamber with absolute authority, can travel outward and return as scathing satire, a dismissive meme, or a puzzled reaction video. Even the most iconic images—"Antarctica is the wall holding the oceans in"—spread far and wide, but the further they move, the more likely they are to be cropped, re-captioned, or remixed into something that carries an entirely different tone. The words may survive; the meaning shifts.

This is message framing theory in action (Entman, 1993; Lakoff, 2004). A message is not defined solely by its raw content; it is shaped by the frame around it. What feels like an unshakable truth in one tightly curated environment can look absurd or unhinged in another, simply because the surrounding cues—the tone, the visuals, the implied audience—have changed. This is the essence of rhetorical resonance drift: the message travels, but its "pitch" changes depending on whose microphone it passes through and which cultural stage it lands on.

Flat Earth rhetoric does not just endure this drift; it exploits it. A viral clip mocked on TikTok? A meme turned into parody? Inside the chamber, that is not failure—it is fuel. The narrative instantly pivots: "If they are mocking us, we must be over the target." What outsiders see as ridicule is reframed as validation, a sign the "system" feels threatened. This is deliberate frame control: a strategic move that turns distortion and hostility into proof. What should weaken the story is transformed into another argument for its truth.

Psychologically, even ridicule keeps the message alive through availability bias (Tversky & Kahneman, 1974). A debunking video, no matter how thorough, cannot erase the phrase it is trying to dismantle. By repeating it—even in the act of refuting it—the debunker makes sure it stays present and familiar in memory (Zajonc, 1968). That is why the chamber rarely abandons a phrase that gets hijacked or mocked. Instead, it doubles down. As long as the words are circulating, the wall is still standing.

And that is the paradox at the heart of distortion: what should, by conventional logic, undermine the narrative often ends up feeding it. Not because the message stays intact, but because the chamber has adapted to survive on the noise as much as the music. Mockery, parody, and criticism all become raw material. Every echo, warped or pristine, still reverberates back into the chamber and gets folded into the story. To its members, the cacophony outside does not sound like rejection. It sounds like confirmation.

Curtain Call

Every compelling performance eventually reaches its end, but the most memorable ones do not just stop when the lights go out—they follow you into the night, lingering in your thoughts and conversations. The Flat Earth echo chamber works in much the same way. What happens inside its walls is not a loose collection of arguments or stray assertions; it is a carefully staged act, built to resonate long after the curtain falls. The shared chorus of mantras, the commanding central voice, and the protective walls holding belief in and doubt out combine to create something far larger than a claim. They build an experience.

Stepping back from the theater metaphor, this chapter has peeled apart the mechanics of that experience in motion. Language drives the engine: repeated slogans serving as powerful ethos builders, memes compressed into portable mini-arguments, and the steady, confident delivery that turns a simple statement into a persuasive performance. Repetition isn't just background noise—it's the structure itself, the scaffolding that holds the entire system together. And even as those messages leak outside the chamber, bending and warping in new contexts, the echo still carries. It carries because this rhetoric is not designed for perfect accuracy; it is designed for survival.

And that durability points to the deeper truth beneath all of it: Flat Earth rhetoric does not endure because of data or airtight logic. It endures because of identity. The elaborate performance is not just telling a story—it is offering the audience a role in it, inviting them to see themselves woven into its fabric. It is a place where doubt is recast as courage, where skepticism feels like clarity, and where the need for certainty finds not just validation but community.

That's where we turn next. Beyond the walls, past the slogans, deeper than the performance itself lies the part that gives the echo chamber its real staying power: the personal. In the following chapter, we move from the stage to the heart, exploring how belief stops being just words or walls and transforms into something far more intimate and binding—a profound sense of belonging, self-affirmation, and a shared identity forged in the unbroken sound of the echo.

Chapter 5 — Rhetorical Sleight of Hand: Tricks, Tropes, and Tactics

When belief wears the mask of identity, it no longer asks for proof — it demands loyalty.

By the time belief becomes deeply personal and intertwined with identity, as we saw in the last chapter, the story is no longer just being told—it is being lived. This is precisely where Flat Earth rhetoric performs one of its most powerful and effective illusions. It understands that it does not need to definitively prove its claim outright; it only needs to make the believer feel like it has been proven.

This is where rhetorical sleight of hand comes into play. Much like a stage magician, the trick is not about what is objectively true, but about what seems true in a fleeting, mesmerizing moment. Flat Earth arguments rarely win by constructing a solid case brick by brick, with verifiable evidence and sound logic. Instead, they succeed by creating the impression of proof: they flood conversations with an overwhelming volume of disconnected details, they frame questions in a way that puts the skeptic perpetually on the defensive, and they leverage powerful emotional weight to tip the scales where concrete evidence simply cannot.

These rhetorical moves are certainly not unique to the Flat Earth community—you can observe the same techniques at work in other conspiracy theories, carefully crafted political spin, and even in everyday arguments. But because the Flat Earth narrative exists in a space where the verifiable evidence is so thin, the tricks of the trade stand out in sharp relief. Emotional appeals are expertly disguised as logic. Well-known logical fallacies are dressed up to sound like common sense. Isolated fragments of "facts" are pulled from vast mountains of unrelated data to build a house of cards that, from the inside, feels like an impregnable fortress.

These rhetorical tricks are most effective because they are designed to work in plain sight. But once you begin to peel back the curtain and see the performance for what it is, the illusion begins to change. The emotional hooks, the clever misdirections, and the carefully chosen fragments of "evidence" all stand out for what they truly are: parts of a captivating performance. What once looked like solid proof starts to feel much more like smoke and mirrors. And when you've finally seen the mechanics behind the show, it becomes almost impossible to unsee them, no matter where they appear.

Emotional Appeals: Fear, Pride, and Belonging

Fear is one of the most powerful emotional levers in persuasion, and Flat Earth rhetoric pulls on it relentlessly. At the heart of many of the movement's arguments is a simple but deeply loaded message: you are being lied to. That idea hits something visceral. No one wants to feel manipulated or kept in the dark—especially not by the very people and institutions we are told to trust. That vulnerability to deception becomes fertile ground for persuasion.

This is what communication theorists call a fear appeal—a technique that deliberately leans on anxiety to drive a change in attitude or behavior (Witte, 1992). But here, the fear is not of a tangible threat like a disease or disaster; it is the far more insidious fear of betrayal. The unsettling suggestion is not just that the Earth might not be what you think—it is that you have been willfully and deliberately deceived on a massive scale. That twist, from a factual question to a personal betrayal, makes the emotional punch land much harder than any simple, data-based argument could.

Flat Earth messaging frames this fear with a consistent story: they are hiding the truth from you. Once that suspicion takes hold, every official source—from NASA photos to peer-reviewed articles—automatically looks suspect. This is a direct appeal to pathos, bypassing logic entirely. It hits the feelings first and lets them quietly override the slower, deliberate process of reason. It also works as a kind of rhetorical inoculation (McGuire, 1964). By warning believers in advance that deception is everywhere and mainstream sources cannot be trusted, it primes them to see any counterargument as part of the lie. Outside evidence does not soften the belief; it reinforces it.

That fear also drives the movement's stark "us versus them" framing. If they—the vague, powerful "elites," the government, the scientists—are lying, then trusting anything outside the circle of believers is not just naive; it is dangerous. This fear of a conspiratorial "other" bonds the group together under a shared sense of vigilance and gives the story moral weight. Inside that frame, questioning science is not just curiosity; it becomes an act of intellectual and personal self-defense. This in-group/out-group dynamic (Tajfel & Turner, 1979) strengthens community ties and solidifies a shared identity.

Psychologists have long noted that fear narrows focus. Under threat, the mind zeroes in on danger and tunes out everything else. In this context, the more the fear of betrayal is stirred up, the less room there is for calm, rational evaluation. The urgency of being lied to drowns out critical thinking, letting the illusion of proof thrive.

Flat Earth influencers often wrap this fear in the language of empowerment so it does not feel like fear at all. Phrases like "Do not let them trick you," "Do your own research," and "Do not be fooled" sound like calls to independence, but they carry the same underlying message: you are under attack from deception. The sleight of hand is that the fear does not register as fear. To the believer, it feels like courage—being awake and alert while everyone else sleeps. That is what makes this appeal so effective. It does not shout, "Be afraid." It whispers, "Be smart. Be careful. They are lying to you." And in that whisper, emotion quietly takes the place of evidence.

Flat Earth rhetoric does not just stir up suspicion and fear; it runs on another, often more potent, emotion: pride. The moment someone starts to seriously question the globe, they are not just asking in a vacuum—they are instantly framed as brave, independent thinkers, the kind of explorers willing to step outside the complacent crowd. That sense of being part of a small, enlightened group who can "see through the lie" is not an accident of community culture. It is a deliberate, effective emotional appeal that turns initial doubt into the foundation of a new identity.

The journey often begins with a single, unsettling thought: What if they really are hiding something? At first, the fear of betrayal dominates. But once that suspicion hardens into the realization that I see what they do not, the emotional tone flips. The initial anxiety and paranoia are replaced with a surge of pride—of being "awake" while everyone else is still "asleep." That shift is what makes the belief so sticky and hard to shake. It is the moment the idea stops being external and becomes an internal source of validation.

This is pathos at work, skillfully flattering the audience. The rhetoric tells them they are sharp enough, courageous enough, independent enough to see a truth billions of others cannot. Phrases like "I see what others cannot" or "I woke up to the truth" are not just statements; they are badges of honor. Once someone puts on that badge, Flat Earth stops being a theory and starts becoming a reflection of who they are. This ties into self-perception theory, where adopting a behavior—in this case, the language of being "awake"—starts to shape personal identity itself (Bem, 1972).

The narrative wraps this in a classic conversion story (Green & Brock, 2000): a journey from blindness to vision, ignorance to awareness. The "moment of waking up" is described in vivid emotional terms—shock at the deception, anger at the betrayal, exhilaration at newfound freedom. Those emotions etch the experience into memory far more deeply than any chart, equation, or photograph ever could.

Flat Earth influencers amplify this by modeling absolute certainty. They become living examples of the "truth-seeker," the virtuous figure worth emulating. That unshakable confidence creates its own persuasion through ethos transfer; even when the argument is thin, the delivery makes it feel solid (Messaris & Abraham, 2001). It is a classic rhetorical move: projecting confidence until belief looks—and feels—like undeniable knowledge.

But there is a hidden cost to this emotional appeal. Once someone defines themselves as "awake" and takes pride in that identity, leaving the belief feels like erasing that courageous, enlightened version of themselves. Changing their mind is not just about evidence anymore; it is a painful act of losing who they think they are. This is cognitive dissonance in action: the clash between "I am an enlightened truth-seeker" and "My core belief might be wrong" is too intense to reconcile, so the identity-driven belief wins (Festinger, 1957).

Unlike fear, which creates urgency and threat, pride feels warm and affirming. It offers strength and belonging all at once (Tajfel & Turner, 1979). That is exactly why it is so effective. Pride does not just reinforce the Flat Earth idea; it reinforces something even stronger—the belief that rejecting it would mean rejecting the person you have become.

Flat Earth rhetoric does not just aim arguments at individual minds; it carefully builds a shared space where the belief feels safe, affirmed, and vividly alive. That sense of connection and belonging is not accidental. It is a deliberate part of how the arguments are presented and repeated.

Belief is rarely held in isolation. As social creatures, we instinctively look to others to validate what we think and feel—a dynamic psychologists call social proof (Cialdini, 1984). This is where the emotional appeal of pathos intersects with what can be described as communal framing: shaping the argument so that accepting it also means joining a group. In Flat Earth spaces, the language reflects this constantly: "Welcome to the truth," "You are one of us now," "We are the ones who see." These phrases do not just affirm the belief itself; they send a powerful message that believing connects you to a rare and courageous family.

That sense of belonging does something rhetorically potent: it makes the belief feel more valid and real. When a newcomer hears others echoing the same arguments, sharing the same "awakening" story, and defending the same positions, it creates a powerful sense of perceived consensus. Even if the group is small compared to the rest of the world, the sheer agreement inside it makes the idea feel weighty and true. Noelle-Neumann (1974) showed how the perception of being in a majority—or in a unified, righteous minority—can profoundly shape belief and expression, creating a self-reinforcing loop of validation.

Flat Earth influencers understand this, whether consciously or by instinct. Livestreams, forums, and comment sections are not just channels for sharing information; they are places where group identity is forged and reinforced through constant interaction. Every "like," every "you are so right," every shared meme becomes a piece of social proof, a small but powerful cue saying, "You belong here. This is your space."

This communal identity also acts as emotional shelter. Outside the group, skepticism and mockery can feel isolating. Inside, those same attacks are reframed as persecution, which strengthens the internal bonds. This is classic in-group/out-group construction (Tajfel & Turner, 1979), but here it is more than labeling enemies. It is about finding a safe, affirming space versus a hostile, dismissive outside world.

The need to belong is such a deep human drive that it often outweighs logic and evidence. When the group becomes where you feel most understood and safe, walking away from the belief is not just changing your mind. It feels like losing a home, a family, and your primary source of validation. That emotional cost is part of what makes this tactic so powerful. It anchors the belief not only in ideas, but in cherished relationships.

At its most persuasive, Flat Earth rhetoric does not just argue that the Earth is flat. It promises that accepting it makes you part of something rare, united, and courageous. That promise of belonging is not just a side effect of the belief—it is a central piece of the persuasion. In the end, it is not only about what you believe. It is about who you believe it with.

This is where pathos does most of the heavy lifting. In rhetorical theory, arguments built on logos rely on careful reasoning, evidence, and logical structure (Aristotle, trans. 2007). Emotional appeals bypass that slow, analytical process and strike directly at what the audience feels to be true. Once a belief is tied to a strong emotion—especially something as visceral as the fear of betrayal or the pride of being "awake"— any counter-evidence has to fight its way through that emotional filter before it can even be considered. That requires immense cognitive effort, which makes emotional appeals far more efficient.

There is also a powerful cognitive shortcut at work. As Daniel Kahneman (2011) explains with his dual-process theory, the brain processes emotional and intuitive information (System 1 thinking) much faster than analytical, logical information (System 2 thinking). That speed gives emotion a decisive head start in any argument. By the time charts, graphs, and evidence show up, the feeling—the fear, the pride, the sense of belonging—has already taken root, shaping how all incoming information will be interpreted. Flat Earth rhetoric exploits this brilliantly. "Do not let them fool you" is not a fact. "You are one of the few who sees the truth" is not a proof. Yet both hit harder and linger longer than a graph or equation because they create urgency and identity. They make the audience feel first and think second.

This is not unique to Flat Earth. Advertisers, political campaigns, and public health messages all lean on emotion because it works. But in a rhetorical space where factual evidence is thin, the imbalance becomes stark. With so few logical proofs to stand on, emotion becomes the scaffolding holding the entire structure together, making a fragile house of cards feel like a solid fortress.

It is also why challenging a belief built on emotion feels so exhausting. A skeptic is not just arguing against a claim or a piece of evidence. They are arguing against someone's fear, their pride, their sense of belonging—the entire emotional core of the belief. Emotional appeals are not just persuasive in the moment; they are incredibly resilient. Facts can be replaced with new facts. Emotions have to be dislodged from the person's identity, which is a much harder, more painful task.

And this is where the rhetorical trick sharpens. Once emotion has built the foundation and framed the story, logic can be imitated. Flat Earth rhetoric often wraps itself in the language of reason and scientific inquiry, with sharp-sounding questions and claims that mimic evidence-based arguments. But beneath that surface, emotion is still doing the real work of persuasion. What follows next isn't just accidental bad logic. It's a deliberate use of rhetoric designed to make emotion all the more powerful when it wears the mask of reason.

Logical Fallacies in Plain Sight

So, if emotion is doing all the heavy lifting, where does "logic" fit in? This is where the sleight of hand gets clever. The rhetoric stops sounding like an emotional appeal and starts wearing a costume borrowed from reason. These are not accidental mistakes; they are deliberate moves designed to mimic a real argument. What follows are the most common tricks you will see in the performance of Flat Earth "logic"—and how they work.

Strawman Arguments

A strawman argument is one of the oldest rhetorical tricks in the book. It takes a real position, distorts it into a weaker or oversimplified caricature, and then attacks that fake version instead of the actual claim. In the world of Flat Earth debates, this move shows up constantly. When the conversation turns to planetary physics or cosmology, you can almost guarantee a strawman will appear, constructed and then knocked down with a flourish. Classic examples include: "So you are saying water sticks to a spinning ball because of magic gravity?" or "You believe we are flying through space at thousands of miles per hour and you do not feel it?" These are not genuine rebuttals of nuanced scientific positions. They are strawmen, built specifically to make the opposing argument sound absurd and easy to dismiss.

What makes the tactic so persuasive is how much it feels like common sense. When an audience hears a position framed in such an obviously ridiculous way, rejecting it feels natural—almost intellectually necessary. It creates a powerful cognitive shortcut (Kahneman, 2011). If the "globe" argument sounds silly in this reduced form, then by comparison, the Flat Earth claim must seem more rational, more grounded, and therefore the "stronger" position. That illusion of victory by default is exactly why the strawman fallacy is so effective.

There is also a second layer to how Flat Earthers use this tactic. They often flip it back on skeptics in a way that shows a fundamental misunderstanding of what the fallacy actually is. When a skeptic explains gravity, atmospheric dynamics, or the Coriolis effect, the retort often comes fast: "Stop building strawmen." In this move, the term itself becomes a defensive shield. Legitimate counterarguments get mislabeled as strawmen so the Flat Earth position can avoid engaging with the actual evidence. It creates the appearance of defending logic while really just sidestepping the debate. This is rhetorical reframing in action—taking a term from logical discourse and re-appropriating it as a tool to control the conversation (Lakoff, 2004).

That misuse is not accidental. It is part of a broader pattern where logical fallacies become weapons rather than concepts with definitions. With strawmen, the effect is doubled: first, the opponent's position is turned into a cartoon version, and then any pushback is dismissed as a strawman itself. The result is a neat illusion of logical superiority without ever touching the real argument.

Rhetorically, this tactic works so well because it simplifies the complex. Nuanced, detailed scientific explanations about planetary physics or cosmology get compressed into easy-to-grasp caricatures that can be effortlessly dismissed. That simplicity plugs directly into the movement's larger emotional appeal: it takes something complicated and makes it look obvious. And once the "obvious" feels undeniable, the argument does not just sound persuasive—it feels unshakably true.

A false dichotomy

False dichotomy is a logical fallacy that frames a complex debate as if there are only two possible answers when, in reality, a wide spectrum of options exists. It creates a narrow, manufactured "either-or" choice, putting rhetorical pressure on the audience to pick a side. In Flat Earth rhetoric, this fallacy shows up everywhere, offering a simple binary framework for an incredibly complex world. Common examples include: "Either the Earth is flat or you believe everything NASA tells you" and "Either you trust your own eyes or you are blindly following mainstream science." By reducing a nuanced scientific question to two extreme, emotionally loaded positions, the argument makes the Flat Earth view appear to be the only independent, rebellious, and credible option.

At its core, a false dichotomy is a framing trick (Lakoff, 2004). It does not add evidence or solid reasoning; it works by shrinking the range of what can even be considered. When the only alternatives are "believe the Flat Earth" or "be a gullible follower," the conclusion feels baked in before the discussion even starts. This frame leans hard on the emotional appeals discussed earlier—the pride of being an independent thinker and the fear of being deceived—to make the choice feel less like logic and more like morality.

Flat Earthers also often misapply this fallacy as a weapon. The dichotomy itself is presented as if it were a legitimate debate structure: "I gave you two options, so pick one." Here, the fallacy is not recognized as a flaw but becomes a deliberate way to corner the conversation so the Flat Earth side cannot lose. This setup guarantees that rejecting the Flat Earth claim automatically means accepting "blind trust," hitting the exact emotional chord the movement plays over and over.

You also see the label thrown back at skeptics. A globe defender pointing to scientific consensus or peer review might be accused of creating a false dichotomy: "So you are saying it is either the mainstream model or nothing?" In truth, the skeptic is not narrowing the field; they are referencing a model supported by centuries of evidence. But once the "false dichotomy" label is dropped into the conversation, it gives the Flat Earth side a convenient shield, letting them claim logical high ground without ever touching the actual argument.

This fallacy works so well because it feels empowering. Offering two stark choices gives the audience a sense of control and decisiveness, even when the options are manufactured. It also leans hard on pathos, turning the decision into a personal statement: "Are you a thinker or a follower?" That emotional frame can override the logical question of whether those were ever the only two choices to begin with.

Moving the Goalposts

The moving the goalposts fallacy occurs when the standard for proof is constantly and arbitrarily changed so that no amount of evidence is ever sufficient. It is a powerful, yet subtle, way to ensure that a debate can never be lost. Each time a Flat Earth claim is addressed with evidence, the rhetorical target subtly shifts: "That is not good enough, show me this instead." In debates with Flat Earthers, this can sound like a conversational loop: "Photos from space are fake, so show me unedited video," followed by, "Video can be faked, so show me live footage," and then, "Live footage is CGI, so show me proof I can see with my own eyes." The finish line is never fixed because the purpose of the tactic is not to genuinely evaluate evidence but to systematically avoid accepting it.

At its heart, this fallacy is a way to keep the debate running in circles, creating the illusion that the skeptic has failed to meet the burden of proof, even when they have comprehensively answered the original question. The ever-shifting standard for what constitutes "real" evidence keeps the Flat Earth claim rhetorically alive by making it functionally unfalsifiable. If no amount of evidence is ever accepted, then the central argument can never be definitively closed, and the belief is immune to refutation. This constant avoidance of a final, disconfirming piece of evidence is a classic defense mechanism against the cognitive dissonance of having a core belief challenged (Festinger, 1957).

Flat Earthers often misunderstand and misframe this tactic as simple persistence or honest inquiry. The behavior is frequently cast as "just asking questions" or "wanting to see more proof." That misunderstanding is a critical part of the illusion. The conversation feels like a relentless and sincere search for truth when, in reality, it's a moving target meticulously designed to prevent any form of resolution. The rhetoric weaponizes the appearance of skepticism to avoid having to confront a contrary conclusion.

This fallacy is also frequently and ironically flipped back onto skeptics. A globe defender who challenges a Flat Earth claim might be accused of "moving the goalposts" when they ask for additional, consistent evidence to support a new claim, even though the request is a consistent application of scientific principles. In this clever reversal, the term itself becomes a rhetorical weapon, allowing the Flat Earth side to avoid scrutiny while claiming the high ground of logical rigor. It's a prime example of how the language of logic is repurposed as a shield.

Rhetorically, moving the goalposts is effective because it feels like a form of intellectual caution and integrity. It plays into the emotional appeal of vigilance that we discussed earlier, directly linking back to the fear of being deceived: "Don't accept anything too quickly; keep demanding more proof." That framing subtly shifts the burden of proof, making the skeptic feel like they are always one piece of evidence away from winning an argument that, by its very design, can never end.

Appeal to Ignorance

An appeal to ignorance (argumentum ad ignorantiam) is a logical fallacy that claims if something has not been definitively proven false, it must be true—or, conversely, if it has not been proven true, it must be false. Flat Earth rhetoric leans on this constantly, using the very absence of evidence as evidence in itself. You hear it in lines like, "You cannot prove the Earth curves, so it must be flat," or "If we cannot see the curvature with our own eyes, it is not there." Rather than offering independent proof for a flat Earth, the argument cleverly flips perceived gaps, scientific uncertainties, or the limits of personal perception into conclusive confirmation of the opposite claim.

That is why this fallacy pairs so neatly with one of the movement's favorite refrains: "Look around you, does it look like a spinning ball?" It sounds like an invitation to reason, but it is built entirely on the absence of data visible to the naked eye. The claim is not supported by evidence; it is supported by what the believer does not see. The same pattern drives their attack on space imagery: "If NASA's photos are fake, the Earth must be flat." Here, the lack of trust in a single source is treated as definitive proof of the opposite claim, with no need to produce any independent, positive evidence for a flat Earth.

As with other fallacies, Flat Earthers often mistake this tactic for sound debate. The underlying assumption is simple: if the Globe model cannot be demonstrated in a way that meets their criteria—criteria often designed to be impossible—their claim wins by default. The key misunderstanding is this: asking for evidence is not the problem. That is an essential part of science. The fallacy lies in treating the absence of proof as if it were proof of the opposite. That critical distinction almost always gets missed, which is why this move feels so definitive inside the narrative.

It also gets flipped back on skeptics. When a globe defender admits uncertainty about a specific scientific detail—say, the precise behavior of atmospheric refraction under rare conditions—Flat Earthers seize on it: "See? You cannot explain it perfectly. That means the Globe is wrong." A natural human or scientific limitation is reframed as a crushing admission of defeat, and that gap is instantly spun into evidence for a Flat Earth, even though it never provides any positive data of its own.

Rhetorically, the appeal to ignorance works because it feels like intellectual caution mixed with common sense. It leans on personal perception: "If I cannot see it, why should I believe it?" That plays straight into pathos and taps into the availability heuristic—the tendency to overvalue what is immediate and accessible to our senses (Tversky & Kahneman, 1974). It also locks tightly to the fear of deception explored in Section 1. If you already believe you are being lied to, every perceived gap in the official explanation feels like proof that the truth is being hidden.

Another reason this fallacy is so resilient is that it demands nothing of the believer. They do not have to build a case; they only have to poke holes in the other side's argument. Presenting evidence is risky—it can be tested and disproven. But demanding proof and turning the lack of it into validation shields the claim from any real scrutiny. In the end, this rhetorical move functions like a mirror: whatever you cannot show becomes their evidence.

Argument from Personal Incredulity / Observation

The argument from personal incredulity is a logical fallacy that claims if something is hard to understand, imagine, or personally observe, it must not be true. In Flat Earth rhetoric, this takes on a particularly visceral shape: the simple declaration, "I see it as flat, so it must be flat." Here, personal observation is not just treated as valid evidence—it becomes the highest standard of proof. Anything that contradicts it—data, models, photographs—is immediately dismissed as lies, illusions, or fabrications.

You hear this argument everywhere in Flat Earth debates and livestreams: "When I look out at the horizon, it is perfectly level." "The ground under my feet is not moving." "The water in the lake does not curve." These statements hit hard because they come from direct, lived experience. They do not sound like abstract theory; they sound like reality itself. That is the power of this fallacy: it bypasses complex data and sophisticated models and instead leans entirely on what feels immediately true in the moment.

Flat Earth content often layers this with a deep distrust of scale. When someone says, "If the Earth were a globe, I would see the curve," they assume their own vantage point is enough to judge something unimaginably larger than human senses can take in. The fallacy is not just in rejecting complex explanations—it is in mistaking the limits of personal perception for the limits of reality itself. The rhetoric frames this mistake as empowerment: "Trust your eyes, not the scientists." That taps directly into naive realism—the belief that we see the world exactly as it is, and those who disagree are biased or misled (Ross & Ward, 1996).

This same move shows up as sheer incredulity: "You expect me to believe we are spinning at 1,000 miles per hour and I do not feel it?" The inability to imagine or physically sense planetary motion is treated as proof it cannot be happening. Again, the error lies in equating personal comprehension with objective truth. Difficulty believing something becomes conclusive evidence against it.

Flat Earthers also flip this tactic onto skeptics. A globe defender explaining orbital mechanics or the use of mathematical models may be hit with, "You are just believing in math you cannot see," reframing calculations and scientific modeling as blind faith. This reversal plays on the same appeal to personal perception: if you cannot observe it with your own senses, it is not real.

Rhetorically, this fallacy works because it taps into something deeply human. We are wired to trust what we can see and feel far more than we trust abstract reasoning or distant data (Kahneman, 2011). It leans heavily on pathos by validating the audience's lived experience and makes rejecting expert consensus feel like an act of intellectual strength. It also connects back to the fear of deception explored earlier: if you believe you are being lied to, your own senses become the last stronghold of truth—and trusting them becomes an act of defiance.

What makes this tactic so resilient is that it feels like the exact opposite of blind faith. To the believer, relying on personal observation seems grounded, independent, and rational. That is the rhetorical sleight of hand: what looks like careful skepticism is actually another form of certainty. The simple statement "I see it flat" becomes more than an observation. It becomes an argument, a belief, and a badge of identity all rolled into one.

The Appeal to Ridicule

The appeal to ridicule (argumentum ad ridiculum) is a logical fallacy that dismisses an argument by making it appear absurd, silly, or laughable, bypassing the need for any factual or logical rebuttal. In the high-energy world of Flat Earth debates, it is one of the most potent tools—and it is used by both sides. You see it when a globe defender brushes off a Flat Earther as an "idiot" or a "moron" without addressing the claim. In that moment, the ridicule is the argument. It's a direct appeal to emotion that bypasses reason entirely (Aristotle, trans. 2007).

Flat Earth rhetoric does not just endure this tactic; it wields it just as powerfully. When an influencer creates satirical "Globe action figures"—tiny caricatures of opponents wearing globes as hats, with captions mocking their "blind faith"—they're using the same fallacy. The figure is not a rebuttal of the globe model; it is pure ridicule, wrapped in performance. A clever rhetorical twist often follows: the influencer frames their own mockery as a neutral observation of "globeheads who come to ridicule and offer no evidence." This move flips the script, casting the influencer as the victim while they are actively deploying the same tactic they claim to expose.

The strength of this fallacy lies in how it works on two levels at once. First, it discredits the out-group, making them look foolish and unworthy of serious consideration. Second, it reinforces the in-group's bonds by creating a shared sense of superiority and validation (Tajfel & Turner, 1979). Ridicule becomes a performance of belonging: laughing at "them" affirms "us." The emotional payoff is immediate—it feels like a clean victory without having to wrestle with complicated arguments or evidence.

It's also a powerful emotional shield. Flat Earth rhetoric uses ridicule as inoculation. When influencers mock "globeheads" in videos and memes, they're not just entertaining their audience—they're preemptively teaching believers how to emotionally process outside criticism. External ridicule gets framed not as a challenge but as a laughably ignorant attack, confirming that "waking up" was an act of courage. The very thing that might have shaken belief instead reinforces it.

Rhetorically, the appeal to ridicule works because it trades substance for impact. It's fast, visceral, and easy to internalize. It doesn't have to prove anything; it only has to make the other side look ridiculous long enough to dismiss them wholesale. Inside that loop, ridicule from skeptics justifies ridicule.

Why Fallacies Feel Persuasive Anyway

Logical fallacies are often described as errors in reasoning, but their real power does not come from logic at all—it comes from how right they feel in the moment. They work because they perfectly mimic the shape of a reasoned argument without carrying any of its weight. And more importantly, they are designed to hit directly at the emotional foundation already laid by fear, pride, and belonging. In Flat Earth rhetoric, this effect is amplified. The fallacies are not accidental slips in reasoning; they are intentional features, a carefully crafted costume that makes the performance of proof look convincing.

Each fallacy offers a different kind of emotional and cognitive reward. A strawman provides the comfort of an easy, decisive victory. A false dichotomy creates the satisfying illusion of control by boiling a complex world down to a simple either/or choice. Moving the goalposts feels like intellectual vigilance—a refusal to be fooled. An appeal to ignorance carries the weight of common sense, a reassurance that what you don't see must speak louder than any external data. The argument from personal incredulity feels like the purest form of truth because it elevates the believer's own direct experience above everything else. Each tactic taps into deep cognitive biases and the human craving to make complicated questions feel simple enough to hold.

That is why these fallacies are not just tolerated inside the movement; they are embraced as a kind of intellectual armor. They give the believer the satisfying sense of reasoning things out and "winning" arguments, even while the emotional frame—

fear of deception, pride in being "awake," the comfort of belonging—is quietly doing the real persuasive work underneath. This dual-layered approach is what makes the rhetoric so effective and, for outsiders, so hard to challenge. When a skeptic points out a logical flaw, they are not just arguing against a mistake in reasoning. They are pushing against the emotional payoff and cognitive comfort that the fallacy provides.

Layer these tactics together, and the effect multiplies. A single fallacy can make an argument feel strong. A steady stream of them can turn a debate into a flood where the sheer repetition starts to feel like proof all by itself. This is where the illusory truth effect comes into play—the well-documented bias where a statement feels more believable simply because it has been heard many times (Hasher, Goldstein, & Toppino, 1977). In Flat Earth rhetoric, that flood of repeated, flawed arguments is not random or sloppy. It is deliberate. The goal is not to prove the claim in the traditional sense. The goal is to overwhelm the conversation until the weight of repetition itself becomes the evidence, and the belief begins to feel like self-evident truth.

The Gish Gallop: Drowning in Details

A single weak argument can collapse under scrutiny. A hundred of them, however, shouted at once can sound like an unassailable wall of proof.

Sometimes persuasion is not about the strength of a single point at all. It is about flooding the room before anyone can take a breath. The Gish Gallop is exactly that—a rapid-fire barrage of claims, questions, and half-arguments delivered so fast that none of them can be examined in detail. The term was first used to describe the debate style of creationist Duane Gish, but it has since become a trademark move in modern pseudoscience debates. The goal is not to prove every claim. The goal is to overwhelm the conversation until the sheer number of statements starts to feel like evidence all on its own.

It begins with a rush. One claim, then another, then three more before the first has even had a chance to land. Facts and half-facts, questions and accusations pile up so quickly the exchange stops feeling like a debate and starts feeling like standing under a firehose. This is no accident. It is a deliberate way to create cognitive overload—a state where your working memory is so swamped with incoming information that it cannot process any of it effectively (Swire, Ecker, & Lewandowsky, 2017).

In Flat Earth debates, this move shows up constantly. A skeptic tries to answer one point and is immediately hit with three more: "If the Earth spins, why don't we feel it? How can water stick to a ball? Why are there no real photos of the globe?" Each question demands an answer, but the rapid pace never gives space for any answer to actually land. The skeptic ends up stuck on defense, chasing claims that multiply faster than they can be addressed.

What makes this tactic especially persuasive is how it feels in the moment. The momentum itself becomes the argument. The side driving the flood looks prepared, confident, and in control, while the opponent appears flustered and behind. It turns the debate into a performance where speed and sheer volume successfully masquerade as quality. This is where the Gish Gallop taps straight into the illusory truth effect: the more times a claim is heard—no matter how flimsy—the more it starts to feel true simply through repetition (Hasher, Goldstein, & Toppino, 1977).

One of the reasons the Gish Gallop works so well is not just the sheer number of arguments—it is the strain it puts on the mind. When too many claims hit at once, the brain's ability to think critically starts to buckle under the weight. This is cognitive overload: the moment when information comes in faster than the brain can process it. In a debate, it feels like trying to juggle too many objects at once. Something is going to drop, and a neutral audience rarely blames the person throwing it. They blame the person struggling to catch them.

Flat Earth debates lean on this effect constantly. Questions like "Where is the curve? Why can we see so far? How can planes land on a spinning ball?" come in waves. Even if each claim is weak on its own, the sheer pace creates a trap. Answer one, and two more are already hanging, leaving the skeptic in a permanent state of catch-up. The conversation blurs, and that blur itself creates the illusion of substance. It looks like the Flat Earth side has more to stand on simply because they have more to say. This is a deliberate way of exhausting the opponent's and the audience's System 2—the slow, analytical part of the brain—and forcing everyone to rely on the quick, intuitive reactions of System 1 instead (Kahneman, 2011).

That shift is not just a debate tactic; it is wired into how we think. Our brains are built to conserve energy. When we are flooded with too many points too quickly, we fall back on mental shortcuts: what sounds confident, what feels familiar, what is easy to agree with (Tversky & Kahneman, 1974). Flat Earth rhetoric exploits that perfectly. The flood creates the overload, and the overload opens the door for emotion to step in exactly when logic should be steering. The questions are not designed to be answered; they are designed to be heard and felt.

For skeptics, it is a frustrating experience in real time. By the time they form a careful, evidence-based response to one question, three more have landed, and the original one has already been forgotten. That imbalance is not a side effect—it is the point. It keeps the skeptic on defense, makes the believer look in control, and turns the exchange into a performance of momentum rather than a search for truth. The Gish Gallop flips the burden of proof on its head, demanding that one person disprove a dozen different claims in rapid fire—an impossible task for anyone.

Rhetorically, cognitive overload is powerful because it does not feel like a trick. It feels like a mountain of evidence. In that state of overwhelm, the brain cannot separate the strong arguments from the weak ones. It just registers the weight of all of them together. At that point, quantity begins to look like quality, and speed starts to sound like certainty. That is the heart of the Gish Gallop's sleight of hand: not winning with proof, but winning by burying the conversation under sheer volume.

Owning the Stage

In a debate, control is not just about the strength of your arguments—it is about who commands the space, the timing, and the audience's attention. Flat Earth rhetoric often pairs the Gish Gallop with another deliberate move: dominating the exchange itself. This can mean talking over a skeptic, cutting them off mid-sentence, or driving the conversation so fast that the other side never gets to finish a single thought. The goal is not necessarily to win on content; it is to win the room—and the audience—through sheer force of presence.

You can see this pattern play out in countless Flat Earth versus Globe debates. A skeptic begins to carefully unpack a complex point, and before the explanation can land, a rapid string of interruptions slices through: "Answer the question! Why do you believe that? How do you know?" The argument itself fades into the background, replaced by the spectacle of control. To a live audience, the Flat Earther comes across as assertive, confident, and unwavering, while the skeptic, no matter how evidence-based their point, can appear hesitant or evasive. That contrast is not accidental—it's a calculated rhetorical move aimed at undermining the skeptic's ethos, or credibility (Aristotle, trans. 2007).

What makes this tactic especially persuasive is how directly it plays into debate as performance. Volume and pace can sound like certainty, and in the moment, certainty often carries more weight than accuracy. A skeptic's measured tone and careful pauses can be flipped to look like weakness, while interruptions and relentless pacing project authority. The stage stops being neutral; it tilts toward whoever controls the tempo. Verbal dominance itself becomes a display of power and perceived expertise (Cappella, 1987).

This tactic also feeds on the emotional energy in the room. A debate charged with constant interruptions and quick-fire exchanges generates tension, and that tension reads as drama. Drama, in turn, makes the subject feel important. Even when the arguments are thin or full of fallacies, the spectacle alone can make the position seem weighty and credible. In that moment, the audience is not just parsing evidence—they are watching a story, and they instinctively gravitate toward the person who seems to own the narrative.

Ultimately, this is less about facts and more about perception. It frames the Flat Earther as the bold, unshakable truth-teller and the skeptic as cautious, evasive, or outmatched, regardless of the actual arguments. Rhetorically, it works because it turns the debate format itself into a weapon. In these exchanges, whoever controls the conversation often ends up controlling the story—and sometimes, that control becomes the only argument that matters.

Confidence is one of the most persuasive tools in any debate, but in Flat Earth rhetoric, it's more than just a delivery style—it is a deliberate strategy. A rapid, unbroken stream of claims delivered without hesitation can make even the weakest, most easily debunked points sound rock-solid. When combined with the Gish Gallop and the tactic of owning the stage, confidence itself stops being a feature of the argument and becomes the argument.

In Flat Earth debates, this often takes the form of absolute, unwavering certainty in the face of complex questions. A bold and confident declaration like "I believe the Earth is flat" can often resonate more powerfully with an audience than a cautious, evidence-based explanation. The assertiveness and certainty behind such statements evoke a compelling psychological impact, leading listeners to think that someone so assured must possess the truth. It's fascinating how conviction can shape perceptions in such a profound way! In this rhetorical performance, the content matters far less than the conviction behind it.

You can see this dynamic play out in debates where the Flat Earth side maintains an unbroken flow of statements, questions, and demands. Even when a claim is directly challenged with data, the delivery doesn't waver. The skeptic might pause to explain or clarify a concept, but the Flat Earther pushes forward without missing a beat. That steady tone of certainty often lands louder than the facts themselves, carrying the implicit message: "I am right because I am sure." This is especially effective for audiences taking what persuasion theorists call the peripheral route, where superficial cues like confidence and delivery weigh heavier than the substance of the argument (Petty & Cacioppo, 1986).

Rhetorically, this tactic works on two levels at once. First, the performance of confidence projects ethos, or credibility (Aristotle, trans. 2007). The audience instinctively reads a steady tone and decisive body language as signs of authority and expertise. Second, it hits pathos, appealing to the deep emotional need for certainty. In a world full of complexity and conflicting information, a confident voice offers something profoundly reassuring: a simple, stable view of reality. That calm certainty can make hesitation look like weakness and doubt look like ignorance. When the debate is framed as "awake truth-tellers" versus "blind followers," that effect becomes even more pronounced.

This is exactly why confidence pairs so seamlessly with the Gish Gallop. A flood of statements delivered with absolute conviction doesn't just overwhelm the skeptic's ability to respond; it overwhelms the audience's ability to separate the strength of the delivery from the strength of the evidence. The debate stops being about what is true and starts being about who sounds like they know it.

The Gish Gallop works because of sheer momentum. It doesn't win by proving a point; it wins by never letting the conversation pause long enough to test a single one. Breaking that relentless rhythm is the only way to expose the tactic for what it really is. When the rapid-fire flood slows to a trickle, the entire performance of overwhelming certainty starts to unravel.

The most effective counter is deceptively simple: isolate one claim and refuse to move forward until it is addressed. It is difficult to do in real time—it feels unnatural to push back against the pace—but it's the only way to take the shine off the tactic. When a single argument is forced to stand on its own without the distraction of ten others lined up behind it, its weakness becomes visible. This momentary pause shifts the audience's thinking from the fast, emotional System 1 mode the Gallop relies on to the slower, more deliberate System 2 mode that evaluates claims carefully (Kahneman, 2011).

Skeptics who manage to slow the pace often describe the dramatic shift that happens. The debate stops feeling like a barrage and starts resembling an actual conversation. The confident performance loses its edge when it is forced to hold still. In that pause, the audience can see the tactic itself instead of being swept up in it. This is a subtle but powerful form of rhetorical inoculation: once people notice the trick, they are better prepared to evaluate the next claim and the one after that with more scrutiny (McGuire, 1964).

At its core, breaking the Gallop is about reclaiming control of the room. The tactic thrives on overload, leaving no mental space to think critically. Slowing it down resets that balance, putting the focus back on the content of a claim rather than the spectacle of delivery.

And when the pace drops, another truth becomes obvious: the mountain of "evidence" is usually the same handful of weak points recycled in slightly different forms. Stripped of speed and volume, the flood stops looking like proof and starts looking like what it really is—disconnected fragments stitched together into something that only resembles evidence from a distance. The performance.

Data Mining and Cherry-Picking

"By stripping away context, the smallest scrap can be made to look like a cornerstone."

When the flood of arguments slows and the debate finally loses momentum, what is often left behind are fragments—single lines, stray quotes, or isolated details pulled from a much larger context. Flat Earth rhetoric excels at turning these fragments into something that looks like compelling evidence. This is the essence of cherry-picking: taking a sliver of information and presenting it as though it tells the entire story. The strength of the argument comes not from what is shown, but from what has been carefully left out.

This tactic works because facts, even when stripped of their context, carry a natural weight and authority. A direct quote from a real document or a number from an official source triggers an automatic sense of credibility (ethos). Our minds tend to register the authority of the source before stopping to ask how that fragment is being used. Flat Earth rhetoric leans hard on that reflex, building entire arguments out of slivers of information that look convincing on their own.

One of the most common examples is the use of phrases like "non-rotating Earth" from engineering manuals or flight training documents. In their proper context, these are not claims about the planet's shape or movement. They are simply reference frames—simplified, local models used to make a specific set of calculations easier. However, once those words are lifted out of their technical background, they are reframed as bombshell admissions from the very establishment that defends the globe. The fragment, recast and isolated, becomes the entire argument (Entman, 1993).

What makes this tactic so persuasive is the powerful illusion of discovery it creates. These cherry-picked facts are often presented as if they were hidden gems unearthed through diligent research. Phrases like "Look what they admit right here in their own document" give the audience the feeling of uncovering a secret, tying directly into the emotional pull of the "awakening" narrative. The isolation of the fact becomes part of the story: the truth was buried by the establishment, and now it has been heroically dug up. That sense of personal discovery taps directly into narrative transportation, pulling the audience into a story where they become active participants in exposing the "truth" (Green & Brock, 2000).

Inside the movement, this tactic is often mistaken for building a solid, evidence-based case. But the argument's real strength does not come from the fact itself; it comes from everything left out around it. The missing context is the shield protecting the claim from scrutiny. Once that context is put back in place, the fragment collapses into what it truly is—one small, often irrelevant piece of a much bigger, more complicated picture.

Rhetorically, this works because it combines the borrowed credibility of ethos with the emotional thrill of pathos. A single line or number, stripped from context, can be framed as a smoking gun—not because of what it actually proves, but because of how convincingly it is presented as proof.

Among Flat Earth talking points, few have the staying power of a single line from a NASA technical document: "non-rotating Earth." It comes from a flight dynamics manual used for guidance and navigation calculations, and within Flat Earth rhetoric, those three words have been elevated to the level of a confession. Entire videos and debates hang on this fragment, presented as undeniable "proof" that NASA itself—the very institution tied to the globe model—has admitted the Earth does not move.

In context, the phrase is nothing of the sort. It's an engineering reference frame, a mathematical simplification used to make certain calculations easier. Engineers and physicists routinely model systems in relation to a "non-rotating" or "flat" Earth when the planet's rotation or curvature is negligible to the specific problem they're solving. But stripped of that context, the three words are reframed as a smoking gun. The sliver of information becomes the whole story (Entman, 1993).

Rhetorically, this is cherry-picking at its sharpest because it leans so heavily on ethos, or borrowed authority (Aristotle, trans. 2007). A NASA manual carries automatic credibility for most people. Seeing that phrase in an official technical document bypasses skepticism and taps into the instinctive belief that written, technical language must represent truth. At the same time, it plays directly to pathos by feeding the emotional thrill of uncovering a hidden admission: "They told you the truth, and you did not even see it." That "gotcha" moment feels far more compelling than any dry technical explanation ever could.

Flat Earth content amplifies this effect by repeating the phrase in isolation, completely detached from the surrounding material. Screenshots are clipped and shared across social media, the words highlighted while the missing context fades away. The argument does not gain its power from what it actually proves but from where it comes from and how it's framed. The phrase is not just evidence; it is turned into a rhetorical prop.

This example also exposes a deeper misunderstanding that runs through much of Flat Earth rhetoric: technical language is not treated as part of a model or calculation, but as a literal description of reality. The crucial difference between a reference frame and an observation gets erased. That gap is precisely where the persuasion lives. "Non-rotating Earth" is not just an isolated phrase—it is a template for the entire strategy. It shows how a single, carefully chosen line, once lifted from its context, can be transformed into the cornerstone of a belief system. It is not the words themselves that convince, but the rhetorical sleight of hand that turns a fragment into a story.

Flat Earth rhetoric does not limit itself to technical documents. It digs deep into history and sacred texts, pulling lines and verses from ancient writings to frame the argument as timeless and foundational. Passages describing the "four corners of the Earth" from the Bible are repeated as if they were literal geography lessons. Quotes from early philosophers like Ptolemy are presented as hard evidence for a stationary Earth. The message is always the same: if the ancients believed it, they must have had a good reason.

This tactic is persuasive because it leans on ethos, or credibility, in two distinct ways. First, it borrows the authority of tradition itself. Ancient voices and ideas carry a sense of inherited wisdom simply because they have endured through centuries. Second, it taps into a deep cultural reverence for the past—the belief that older knowledge is somehow purer, less corrupted, and closer to fundamental truth than anything born of modern technology. This is a subtle but potent version of the argument from tradition fallacy.

Flat Earth content uses this strategy with surgical precision, pulling single lines from larger works and stripping away their original context. A verse about a "firm, unmoving Earth" in scripture is presented as literal cosmology rather than the symbolic, poetic language it was likely intended to be. A description of a domed sky from ancient Babylonian tablets is reframed as factual proof that "they knew the truth before it was hidden." Just like the "non-rotating Earth" example, the persuasion lives not in what is included but in what is deliberately left out. Context disappears, and the fragment is elevated into irrefutable evidence.

What makes this tactic especially effective is that it does not feel like a blunt appeal to authority. It feels like honoring forgotten wisdom. Quoting an ancient source creates the impression of respect for a sacred lineage, and that emotional appeal ties directly into the Flat Earth narrative of rediscovery: "We are not creating something new; we are uncovering what was always known." This also plugs directly into the emotional framework built earlier in the chapter—the fear of deception, the pride of awakening, and the powerful need to belong. Invoking the ancients does not just support the belief; it gives the believer a sense of identity as part of an unbroken chain stretching back through time (Tajfel & Turner, 1979).

Rhetorically, this is cherry-picking with a different source of authority. Instead of pulling from the credibility of a technical manual, it pulls from the immense weight of history itself. A single sentence does not become a cornerstone because of what it says, but because of the age, reverence, and perceived wisdom it carries.

Flat Earth rhetoric thrives on the appearance of being deeply researched. Hours of video and endless pages of screenshots are often built around the same core tactic: digging through mountains of material to find one usable line. NASA reports, flight manuals, physics papers, historical archives—all of it becomes a quarry to sift through, not to explore a question, but to confirm a conclusion that has already been decided. The hunt is not for understanding; it is for a fragment.

One of the most visible signs of this tactic is the flood of charts and documents that often accompany the claims. Screenshots from technical manuals flash on the screen. Graphs and diagrams are dropped into conversations. Links to PDFs stack up in comment threads. The sheer weight and quantity of citations, rather than their quality or relevance, create the illusion of credibility. It looks like a mountain of evidence when, in reality, it is often a handful of out-of-context lines surrounded by noise. This is a deliberate strategy to exploit the cognitive bias that makes quantity feel like quality (Hasher, Goldstein, & Toppino, 1977).

What makes this approach work isn't only what gets highlighted but what gets cut away. Entire sections of reports and pages of surrounding context disappear so that a single line can stand on its own. Unlike genuine research, which digs into that surrounding context to understand how each piece fits into the whole, this tactic relies on a willful absence of it. The fragment only appears strong because the rest of the picture is missing—a tiny piece framed as if it carries the weight of the entire document. This is cherry-picking at its core: turning a sliver into the story.

Flooding a conversation with citations accomplishes two things at once. First, it overwhelms the skeptic, making it impossible to challenge every source in real time, creating cognitive overload. Second, it frames sheer volume as proof. In this way, the impressive stack of documents is not an invitation to dig deeper. It's meant to project the intimidating impression that the case is already airtight.

The real rhetorical power of this tactic lies in how convincingly it can pass for actual research. It borrows the surface features—citations, technical documents, official formatting—while deliberately sidestepping what makes research meaningful: building context, cross-referencing, and inviting scrutiny. Real research opens the door to deeper understanding. This performance of research closes it, replacing inquiry with spectacle. That is the crucial difference between a persuasive illusion and an honest investigation.

Cherry-picking is not just a way to build an argument; it is a way to skip the hard work of research altogether. A single fragment, lifted from a larger whole, is held up not as one piece of evidence to weigh but as if it represents the entire truth. It is the shortcut to a conclusion: find one line that appears to agree with you and present it as definitive proof. In doing so, the tactic sidesteps the slow, methodical work of real research and jumps straight to the desired end point.

This approach leans heavily on confirmation bias—the natural human tendency to seek out and interpret information that reinforces what we already believe (Tversky & Kahneman, 1974). When a fragment aligns with what the audience wants to hear, the mind eagerly fills in the rest. The missing context goes unquestioned because the sliver feels complete and emotionally satisfying. Instead of being one thread in a larger, complex fabric, the fragment is framed as if it is the whole cloth.

Rhetorically, the move is subtle but potent: it creates the powerful illusion that the research is already done. By labeling a single line as "proof," the argument avoids the need to explore the source fully or grapple with contradictory information. This also serves another function: it eases cognitive dissonance—the discomfort of holding conflicting ideas—by providing a neat, simple piece of "evidence" that justifies the core belief (Festinger, 1957). It closes the conversation before it even starts by making the audience feel as though they have already seen enough.

Flat Earth rhetoric uses this move repeatedly with technical documents and historical texts. A phrase like "non-rotating Earth" or a scriptural reference to an "unmoving world" stops being a detail to unpack and instead becomes the conclusion itself. The fragment is no longer a piece of evidence; it becomes the verdict.

What makes this strategy so convincing is how neatly it ties into the emotional scaffolding built throughout the narrative: the rush of discovery, the pride of awakening, the sense of holding a secret truth that "they" want to hide. A single highlighted line becomes more than an argument; it becomes a badge of belonging (Tajfel & Turner, 1979). And once a fragment has been crowned as "proof," the dynamic of the conversation shifts. The questions stop testing the fragment and start forcing others to answer to it. The fragment does not have to hold the weight of the world—it only has to make someone else carry it.

Question-Framing and Shifting the Burden of Proof

"I would rather have questions that cannot be answered than answers that cannot be questioned." — Richard Feynman

In Flat Earth debates, questions are not always about curiosity or a genuine search for truth. More often, they are used as a rhetorical tool to control the flow of conversation. A single, sharply delivered challenge—like "How do you know the Earth curves?"—can flip the entire dynamic. Suddenly, the skeptic is no longer presenting evidence. They are on defense, scrambling to justify something that had been taken as a settled fact.

That is the trick. A question sounds harmless—even fair—on the surface. But when it is framed to shift the spotlight away from the person making the claim and onto the person challenging it, it becomes something else entirely. It quietly shifts the burden of proof. Instead of the Flat Earther needing to back up their extraordinary claim, the skeptic is made to carry the weight of disproving it. In that moment, the debate stops being about what is true and becomes about who has to answer. It is a subtle, effective way of flipping the structure of the conversation, even though, by basic standards of argument, the person making the claim is the one responsible for proving it (Ross & Ward, 1996).

You can see this play out in Flat Earth conversations all the time. A skeptic begins to explain orbital mechanics or light refraction, and just as they build toward a point, they get cut off: "Where is your proof of motion?" That question acts like a roadblock. The skeptic has to stop, reset, and answer—otherwise, they risk looking evasive. No new evidence has been offered, but the question has already done its job: it has stalled the argument and shifted the pressure.

This tactic works so well because it feels natural. Questions create tension. They open a gap in the conversation, and our instinct is to close that gap. That built-in pressure is precisely what Flat Earth rhetoric exploits. The moment the skeptic leans in to respond, the rhetorical win is already in motion. The question now feels like a checkmate—because it got answered.

There is also a deeper psychological layer here. A question like that does not need to stump the expert to work on the audience. It creates a brief but effective moment of cognitive dissonance—the mental discomfort that comes from holding conflicting ideas—especially when the audience is faced with a question they cannot answer easily themselves (Festinger, 1957). It makes people pause, wonder, and second-guess. The question is not really aimed at solving anything. It is meant to unsettle. And often, that is enough.

Not every question is neutral. Some are crafted so that, no matter how you answer, you lose ground. Flat Earth debates use this tactic often, dropping challenges like, "When did you start believing NASA's lies?" or "Why do you trust what the government tells you?" The question itself carries a hidden accusation. Unless the premise is rejected outright, any response sounds, to an audience, like agreement with the charge behind it.

This is the classic loaded question, a logical fallacy that hides a flawed assumption inside what looks like a simple inquiry. Rhetorically, it is a trap: the questioner defines the battlefield before the discussion even begins. Answer it directly, and you implicitly validate the hidden claim (for example, that NASA is lying). Step back to dismantle the question and explain why it's flawed, and you risk looking evasive or defensive. Either way, the frame has already been set. That's the power of a loaded question—it simultaneously accuses and demands a response, forcing the other person into a position where every answer feels like sinking deeper into quicksand.

In Flat Earth debates, this tactic shows up most clearly when evidence is on the table. A skeptic might present satellite data, and the immediate reply comes: "Why would NASA fake all of this?" The question does not touch the evidence itself. Instead, it sidesteps the point entirely and reframes the conversation around a conspiracy. In an instant, the burden of proof flips. The debate is no longer about the data—it's about the motives of the source. This is framing at work, pulling the discussion away from facts and into emotionally charged territory (Lakoff, 2004).

Loaded questions are effective because they feel so natural in conversation. To someone listening, it often sounds like the skeptic is dodging when they pause or try to challenge the premise. The tactic hides behind the rhythm of dialogue—questions demand answers—making the trap invisible to the casual ear. Rhetorically, it leans on both framing and pathos at once. The framing forces the discussion into the Flat Earth narrative, while the emotional weight of the accusation puts the skeptic on the defensive before a single piece of evidence is even considered. The question is not asked to seek truth; it's designed to plant a story inside the question itself.

One of the oldest moves in Flat Earth rhetoric is making someone else carry the weight of their claim. Instead of presenting evidence for a flat Earth, the argument flips into a demand: "Prove to me that the Earth curves," or "Show me that it spins." To an audience, it can sound like a fair challenge. Underneath, it rewrites the rules of debate entirely by leaning on the fallacy of shifting the burden of proof.

In any argument, the burden of proof belongs to the person making the claim. When someone challenges something as well-established and empirically verified as the globe model, the weight of evidence naturally falls on the side introducing the radical alternative. This is not a question of which side is "right"; it is a basic principle of logic and epistemology. Without that starting point, the conversation quickly devolves into defending against questions instead of scrutinizing the claim being made.

Flat Earth rhetoric exploits this by pushing that weight onto the skeptic. The skeptic is then left trying to disprove a negative or re-prove a fact that has already been demonstrated countless times. This reversal creates the illusion of strength while standing on nothing. When Flat Earthers declare, "There is no proof for the globe," it sounds like a devastating blow, but it is really just a rhetorical maneuver. The evidence for a spherical, rotating Earth is not an absence of proof; it's the accumulated, peer-reviewed consensus of centuries of scientific work. The Flat Earth claim has no such foundation, which means the burden to support it lies entirely with the Flat Earther.

This tactic works because of framing. By forcing the skeptic to "prove the globe," the conversation starts from a false balance, as if both positions are equally unproven and in need of equal defense (Entman, 1993). That framing taps into the natural instinct to answer a direct challenge and masks the fact that the extraordinary claim has not provided any evidence at all. It also plays on naive realism by demanding direct, personal proof for complex scientific phenomena, ignoring the scale and context those phenomena require (Ross & Ward, 1996).

You can see this pattern in nearly every debate clip. A skeptic begins laying out satellite data or geodetic measurements, and the interruption lands: "Where is your proof of curvature?" In an instant, the skeptic is no longer presenting their case—they are carrying both theirs and the one the Flat Earther never made.

Rhetorically, the tactic works because it looks fair. To someone listening, it sounds like the Flat Earth side is simply asking for evidence. In reality, it is a way to avoid offering any. The lack of proof becomes the illusion of victory because the wrong side is carrying the load.

Questions carry a built-in weight. Even without answers, they create momentum in a conversation, and the person asking them appears to be steering the exchange. In Flat Earth rhetoric, that effect often becomes a stand-in for evidence. A rapid series of questions can feel powerful, not because it proves anything, but because it forces the other side to respond and defend.

Framing is at the heart of this tactic. When the skeptic is pushed into a reactive role, scrambling to answer a barrage of challenges, it creates the impression that the Flat Earth side holds the higher ground. That perception alone can feel like a win, even when no point has been substantiated. The question does not have to be resolved; it only has to control the flow. In that moment, the Flat Earther's silence, broken only by pointed challenges, projects a false sense of ethos and confidence (Aristotle, trans. 2007).

This is why so many Flat Earth exchanges lean more on questions than on direct statements. A single, well-placed challenge can shift the entire tone of a conversation, turning a debate over facts into a subtle struggle for control. The persuasion doesn't live in the answer—it lives in the pressure of having to give one.

That sense of control extends beyond the words themselves. In debates and videos, the illusion of victory is amplified through body language, tone, and pacing: the calm, composed questioner against the reactive, flustered skeptic. That visual story, told as much through performance as through dialogue, sets the stage for the final layer of persuasion—the power of images and presentation.

Visual Rhetoric: Memes, Maps, and Diagrams

A picture does not just say a thousand words — it sets the stage for how we hear them.

There is a reason the phrase "seeing is believing" has lasted for centuries. Our brains are wired to give what we see priority over what we are told. In a single instant, an image can bypass the slow, careful process of weighing data or questioning evidence and go straight to the part of us that says, "I saw it with my own eyes." It is not that we stop thinking; it is that the picture quietly tells us how to start thinking before we even realize it.

Visuals carry a unique kind of authority that words rarely match (Messaris & Abraham, 2001). A claim can be debated. A chart can be questioned. However, when a photograph or diagram appears, it feels less like someone's argument and more like reality itself entering the conversation. Flat Earth rhetoric leans hard into this instinct. A single photo of the horizon appearing perfectly flat lands with more immediate weight than a detailed explanation of atmospheric refraction or curvature math. A meme showing a P1000 camera "pulling a ship back into view" is not just making a claim—it creates the powerful feeling that you have seen proof with your own eyes, even if it is only a carefully chosen and deliberately framed moment.

The strength of images lies in what they skip. Words and graphs require decoding, a step that demands effort and critical thought. A picture arrives already loaded with mood and story. That is why a single frame can feel more convincing than a thousand words; it is processed almost instantly and with far less cognitive strain (Kahneman, 2011). It is also why images can slip so easily past our critical filters. Our brains evolved to treat sight as the most reliable sense for survival, and that same wiring can make a well-crafted picture feel "true" before the rational mind has even caught up.

Flat Earth content creators know this, sometimes consciously and sometimes simply by following what resonates. A video clip of a rocket hitting "something" in the sky, looped over and over, does more than argue for a dome; it lets you experience the impact as if you were behind the camera. A homemade map drawn with clean lines and bold colors does more than suggest a model; it tells your brain, this is official. Even simple memes play the same game. The image carries the argument long before the words ever get a chance to.

That is why the "power of the image" in Flat Earth rhetoric is not just about pictures being persuasive. It is about how they quietly set the stage. An image does not argue the way a debate does; it frames the scene, sets the mood, and establishes a starting point. By the time the words or captions arrive, the picture has already told your brain what kind of story it is in. In this rhetoric, that stage-setting is everything. Before any facts are discussed, the image has already whispered: look, you have seen the truth. And once that stage is set, even the smallest details—the colors, the polish, the framing—can shape how that "truth" feels.

Design is never neutral. Every choice—from color and typography to framing and polish—communicates meaning before a single word is read. In Flat Earth rhetoric, those choices often matter as much as, or even more than, the content itself. A homemade diagram drawn with precise lines and professional-looking labels feels instantly more credible than a rough sketch, even if both are equally wrong. A video clip framed in deep blues and stark contrasts can make an ordinary horizon feel like a profound discovery. The way something looks becomes part of the argument itself, lending an immediate sense of ethos and authority before a claim is ever explained (Aristotle, trans. 2007).

Color is one of the most subtle but powerful tools in this process. Dark palettes carry a sense of mystery and hidden knowledge; light palettes can suggest openness or revelation. Cool tones—blues, silvers, whites—borrow the visual language of science and precision, tapping into decades of association with NASA images, lab coats, and technical diagrams. Flat Earth visuals lean into this instinct, sometimes deliberately, sometimes subconsciously. A black sky over a glowing flat horizon does more than show a model; it evokes the feeling of cosmic truth. A map rendered in bold reds or golds taps into authority and permanence, colors long linked with power and tradition.

Texture and shading add another layer of persuasion. A map with soft gradients and subtle shadows feels dimensional, which our brains often interpret as "more real" than a flat graphic. Clean typography and orderly labels suggest professionalism and attention to detail. Even small touches—a glow behind text, a vignette at the edges—can shift an image from "homemade experiment" to "official model" in the viewer's mind. This is not accidental; it is the psychology of design at work. Our brains are wired to equate polish with competence. Something that looks finished feels credible.

That credibility is amplified through cognitive fluency—the brain's preference for information that is easy to process. Clean lines, clear contrasts, and consistent symbols reduce visual noise, making the message feel more "right" and believable even before it is examined. This is why a Flat Earth map rendered in smooth 3D with elegant labels can carry more weight than a page of complex data (Kahneman, 2011). The design itself becomes a shortcut to belief.

Symbols do their own heavy lifting alongside polish. Flat Earth imagery circles back to the same icons again and again: the UN-style azimuthal map, the domed firmament, the sun circling overhead. These are not just aesthetic choices; they are powerful visual cues. Symbols bypass logic and work on identity and familiarity. The more often the UN map is presented as "the Flat Earth map," the more it stops feeling like one model among many and starts feeling like the model (Tajfel & Turner, 1979).

Repetition strengthens this effect. Each time the same map or dome image appears, it reinforces a sense of shared knowledge and belonging. Over time, that repeated icon stops being a claim to test and starts feeling like a fact to remember. This is the illusory truth effect at work, where things encountered frequently are more likely to be believed (Hasher, Goldstein, & Toppino, 1977). That shift—from image as argument to image as identity—is where Flat Earth visual rhetoric does its quietest, but most powerful, work.

This is why design in Flat Earth rhetoric is not just decoration; it is persuasion in another form. The colors, the shading, the familiar symbols—all of them set a tone before the first caption is even read. They quietly suggest that what you are seeing is polished, trusted, and shared. Even when the claim underneath is weak, the presentation lends it weight. Once that weight settles in, the image no longer has to argue loudly. The design has already done the talking, leaving only a label or a meme to carry the message forward. From there, it is only a small step to the next layer of persuasion: not what is placed inside the frame, but how the frame itself can change what we believe we see.

Zoom changes more than distance. It changes perception. In Flat Earth rhetoric, it is not just a camera feature; it is stagecraft dressed up as science. At the center of this is the Nikon P1000, a consumer camera with an extreme optical zoom that has become a kind of folk laboratory for "experiments." Technically, the process is simple: a narrow field of view magnifies a small section of the horizon, pulling distant objects into apparent closeness. But in the hands of Flat Earth creators, that basic function becomes something else entirely: a visual argument that feels undeniable because it is seen, not explained.

One of the most iconic examples is the "disappearing ship" video. A boat vanishes hull-first over the horizon, appearing to confirm curvature. Then the P1000 zooms in and "brings it back." To the untrained eye, it feels like the curve itself has been exposed as an illusion. In reality, the camera has simply compressed distance. Optical zoom does not flatten the Earth; it magnifies a thin slice of the scene, reducing atmospheric distortion and making details visible again. The boat never "returned." The camera only changed the scale of what was already there.

However, the emotional impact of that moment—the boat sliding back into view—is powerful. It does not feel like a technical artifact; it feels like a revelation. This is where pathos does its quiet work. That flash of wonder, tinged with the sense that something hidden has just been uncovered, carries more weight than any explanation. It creates what you call the Pathos of Revelation, the emotional swing that gives the illusion its staying power.

The camera itself becomes part of the persuasion. A P1000 on a tripod is more than a tool; it looks like science in action. This is Ethos by Proxy—the credibility borrowed from the symbols and tools of authority (Aristotle, trans. 2007). Even when the person behind the lens has no training in optics, the hardware cues expertise. The equipment does not just record the argument; it becomes part of it.

Zoom is only one piece. Framing and cropping do the rest (Entman, 1993). A P1000 clip rarely starts with a wide shot. The viewer is not shown the larger horizon or the cues that reveal scale and curvature. The frame isolates a narrow slice, stripping away context until the world looks exactly as flat as the argument needs it to be. This is not an accident; it is visual framing as persuasion. By choosing what stays inside the borders and what gets cut away, the creator is not simply showing reality—they are editing it.

Still images work on the same principle. A photo of an ocean taken at eye level with no landmarks will almost always look flat. Our brains expect it to. Without reference points, water forms a plane in perception. Flat Earth content leans into this by cropping out anything that hints at scale or curve. The frame itself becomes the argument: look, it is flat. Furthermore, because the image arrives whole and seamless, most viewers never stop to ask what was left outside it.

Language often rides alongside the visuals to reinforce the effect. Captions or narrators repeat words like "look," "see," or "there it is" as the zoom tightens. This is simple anaphora—the deliberate repetition of a word or phrase to drive a point home. Synced with the image, it creates a rhythm: you are not just seeing the boat; you are being told to see it. The words and the reveal fuse into a single experience of discovery.

This is where the rhetorical power of zoom and scale manipulation lives: turning a camera feature into a story. The boat over the horizon becomes less about optics and more about hidden truths revealed, a parable about what "they" do not want you to see (Green & Brock, 2000). The camera frame becomes a curtain, and when the zoom "pulls it back," it feels like revelation. That feeling is the payload. The technical content is secondary to the emotional experience of "seeing through the lie."

Zoom and framing here are not scientific arguments; they are performances. And like all effective performances, they rely on stagecraft—controlling scene, perspective, and timing so the audience feels they are witnessing something extraordinary. Once the performance lands, it condenses into its most shareable form: a meme. A single frame with a single line of text carries the entire story forward.

Memes are not just jokes or internet wallpaper. In the Flat Earth space, they are compact arguments, perfectly designed to be carried, shared, and believed. A single image with a single line of text can pack more persuasive weight than a thousand-word post because it delivers its punch in one glance. No buildup, no debate—just instant impact.

Memes work because they collapse complexity into simplicity. A photo of a flat horizon with the words "Where is the curve?" does not simply ask a question. It frames the entire debate in five words and one image (Lakoff, 2004). It is not trying to spark conversation; it is setting the terms of the conversation before it even starts. This is why memes are not casual commentary—they are rhetorical weapons disguised as quick observations.

Humor gives them their first edge. Laughter lowers defenses, creating a gap where the message slides in without resistance. A meme that mocks "globe believers" as naïve or blind is not just making a joke; it is framing the opposition as foolish while letting the in-group share a laugh. That shared humor reinforces belonging and social identity, turning one image into a communal signal: we get it; they do not (Tajfel & Turner, 1979).

Memes also rely on sheer volume. The same images and captions circulate endlessly, often with only slight variations. This is not laziness; it is strategy. Repetition in rhetoric is a form of anaphora—the deliberate echoing of words or images to make a message stick. Each time the same meme pops up in a new thread, it reinforces itself like a chorus. Eventually, a line like "Where is the curve?" stops functioning as a question and starts functioning as a mantra.

This constant repetition taps into cognitive fluency. The more the brain sees the same pairing of image and message, the easier it becomes to process—and the easier something is to process, the more "true" it feels (Kahneman, 2011). That mental shortcut is why Flat Earth memes rarely get complicated. Simplicity plus repetition creates a sense of obviousness, and that sense of obviousness quickly turns into belief.

Most Flat Earth memes are not built on data; they are built on pathos. They aim to spark humor, ridicule, or a flash of righteous anger against a supposed deception. A meme with the NASA logo captioned "Never A Straight Answer" does not present evidence; it delivers an emotional verdict. What sticks is not a fact but a feeling, and that feeling is what spreads.

Memes are also built for the echo chamber. They are frictionless: easy to copy, share, and repeat without attribution or explanation. Every repost serves as both reinforcement and recruitment. Their anonymity strips away questions about the source and makes the message feel universal. A successful meme does not sound like one person speaking; it sounds like the internet itself talking.

This is why memes in Flat Earth rhetoric are not filler. They are the delivery system. They distill the entire narrative into simple, repeatable visuals that move faster than explanations and linger longer than facts. And once a meme lands, the same visual style often gets repurposed into a different costume—a map, a chart, or a diagram that trades humor for the appearance of evidence.

There is something about a map or a technical diagram that makes people pause. Even in an era of deepfakes and endless digital edits, our brains still give anything with grids, labels, and measurements a special weight. Flat Earth rhetoric leans hard on this instinct. A homemade map with crisp lines and a bold compass rose does more than suggest an alternative model—it carries the quiet authority of something official. A diagram filled with arrows and angles looks less like an argument and more like documentation.

The psychology behind this is simple. Maps and diagrams signal structure and precision. They use the visual language of expertise: order, labeled parts fitting neatly into a system. This taps into what communication scholars call authority cues—subtle signals that tell the brain, "this is information you can trust" (Messaris & Abraham, 2001). When Flat Earth maps mimic navigation charts or scientific schematics, they are not just presenting a claim; they are borrowing the credibility of an entire tradition of technical illustration.

Polish itself becomes persuasion here, just as it does in other areas of design. A Flat Earth map rendered with clean lines and digital shading does not need to be accurate to feel convincing. Smooth gradients and balanced typography create a sense of professionalism, and professionalism creates a sense of truth. This is cognitive fluency in action: the easier something is to process visually, the more our brains lean toward accepting it (Kahneman, 2011). A cluttered sketch looks like an idea. A polished diagram looks like evidence.

Flat Earth content exploits this gap repeatedly. A "model" of the sun moving over a disk, rendered with glowing trails and smooth animation, carries weight before anyone even asks if the model works. It is not just the claim that persuades—it is the way the claim is dressed. The polish itself whispers: someone has solved this. Someone has tested it. Even if no testing has ever been conducted, the design effectively makes the argument for them.

Many of these maps and diagrams are made in home offices, stitched together with free software or even hand-drawn before being digitized. However, once they are framed with a grid, a compass point, and a title, they take on the aura of official documentation. This is the visual version of Ethos by Proxy. Instead of borrowing credibility from a piece of equipment, the diagram borrows it from the entire history of technical illustration. It looks like science, so it feels like science.

Maps also play another role in Flat Earth spaces: they are not just claims; they are emblems. The UN-style azimuthal projection shows up so often that it has become more than a diagram. It functions as a symbol of the belief system itself. When that map appears in a meme or a video, it does not matter whether anyone checks the math behind it. It works as an icon, a shorthand for belonging and identity (Tajfel & Turner, 1979). This is why the same map appears again and again with only minor tweaks. Each repetition does more than reinforce the argument—it reinforces the group.

When a Flat Earth diagram is shared online, it often travels without debate. People do not pick apart the angles or question the measurements. They react to the look of it. A technical diagram feels like a conclusion rather than a starting point. That is where the persuasion lives: not in the data it claims to show, but in the visual authority it projects. The map or chart becomes an argument without words, a picture that tells the brain: this is how the world works.

This is also why maps and diagrams serve as a bridge between humor-driven memes and more serious-looking "evidence." They take the same ideas and dress them in the trappings of documentation. A joke becomes a chart. A slogan becomes a labeled map. And once an image crosses that line into "proof," the persuasion has already done its quiet work. The trick has been performed, and what comes next feels less like argument and more like revelation.

When something is shown instead of explained, the brain takes a shortcut. Sight has always been our most trusted sense; long before written language or formal argument, survival depended on believing what we could see. Flat Earth rhetoric leans into that ancient wiring. A well-crafted image does not just make a point—it feels like proof. And that feeling is where the persuasion lives.

Visuals carry a kind of authority that words alone cannot match (Messaris & Abraham, 2001). A meme can skip the debate entirely and deliver its verdict in a single glance. A map dressed in technical polish can shift from "claim" to "evidence" before the first label is even read. A P1000 zoom video can turn a simple optical effect into what feels like a revelation. None of these are about data by themselves; they are about the experience of seeing. Once the image lands, the argument has already begun.

This taps directly into the illusory truth effect—the cognitive bias where familiar, easy-to-process information is more likely to be accepted as true (Hasher, Goldstein, & Toppino, 1977). Flat Earth content creators, consciously or not, lean on this bias. They understand that a picture can carry more weight than an explanation because the picture arrives already speaking to the part of the brain that trusts its own eyes. The argument does not have to be airtight. It only has to look airtight.

This is where the sleight of hand comes full circle. Visual rhetoric is not just about what appears inside the frame; it is about how the frame itself is crafted—the stage it sets before a caption or a single word ever appears. The strongest Flat Earth images are not evidence in the scientific sense; they are performances. They create a scene, evoke a feeling, and let the viewer supply the conclusion. By the time the text shows up, the persuasion has already happened.

That is why seeing feels so much like believing. A diagram, a meme, a zoomed-in video—each is its own kind of visual spell, cast not on the eyes but on the story the mind builds around what the eyes deliver. And when the story feels real enough, the image does not need to argue at all. It only has to let you believe you have seen the truth yourself.

In the end, this is why visual rhetoric fits so neatly into the larger pattern of Flat Earth persuasion. Every meme, every polished map, every carefully cropped video is not just an argument; it is a performance. Each one hides its mechanics while letting the effect land, the way a magician's flourish draws your eyes away from the trick itself. Seeing may feel like believing, but in rhetoric, what we believe often has less to do with what our eyes reveal and far more to do with how the scene was staged for them.

The Residue of Persuasion

Every tactic in this chapter has shared one common thread: the ability to shape perception without ever admitting that perception is being shaped. Emotional appeals that feel like conviction. Logical fallacies dressed up as airtight reasoning. Questions that sound harmless but quietly shift the burden of proof. Memes, maps, and diagrams that can carry more weight in a single glance than a page of explanation ever could. Each one is a small act of misdirection, guiding the audience so they see the conclusion first and only later—if ever—notice how they got there.

This is why "rhetorical sleight of hand" is more than just a metaphor here. Flat Earth persuasion thrives on performance. These tactics work not because they win arguments in the traditional sense, but because they create an experience: a flash of discovery, the thrill of uncovering a hidden truth, the comfort of belonging to the few who can "see through the illusion." Like any skilled illusionist, the creator is not merely offering information; they are constructing a scene, carefully setting the stage so the audience supplies the proof themselves.

And beyond that stage, another layer quietly hums. The repeated memes, the polished diagrams, the endless livestreams and debates—they are not only about belief. They are also about keeping the performance alive, feeding the attention and affirmation that keep the lights from dimming. That part is not always visible from the seats in the audience. Sometimes you can only catch it in the silence between acts.

Chapter 6 — The Grift Beneath the Globe: Flat Earth as a Business

"90% of selling is conviction and 10% is persuasion."
— Shiv Khera

There is a real difference between sharing an idea and selling one. Sharing invites open discussion; selling demands a transaction. In the Flat Earth world, that transaction is not only about money. It is about loyalty. It is about belonging. It is about turning a listener's doubt into certainty — and then turning that certainty into a kind of currency.

What might look like a grassroots search for truth is, just beneath the surface, a marketplace. Belief is the product. Conviction is the packaging. And the currency is not only financial — it is emotional and social. Every slogan, every livestream, every carefully timed "aha moment" comes with a price tag. Sometimes that price is printed on a T-shirt, sometimes it is hidden behind a donation button, and sometimes it is woven into the quiet exchange between a magnetic personality and the people hanging on their every word. This is the commodification of belief — the packaging and selling of an ideology as if it were a product (Arvidsson, 2006).

The machinery behind that sale is not always obvious. It hides in the emotional hook that draws a listener in, pulling them into a parasocial relationship — a one-sided bond that feels intimate and personal (Horton & Wohl, 1956). It lives in the persona of the confident guide, a charismatic voice that seems too sure to question, acting as the leader of a new, enlightened community. This dynamic makes the audience feel like they are part of a special, exclusive group, which only deepens their loyalty (Tajfel & Turner, 1979). It thrives in the small rituals —

the repeated phrases, the secret groups, the "support the cause" banners that make giving feel less like a transaction and more like an act of courage. It even gains power from resistance; few things sell better than the story of a silenced truth.

Strip away the slogans and the stage lights, and what remains is a trade as old as persuasion itself: turning belief into something that can be sold. This chapter steps into that marketplace — into the incentives, the profit systems, and the business models that have turned a fringe belief into a thriving, self-sustaining industry. It is where the performance of Flat Earth rhetoric becomes a business, and where its most successful voices have learned how to turn skepticism into their most valuable asset.

The Psychology of the Grift

Conspiracy spaces are fertile ground — not only for ideas, but for people who know how to package them.

The barrier to entry is almost nonexistent. With a camera and a confident tone, anyone can step into the role of "truth-teller." In these spaces, authority is rarely earned. It is performed. A steady voice, repeated often enough, can pass for expertise. What matters is not credentials but presence — a form of charismatic authority built on the speaker's perceived exceptional qualities rather than any formal position or evidence (Weber, 1947). In a movement built on distrust of mainstream authority, that performance often outweighs proof.

These spaces also come with a ready-made audience. Many who arrive carry deep skepticism toward institutions and are actively searching for someone outside the mainstream to follow. That skepticism, rooted in a desire for control, leaves a void — and a charismatic voice can fill it quickly. Every statement that echoes what they already suspect lands as confirmation, a textbook case of confirmation bias. A small spark of agreement grows into loyalty. In a place where trust forms through echoes rather than evidence, loyalty becomes its own currency.

Conspiracy narratives make the setup even easier by casting the story in familiar roles. There is always a hero to follow and a villain to fight. A would-be leader only needs to step into that script and claim the role of protector, standing between the audience and a shadowy "they." That claim does not require proof — only framing. By presenting themselves as the shield against a hostile outside world, the speaker creates belonging and fear in the same breath. Both emotions are powerful motivators — and powerful sales tools. This dynamic is central to social identity theory, where the in-group (those who know the "truth") defines itself against the out-group (the "they") (Tajfel & Turner, 1979).

The engine behind this exchange is not data but feeling. Fear keeps people listening. The promise of rare, hidden knowledge keeps them leaning in, building a parasocial relationship — a one-sided connection that feels personal and intimate (Horton & Wohl, 1956). When something is framed as secret or scarce, it carries value before it is tested. That sense of urgency is the first transaction, long before any money changes hands. Once trust takes hold, emotion becomes currency. And when emotion can be traded, belief does not simply spread — it begins to harden into a business.

Doubt may serve science well, but in the business of belief, it is a liability. In conspiracy spaces, the moment a figure hesitates or admits uncertainty, the performance begins to crack. And when the performance cracks, the income stream follows. What keeps the grift alive is not just the message — it is the posture of absolute conviction. Certainty sells. The more unwavering it appears, the more valuable it becomes.

Money locks that certainty into place. Once an audience starts donating, subscribing, or paying for content, every transaction reinforces the need to deliver what they came for — affirmation. At that point, belief is no longer what is being sold. What is really for sale is consistency. Backtracking or showing doubt risks snapping the thread that holds the support system together. The business model rewards staying the course, no matter how deep the cracks run beneath it.

Subscription models and paywalls amplify the effect. Recurring income depends on return — an audience that shows up again and again, expecting the same strength of conviction every time. That rhythm creates a feedback loop: the creator's income becomes tied to certainty, and the audience's sense of identity becomes tied to supporting it. What begins as content becomes an unspoken contract: *I will keep giving you the truth, if you keep believing it.* That kind of tie-in turns a simple echo chamber into a monetized engine that runs on belief.

You can see it in the architecture. Free content reels people in, but the "real" material — the dangerous, high-value truths — are locked behind a paywall. Access becomes a loyalty test. Paying does not just unlock information; it affirms identity. Even a small recurring payment is not just financial — it is emotional. Every transaction raises the cost of doubt, a pattern rooted in cognitive dissonance (Festinger, 1957). The more someone invests, the harder it becomes to admit they were wrong. Instead, they double down. Walking away no longer feels like losing money — it feels like losing community, purpose, and the certainty they paid to protect (Tajfel & Turner, 1979).

Algorithms tighten the grip. Platforms like YouTube reward what drives engagement — and nothing pulls clicks like outrage delivered with confidence. That reward system pushes creators toward louder voices and sharper claims, stripping away any space for subtlety or second-guessing. Over time, the incentive shifts. It is not just about selling belief — it is about selling it in its most absolute, most polarizing form. For the audience, that certainty does not feel like a sales pitch. It feels like belonging. And it is that emotional charge — more than any individual argument — that turns curiosity into commerce, and belief into business.

Every sale begins with a feeling. In conspiracy movements, that feeling is rarely excitement. More often, it is belonging — or fear. When someone encounters a message that mirrors their suspicion or explains their unease, it does not feel like discovering a product. It feels like finding a home. Buying into the movement — literally and figuratively — becomes part of shaping identity. A T-shirt or a book is not just merchandise. It is a badge. A public declaration of self. It signals membership in an in-group defined by shared knowledge (Tajfel & Turner, 1979). When belief and self-image merge, pulling out a wallet no longer feels like making a purchase. It feels like reinforcing who you have chosen to be.

One of the strongest levers in this exchange is reciprocity. Hours of free videos or neatly packaged "proof" do more than inform. They create a quiet sense of debt. Viewers begin to feel they owe something to the person who "opened their eyes." A donation or subscription becomes more than a payment; it feels like balancing the scales. This reflects a fundamental principle of influence: people are more likely to comply with a request when they feel a sense of obligation to the person making it, especially after receiving a gift or favor (Cialdini, 1984). It is rarely a conscious calculation. It is an emotional reflex.

Scarcity adds urgency. When content is framed as exclusive, when access is limited, or when information is pitched as "what they do not want you to know," scarcity takes over. This is another classic persuasion principle: things that appear rare or limited are perceived as more valuable (Cialdini, 1984). Urgency makes the offer feel precious — even fragile. In that moment, the question shifts from *Is this true?* to *Can I afford not to have it before it disappears?* That pivot can turn even a cautious skeptic into a customer with a single click.

And then there is hope — the most potent product of all. Conspiracies do not only sell fear; they sell the promise of control. The sense that you can see what others cannot. That you are on the inside track to hidden knowledge. It offers safety and agency in an uncertain world. Supporting the movement becomes a way to protect that hope — to keep it alive. When fear, belonging, and hope all tie to a single source, payment no longer feels like commerce. It feels like preservation — a way to keep a piece of yourself intact.

That is why the people at the center of these movements matter so much. The emotional pull is not only about the ideas themselves, but about who delivers them — and how. The hooks work because someone is holding them, shaping them into something that feels personal. What begins as a message becomes a persona. And that persona, wrapped in belonging, fear, and hope, becomes the most marketable product of all.

Crafting the Face of the Movement

In the economy of belief, the voice selling the story is always the first product.

Every movement needs a voice. In conspiracy spaces, that voice rarely stays a simple messenger — it becomes a brand. In Flat Earth circles, those who step forward are not just making an argument; they are packaging themselves as living symbols of "truth." That is part of the grift's pull: the audience is not only buying into an idea about the world — they are buying into the person who delivers it. This is the commodification of belief in its most personal form (Arvidsson, 2006).

Charisma and certainty are the currency here. Doubt does not sell. A confident tone, a steady gaze, and the refusal to flinch under criticism become their own form of proof. In this space, performed authority often outweighs evidence. This is charismatic authority at work — influence rooted not in credentials but in personal magnetism and unwavering conviction (Weber, 1947). The persona becomes the product, and the more authentic it appears, the more value it carries.

Authenticity itself becomes a sales tool. The "real" and "unfiltered" personality plays directly to the emotional side of persuasion. When someone frames themselves as the everyman, the outsider who is "just asking questions," they are building a bridge of trust. That trust becomes the foundation for everything else — from shared identity to financial support. It is not accidental; it is constructed, even when dressed to look spontaneous. This is the building of ethos — credibility — not through expertise, but through a relatable persona (Aristotle, trans. 2007).

That pattern did not appear by accident. The first wave of Flat Earth content laid the blueprint. A handful of personalities saw that belief alone would never be enough; it had to be wrapped in a story. A simple series of videos, framed as "clues," turned a fringe theory into a serialized mystery. Each installment built anticipation, making viewers feel like participants in a discovery rather than passive spectators. This is narrative transportation — the psychological state that makes a message more persuasive and more memorable (Green & Brock, 2000). When the formula expanded into livestreams and direct conversation, the model was complete. Belief became a story you could join — and joining became the first investment.

This is why the faces of these movements matter as much as the ideas they promote. The voice does not just carry the message — it is the message. The persona becomes the lens through which belief is shaped, reinforced, and sold. When fear, belonging, and hope are tied to a person instead of an argument, belief stops being abstract. It becomes personal. And once belief feels personal, it becomes the most marketable product of all.

The Repetition Strategist

For some voices, authority is not claimed in a single moment but built layer by layer, until the sheer weight of what has been said makes the foundation feel solid — whether or not it truly is. These are the builders of belief, the ones who do not simply present ideas but surround the audience with them. Their strategy is not about a single breakthrough argument. It is about immersion. When every video, post, and conversation points in the same direction, doubt begins to feel out of place — not because it has been answered, but because it has been drowned out.

Repetition is the cornerstone. A single line dropped once can be ignored. That same line, repeated across dozens of videos, echoed in livestreams, mirrored in memes, and parroted in comment threads, begins to take root. The shift is subtle but powerful. It stops sounding like persuasion and starts feeling like recognition — as if the audience has always known it. This is no accident. Repetition bypasses debate and goes straight to memory. This is the illusory truth effect in action, where repeated information is more likely to be believed (Hasher, Goldstein, & Toppino, 1977). Belief begins to feel familiar — and familiarity often passes for truth.

Volume creates its own illusion of depth. A catalog of "proofs," no matter how weak each one may be on its own, gains weight through sheer accumulation. In the peripheral route to persuasion, audiences often rely on simple cues — like the number of arguments — rather than their strength (Petty & Cacioppo, 1986). The goal is not to have every piece scrutinized.

It is to have the audience stand back, take in the wall of evidence, and feel its weight without testing its structure. That wall becomes a monument, and the person building it becomes its architect. In time, the persona and the foundation merge so completely that to challenge one feels like attacking both.

Repetition does more than reinforce facts — it shapes identity. Familiar phrases turn into a shared language. When a movement begins to echo the same lines in unison, it stops feeling like following someone else and starts feeling like speaking in your own voice. This is social identity theory at work once again (Tajfel & Turner, 1979). That sense of ownership is the final step. The Repetition Strategist does not simply create content — they create a chorus. And once the song is in everyone's head, the person who wrote it becomes more than a messenger. They become the pulse of the belief itself.

The Digital Showman

Not every persona builds belief brick by brick. Some light up the stage all at once. The Digital Showman sells conviction the way a performer sells a performance — through spectacle. Their authority does not come from stacking proofs but from projecting energy. In their hands, persuasion is not just a message. It is an event.

Technology is their favorite prop. Interactive maps, flashy visuals, live-streamed experiments, and custom-built apps are less about accuracy and more about creating the feeling of innovation. When a tool looks complex, it feels credible — even when its foundation is weak. This is Ethos by Proxy in action, where credibility is borrowed not from personal expertise but from the technology itself. The Showman understands this instinctively. Tech becomes part of their ethos, positioning them as the cutting edge of the movement. The result is not simply information, but performance — a fusion of charisma and gadgetry that makes belief feel alive. For an audience following the peripheral route to persuasion, these visual and technological cues can carry more influence than the content itself (Petty & Cacioppo, 1986).

Where the Repetition Strategist surrounds the audience with a slow build, the Digital Showman creates immediacy. A livestream, a dramatic reveal, a "you have to see this" moment — each one is crafted to pull people in right now. That urgency feeds on emotion: excitement, belonging, and the rush of being part of something unfolding in real time. When hundreds of viewers are watching together, comments flying in unison, belief shifts from private conviction to shared experience. This dynamic strengthens parasocial relationships with the creator while also reinforcing social identity within the group (Horton & Wohl, 1956; Tajfel & Turner, 1979). The performance does not simply deliver a message — it builds a community.

Even setbacks become part of the act. A banned video or removed channel is not treated as a loss but as proof. "They are trying to silence us" turns a platform strike into a rallying cry. This is a deliberate act of narrative framing (Entman, 1993), reframing a negative event as confirmation of a conspiracy. Persecution becomes marketing. Every obstacle becomes evidence that the message is dangerous to the establishment. It also triggers psychological reactance — when people feel their access to information is being threatened, they often double down in support of the source being targeted (Brehm, 1966). In the hands of the Digital Showman, even failure sells.

Beneath the spectacle, the tactic is straightforward: make conviction feel like a show no one can afford to miss. When belief comes wrapped in performance, the audience does not just consume content — they participate in it. And that participation is what brings them back, supporting and paying for the next act.

The Visual Rationalist

Some personas do not rely on spectacle or sheer volume. Their authority is drawn in cleaner lines — minimal words, strong visuals, and an analytical tone that promises reason over rhetoric. The Visual Rationalist sells belief as if it were science. Their memes, diagrams, and carefully composed graphics are designed to look objective, to signal that this is not a movement built on emotion but on evidence. That presentation is part of the persuasion. The polish itself becomes proof.

This archetype thrives on what looks like logic. Charts, labeled images, and "experiments" are presented with the detached voice of analysis — even when the conclusions are already built in. The goal is not debate. It is the performance of reason. A viewer scrolling past a polished graphic or neatly formatted "proof" absorbs the message differently than from a rambling livestream. It feels measured. Precise. Undeniable. But in reality, it is the same appeal to belief as every other strategy — simply wearing the mask of critical thinking. For audiences using the peripheral route to persuasion, the aesthetics of a professional-looking diagram act as a shortcut, bypassing deeper analysis of the content itself (Petty & Cacioppo, 1986).

Anonymity often amplifies this effect. A name can be questioned. A face can be criticized. But a clean logo or untraceable username feels larger than a single person — a voice of reason rather than a personality. That distance builds mystique and reinforces the impression of objectivity. It also allows the content to move more freely. A meme without an author is easier to adopt as "everyone's truth."

The Visual Rationalist understands the economy of shareability. Quick-hit visuals spread faster than long explanations, and every repost drives the message deeper into the echo chamber. This is where rhetoric meets design: each image bypasses argument and goes straight to recognition. When a diagram or quote appears across dozens of pages and threads, it stops feeling like one person's idea and starts feeling like common knowledge. This repetition fuels the illusory truth effect, making each exposure feel more familiar, and therefore more believable (Hasher, Goldstein, & Toppino, 1977).

Beneath the clean lines and composed formatting, the same emotional hooks are at work. The promise has not changed: to be on the inside, to see what "they" will not show you. The Visual Rationalist frames belief as bravery and skepticism as weakness. The message is not "look at this evidence," but "be the kind of person who can see it." That subtle shift turns a diagram into a mirror. The audience does not simply see a claim — they see themselves as the enlightened ones who understand it. This is a core mechanism of social identity theory, where belief and self-concept become intertwined (Tajfel & Turner, 1979). Once belief becomes part of who you are, defending it feels like defending yourself. And that is the moment when identity stops being abstract and starts carrying value — the kind of value people will defend, share, and eventually pay to keep alive.

Building the Marketplace

Once belief carries value, it rarely stays in the abstract for long. Sooner or later, value finds a price tag. In Flat Earth spaces, that price tag appears everywhere: books, maps, T-shirts, DVDs, and digital downloads. Each item is framed not as simple merchandise but as proof — as if buying it is not a transaction, but an act of loyalty. Conviction gets printed, bound, or stitched into something tangible. And holding it feels like holding the truth itself.

Merchandise becomes more than memorabilia. A shirt or a mug becomes a public declaration: *I see what they do not.* That shift turns a purchase into a signal of belonging. It is not only buying into an idea — it is wearing your identity. Social identity theory plays out here in fabric and ink. The more visible the product, the stronger the in-group pride (Tajfel & Turner, 1979). Every item purchased reinforces not just the belief, but the buyer's place within the movement.

The language surrounding these sales rarely sounds like commerce. "Support the truth." "Keep the movement alive." "Help spread awareness." Each phrase frames the purchase as activism, not consumption. That rhetorical shift matters. It turns what could feel like a financial exchange into a moral one. A book is not just a book — it is a tool to "wake people up." A DVD is not simply content — it is "evidence preservation." The transaction is wrapped in purpose. And purpose sells better than product. This framing, central to the grift, bypasses the guilt of consumption by tying it to a higher, altruistic cause.

Even the archetypes feed this cycle. The Repetition Strategist turns their "foundational" content into guides or collections, selling the message in a form meant to be shared. The Digital Showman offers exclusive merchandise tied to livestream moments, selling the chance to "own a piece" of the performance. Belief becomes something that can be packaged — and packaging becomes part of the persuasion.

When conviction takes physical form, it gains weight. A theory on a screen can be swiped past. A book on a shelf or a shirt on someone's back lingers. It turns belief into something that can be seen, touched, and shared. And that is where the line between belief and business quietly disappears — not with a hard sell, but with a soft shift. Until the movement becomes as much a marketplace as it is a message.

For all the talk of "truth movements" and grassroots awakening, the machinery that keeps the Flat Earth economy running looks far less like rebellion and far more like business. Behind the polished livestreams and hand-lettered slogans, there are affiliate networks, ad revenue strategies, cross-promotions, and carefully negotiated partnerships. The rhetoric is anti-establishment, but the structure mirrors the very systems it claims to reject.

Much of this infrastructure stays hidden by design. A creator's public persona leans heavily on authenticity and outsider status, while the backend runs like a small marketing firm. Sponsorship deals are tucked into "resource lists." Merch platforms are white-labeled to appear homemade. Affiliate links are wrapped in the language of "sharing tools" rather than earning commissions. That deliberate invisibility serves the grift: if the money flow appears too professional, the illusion of grassroots passion begins to crack. This is stealth marketing — commercial activity disguised as authentic, non-commercial behavior to preserve audience trust (Balakrishnan & Al-Aswad, 2021).

The platforms themselves play a central role in this hidden economy. YouTube monetization, Patreon tiers, and ad-driven revenue models convert attention into currency — a defining feature of the attention economy. Algorithms reward consistency and engagement, pushing creators toward structured content schedules and narratives designed to keep audiences coming back. The so-called "truth teller" starts to look less like a lone voice in the wilderness and more like a brand manager working inside a system that thrives on polarizing, high-engagement content (Benkler et al., 2018). The business model does not just coexist with the belief system — it shapes it.

Cross-promotion strengthens this web. Influencers guest on one another's livestreams, trade mentions, and link to each other's products to expand their reach. These collaborations are framed as unity within the movement, but the effect is unmistakably commercial: audiences are shared, markets are widened, and loyalty is monetized across multiple channels.

What looks like community-building doubles as a revenue strategy, turning belief into business.

For the audience, none of this is presented as commerce. The language stays grounded in mission and movement: "support the cause," "keep the truth alive." This rhetorical layer keeps the machinery out of sight, allowing participation to feel like activism instead of consumption. It is a sleight of hand — one that depends on performance as much as any livestream or speech. The product is not just content or merchandise. The product is the system itself — the machinery that keeps belief packaged, priced, and circulating.

And that is the quiet irony. A movement that claims to reject "manufactured narratives" relies on one of its own: the story that what you are funding is a fight, not a business. It is a curtain that cannot be pulled back, because once the machinery is seen, the spell begins to break. So the show goes on — carefully staged, tightly managed, and always selling.

Merchandise can put belief in someone's hands, but conferences put it under their feet. When a movement gathers in one place, conviction takes on a new form — not just an idea or a product, but a shared experience that can be stepped into. These events do more than spread a message; they turn it into a living marketplace of loyalty and access. A ticket is not simply entry to a venue. It is entry into the heart of the community — a way to prove not only what you believe, but who you belong to.

Conferences sell more than information. They sell proximity — to the movement, to the personalities who define it, and to the feeling of being surrounded by people who "see the truth." That emotional high is the real product. It turns belief from something fragile into something that feels inevitable. Online spaces can imitate that unity, but they cannot match the moment when hundreds chant the same lines or nod together at the same "proofs." This kind of physical gathering is a powerful reinforcement of social identity theory, solidifying the in-group and amplifying its shared purpose (Tajfel & Turner, 1979).

Exclusivity pushes the price higher. Access to influencers is framed as a rare opportunity — a signed book, a photo, a brief moment of direct contact with the voice you follow online. That contact is not just personal; it is transactional. It transforms a parasocial relationship — a one-sided emotional connection — into something physical, and therefore, something that can be sold (Horton & Wohl, 1956). The Digital Showman thrives in this space. Performance becomes presence, and presence becomes profit.

These gatherings also sell the movement back to itself. Merch tables line the halls, workshops promise deeper "insights," and tickets for the next event go on sale before the current one has even ended. Scarcity amplifies the draw. The fear of missing out makes each gathering feel monumental — a piece of history that cannot be skipped (Cialdini, 1984). The event becomes more than a meeting. It becomes a ritual. And rituals are powerful anchors for belief.

In the end, the conference economy does not just monetize the message — it monetizes the experience of belonging. People do not leave with only notes or souvenirs. They leave with the memory of being part of something larger than themselves — and that feeling is what ensures they will buy their way back into the room next time.

Buying Into Belief

Money does not just sustain belief; it seals it. Every payment is a small vow not to let go.

When belief becomes a steady source of income, certainty stops being only a stance and turns into a business model. Subscriptions and paywalls transform conviction into something that can be measured out in monthly installments. The promise of "deeper truths" locked behind a recurring fee does more than fund the movement — it reinforces the idea that belief has layers, and that access to the "real" answers must be earned.

Exclusivity does the heavy lifting. Content framed as "too valuable for public release" takes on an instant sense of importance. Restriction alone makes information feel weightier, whether or not it offers anything new. Paying for that access feels less like buying content and more like passing a test of loyalty. Even small recurring donations become proof of commitment — a tangible way to show membership in an inner circle. This is a potent combination of scarcity and social proof, as the "inner circle" becomes a visible community others aspire to join (Cialdini, 1984).

The psychology is subtle but powerful. Once someone invests money on a regular basis, even in small amounts, they begin to invest emotionally to match. This triggers cognitive dissonance — the discomfort of holding conflicting beliefs (Festinger, 1957). Doubt now carries a cost, not just in belief but in identity: admitting error means admitting you paid for the wrong thing. That quiet pressure keeps people subscribed long after the novelty fades. What begins as support becomes ritual — a monthly renewal of both the message and the self.

Creators understand this instinctively. The Repetition Strategist uses tiered memberships to turn mantras into purchasable "levels" of understanding. The Digital Showman turns paywalls into VIP communities, framing access as belonging as much as information. Even the Visual Rationalist leans on crowdfunding platforms, packaging anonymity as "community-supported truth preservation." In every case, the mechanism is the same: belief as subscription, identity as invoice.

Recurring income does more than sustain a movement — it locks it in place. When certainty pays the bills, doubt is no longer just inconvenient; it is expensive. The audience learns to avoid it. The creator learns to perform around it. Together they build a system in which belief is not only held but renewed on a schedule, each payment reinforcing a story both sides are invested in keeping alive. And as the movement searches for new ways to package that story, the next evolution comes not in content or conferences, but in tools designed to make belief itself look digital, portable, and permanent.

Money changes the shape of belief. The moment someone spends even a small amount to support a movement, conviction stops being only an idea in their head and becomes a stake they have planted. Payment carries weight because it makes belief tangible. And once it is tangible, it becomes something to defend.

This is where psychology and economy meet. Spending money does not just buy access — it forges identity. A few dollars for a subscription or a one-time donation might feel minor, but it creates what behavioral economists call sunk cost pressure. This is the sunk cost fallacy in action: the more a person has invested — time, money, or effort — the harder it is to walk away, even when the evidence says they should (Staw, 1976). Walking away no longer means simply changing your mind. It means admitting you paid for the wrong thing. With every transaction, the emotional cost of doubt rises, until leaving feels heavier than staying.

Creators understand this instinctively. They frame payments not as purchases, but as acts of support: *You are helping keep the truth alive.* That framing bypasses consumer skepticism and turns a transaction into a moral act. It is no longer about what you are buying. It is about the person you are proving yourself to be. Each payment becomes less a receipt and more a certificate of identity.

Over time, paying becomes a ritual. Monthly subscriptions stop feeling like bills and start to feel like renewal ceremonies — a quiet, recurring way to say, *I still believe.* This ritual reinforces not only the message, but the self. When belief is tied to who you are, renewing it feels less like a financial choice and more like protecting a piece of yourself.

Payment also does more than bind an individual to the message. It ties them to the community. When everyone around you is paying too, the act itself becomes a shared signal — a currency of loyalty. Each contribution, no matter how small, says *we are in this together.* That shared investment sets the stage for the next layer of the economy: when payment turns the audience into something more than supporters. It turns them into stakeholders. And once you hold a stake, you are not just following a movement — you are helping build it.

When money moves from casual support to shared investment, the audience stops being just an audience. They become stakeholders in the story. Every donation, subscription, and purchase feels less like buying a product and more like buying into the movement itself. And with that investment comes a subtle but powerful shift: when you help build something, you have a reason to keep it standing.

This is the unspoken contract of the belief economy. Supporters are not only funding a message; they are underwriting an identity. Each contribution — no matter how small — acts like stock in the narrative. The more you pay, the stronger the pull of psychological ownership, the feeling that you own a piece of it (Pierce et al., 2001). That sense of ownership creates its own gravity. Doubt is no longer just a private thought — it begins to feel like betraying something you helped create.

The effect goes beyond money. In conspiracy spaces, unpaid labor becomes another form of currency. Fans share videos, create memes, moderate comment sections, and recruit new followers — not because they are told to, but because investment has fused with identity. This is prosumerism in action, where the line between producer and consumer blurs and the audience actively participates in creating and spreading the content (Ritzer & Jurgenson, 2010). Every share increases the perceived value of what you have a stake in. It is a feedback loop: belief reinforcing belief, with the audience doing the work of keeping the market alive.

Rhetorically, this dynamic is framed as empowerment: *You are part of the movement. You are helping spread the truth.* The language recasts audience labor as activism, turning every act of promotion into something meaningful. Psychologically, it taps into the principle of commitment and consistency — once someone has put in effort or money, their behavior bends to match that choice (Cialdini, 1984). Walking away does not feel like changing your mind; it feels like abandoning your own work.

This is why the most successful grifts make the audience feel like co-creators. The persona at the center provides the spark, but the community carries the flame. And the more that audience believes they are helping shape the story, the more willing they are to protect it — and to fund it. In the economy of belief, the audience is not just the market. They are the investors who make sure the market never closes.

As the movement searches for new ways to package its story, the next evolution does not come in content or conferences but in tools designed to make belief look digital, portable, and permanent. Apps and online platforms turn conspiracy into something you can carry in your pocket. A map on a screen, a "truth calculator," or a location-based experiment creates the impression that belief has moved beyond words into hard, interactive proof. The interface itself becomes part of the persuasion: if it looks technical, it feels credible. For a user operating on the peripheral route to persuasion, sleek design and the appearance of complexity can be more convincing than the actual substance of the tool's output (Petty & Cacioppo, 1986).

These tools are often riddled with problems — data pulled from the very systems they claim to reject, calculations bent to fit a conclusion — but flaws rarely matter. The presence of an app alone creates an aura of legitimacy. It signals organization, innovation, and most importantly, resistance. Using the tool becomes an act of defiance, a way to feel like you are "fighting the system" with technology designed to subvert it. In that framing, even a broken compass can feel like a weapon.

Gamification adds another layer. Interactive features — tracking flights, plotting routes, comparing "real-time" data — turn belief into participation. The act of using the app becomes a performance of loyalty, a ritual the user can repeat every day. Each click and calculation reinforces not just the message but the feeling of being on the inside of something important. It is less about what the tool proves and more about what using it says: *I am part of this.*

The personas feed into this market in different ways. The Digital Showman leans on flashy features and claims of censorship, framing every update as a battle against suppression. The Visual Rationalist uses crowdfunding to present apps as "community-built truth preservation," turning anonymity into collective effort. Even the Repetition Strategist folds tools into their foundation-building, offering digital "evidence kits" that make belief feel organized and scientific.

At their core, these apps are not about technology. They are about packaging conviction into something you can tap, swipe, and hold. They turn belief into an object, a daily interaction, a habit disguised as proof. And once belief becomes a habit, it does not just live in the mind — it lives in the hands. That makes it harder to let go.

But the real product is not the tool itself. It is the connection the tool represents — the sense of access to the movement, to its message, and to the people who carry it forward. Each update, each login, is a small act of proximity. That is the quiet shift these platforms create — turning belief from something you consume into something you feel you are touching. And once proximity can be packaged, the next step is inevitable: selling access itself.

When access becomes the commodity, what is really being sold is not content or tools — it is the people themselves. In conspiracy movements, the faces at the center are not just delivering a message; they are performing a relationship. Livestreams, Q&As, personal updates, even casual "behind the scenes" moments all carry a subtle price tag: emotional proximity.

The audience is not simply paying for information. They are paying for the feeling of being seen by the person they have invested in. This is where parasocial connection turns into currency (Horton & Wohl, 1956). A private chat, a personalized shoutout, or a tier that promises "direct contact" frames closeness as something you can buy. The message becomes secondary. The emotional access is the real product.

Creators lean into this because it works. A livestream is not just a broadcast; it is a room filled with people who feel they are in conversation with the persona they follow. Every thank you, every name read aloud in a donation list, reinforces the bond. The more the creator performs intimacy, the more the audience performs loyalty — and both sides understand the exchange, even if no one says it out loud.

Psychologically, this trade is powerful because it taps into reciprocity and belonging at the same time. When someone believes they are part of the creator's "inner circle," supporting them stops feeling optional. It becomes an emotional duty. Walking away does not feel like canceling a subscription; it feels like abandoning a relationship. That quiet weight is what makes emotional labor one of the most lucrative products in the belief economy. The high emotional cost of leaving — a mix of sunk cost and the loss of a social bond — is a powerful force in maintaining commitment.

The personas all use this dynamic in different ways. The Digital Showman sells "backstage access" to the performance. The Repetition Strategist turns loyalty into mentorship, offering guidance in exchange for deeper commitment. The Visual Rationalist trades on mystique, making a glimpse behind the curtain feel rare and therefore valuable. No matter the tactic, the economy is the same: proximity as product, intimacy as invoice.

This is the final step in the marketplace of belief. It is not just about selling ideas or tools — it is about selling connection itself. When the movement can package closeness and call it truth, the transaction is no longer about evidence at all. It is about identity wrapped in relationship. And once belief and belonging fuse into that kind of bond, the business does not just sustain the message — it sustains the people who carry it, one emotional transaction at a time.

The Martyr Narrative: Silenced or Selling?

A threatened story doesn't just gain weight—it gains worth.

In the economy of belief, nothing raises the value of a message faster than the appearance of being suppressed. A takedown notice, a shadowban, or a missing video is not treated as a loss — it is rebranded as evidence. In Flat Earth spaces, persecution is not just endured; it is performed. The logic is simple and powerful: if "they" are trying to silence this, then it must be true. The strike itself becomes the proof.

This framing is deliberate. The language around these moments is crafted to ignite a reflex: screenshots of bans are shared like trophies, hashtags rally supporters, and every platform action is reframed as a desperate attempt to bury the truth. The emotional effect is immediate. Anger surges first, but beneath it comes something stronger: loyalty. The audience is not simply defending content; they are defending the story and, by extension, themselves. This deliberate shaping of the narrative around negative events is a textbook example of framing (Entman, 1993).

The psychology runs deep. Once a belief is tied to identity, any attack on it feels personal. When the "system" pushes back, it triggers the us-versus-them framing that binds the movement together, reinforcing in-group boundaries (Tajfel & Turner, 1979). Every strike reinforces the sense of being under siege, and that siege raises the price of belonging. It also activates psychological reactance — when people feel their freedom to access information is threatened, they often double down on their belief (Brehm, 1966). In this frame, donations stop being about supporting a creator and become contributions to the "defense of truth." Giving money no longer feels like commerce; it feels like resistance.

Creators understand the pull of this narrative. Some lean into it instinctively; others build it intentionally. A platform ban becomes a rallying cry. A takedown turns into a campaign. Even small restrictions can be spun into signs of danger, each one inflating the perceived value of the message. Persecution does not just protect belief — it sells it. It turns the abstract into a currency backed not by evidence, but by the cost of defending it.

And once persecution itself becomes proof, the next step is inevitable: even the smallest crack, the tiniest flaw, can be reframed as another attack. When everything is cast as a siege, imperfection does not weaken the story — it raises the stakes.

In the economy of belief, mistakes are rarely left as mistakes. A broken feature, a misaligned chart, a poorly edited video — any flaw can be spun into something larger: not an error, but an attack. When technical issues or criticism are reframed as deliberate sabotage, the flaw itself becomes part of the proof.

Apps that glitch are presented as victims of tampering. A missing video is not oversight but evidence that "they" are trying to erase the truth. Even negative reviews or fact-checks are folded into the story as attempts to discredit the movement. Imperfections in books, maps, or tools are no longer weaknesses; they are framed as scars from the battle. The message is clear: the content is so dangerous that outside forces are desperate to destroy it.

This tactic shifts attention away from the flaw and onto the supposed injustice behind it. A factual error is not examined or corrected; it is buried beneath a new narrative that appeals to pathos rather than logos (Aristotle, trans. 2007). The audience is not being asked to forgive a mistake — they are being asked to defend against an attack. That pivot sparks loyalty. Anger comes first, then solidarity. Criticism becomes the enemy, and the creator becomes the embattled defender of truth.

There is calculated psychology at work. Scapegoating creates a common foe, reinforcing the us-versus-them frame that keeps the movement unified (Tajfel & Turner, 1979). Authenticity is paradoxically strengthened: the content feels more "real" precisely because it appears to be under fire. The flaw becomes a badge of honor, a sign that the message matters enough to be targeted. This constant sense of siege also activates psychological reactance, prompting the audience to cling more fiercely to the content they believe is being suppressed (Brehm, 1966).

When flaws are reframed this way, the movement takes on a self-sealing quality. Every error, every challenge becomes fuel for the story instead of a crack in it. And when even the mistakes can be sold as evidence, the stage is set for the next — and most profitable — move: turning that constant sense of siege into a product of its own.

In Flat Earth spaces, the story of being silenced often outperforms any claim of proof. A chart can be debated. A video can be fact-checked. But a narrative of persecution bypasses argument entirely. It does not ask the audience to weigh evidence; it asks them to feel injustice. That emotional pull is stronger than data because it reframes belief from a question of facts to a question of loyalty.

Victimhood sells because it creates urgency. When a creator frames themselves as under attack, every donation or purchase becomes more than support — it becomes defense. The language shifts: you are not buying a DVD or funding a livestream; you are "keeping the truth alive." That framing works because it casts the audience as active participants in the fight. Each contribution feels like a stand against suppression, a small act of rebellion wrapped inside a transaction.

This tactic taps into deep psychological levers. Pathos-driven persuasion stirs emotion first, and social identity theory does the rest. An attack on the message is framed as an attack on the group, and the group rallies to protect itself (Tajfel & Turner, 1979). Emotional contagion magnifies the effect: fear and outrage spread quickly, and each wave of feeling is converted into renewed commitment (Hatfield et al., 1994). Creators understand this balance instinctively. Evidence can persuade a few. Persecution can bind a crowd. It forges an in-group by defining an enemy on the outside. Meanwhile, the scarcity principle hums in the background: if the message is always "at risk of being erased," then every piece of content feels rare, every moment to act feels fleeting (Cialdini, 1984). That urgency is not just emotional; it is profitable.

When persecution becomes the product, belief stops being about what you know and starts being about what you are willing to defend. And in a marketplace built on conviction, the most valuable thing you can sell is the story that the truth itself is under siege.

In the world of conspiracy movements, the line between genuine conviction and calculated performance is razor-thin. A creator may start with sincere belief, but the moment persecution proves profitable, authenticity becomes both a persuasion tool and a product. What begins as defending an idea can quietly shift into defending a brand.

Persecution becomes a performance. Each strike, ban, or criticism is not simply endured — it is staged, replayed, and amplified. What might be a setback in another context turns into a campaign here. The story of being silenced does not just keep the message alive — it keeps the business alive. The martyr narrative stops being a side effect and becomes a tactic, blending pathos-driven persuasion with the reliability of a business model.

The audience rarely questions the sincerity behind the suffering. Confirmation bias fills in the gaps: if they already believe the message, the performance of persecution feels not only real but inevitable. Emotional contagion spreads the story until it becomes part of the group's identity (Hatfield et al., 1994). In-group bias, a core component of social identity theory, seals it off from scrutiny — questioning the narrative would mean questioning the movement itself, and few are willing to cross that line (Tajfel & Turner, 1979).

This leaves the movement in a constant state of tension: a marketplace built on conviction, yet shaped by performance. The faces of the movement are both believers and sellers, both voices of faith and architects of the grift. That duality is not a flaw in the system; it is the system.

And it is here, at the edge where belief meets business, that the cost of the grift begins to show — not just in money exchanged or products sold, but in the way conviction itself is bent, packaged, and traded until it is hard to tell where the truth ends and the performance begins. That tension is not confined to a single persona or tactic; it runs through the entire economy of the movement. When the performance becomes the product, the question is no longer just who believes — it is what that belief is really worth.

Every economy has its currency. In this one, the coin is conviction. It changes hands in livestreams and conference halls, in merchandise and monthly subscriptions, in quiet moments of loyalty whispered through a donation screen. But what sustains it is not just money. It is the performance of belief, repeated until it stops feeling like performance at all.

Flat Earth spaces sell more than maps or theories. They sell identity, belonging, and the comfort of certainty in a world that feels unstable. They wrap fear and hope into something you can hold, wear, or pay to keep alive. In doing so, they reveal the grift beneath the story — not as an accident, but as the structure itself.

That structure is not built on evidence. It is built on exchange. Every claim, every emotional hook, and every product offered is part of a transaction where the line between belief and business fades until it is almost impossible to see. The faces at the movement's center are not just selling ideas; they are performing parasocial relationships and shaping narratives through strategic framing. They turn conviction into commodity and commodity back into conviction in a self-sustaining loop. As sunk cost pressure and cognitive dissonance grow, the audience becomes both the market and the emotional investors, doing the work of keeping the market alive.

And yet, beneath the performance, there are still people — audiences searching for meaning, creators navigating the space between faith and survival. That tension hums through every livestream and every sale: is this belief, or is it business? In the end, the grift does not erase sincerity. It bends it, packages it, and sells it back, until even the true believers are caught in a marketplace where the most valuable product is not the message itself, but the story of what it costs to believe it.

Chapter 7 — Beyond the Vanishing Point: What This Teaches Us

Flat Earth is not just a belief—it is a window into the heart of human nature. It reveals how we search for meaning, how we shape our identities, and how rhetoric can reshape our sense of reality.

Beneath the surface of wild claims and heated arguments lies something more familiar: the universal struggle to find certainty in an uncertain world. In that sense, the Flat Earth movement becomes a living case study in narrative transportation—a story so compelling that people can lose themselves inside it (Green & Brock, 2000).

This is not just about a fringe theory. It is about the powerful forces that tether us to belief, even when reason and evidence point the other way. The ongoing tension between new information and what we already believe often sparks cognitive dissonance, keeping individuals locked in a feedback loop of self-justification (Festinger, 1957). It is the tug between conviction and doubt—and the way we cling to comforting ideas, even when those ideas begin to fall apart.

Somewhere in that space between certainty and uncertainty, we find the real power of persuasion. We have looked at how framing influences perception, how social identity theory creates insular communities, and how the attention economy reinforces thought patterns we may not even realize we are stuck in. And still, change is possible. Some do find their way back—stepping away from deeply held beliefs to see the world differently.

Those stories remind us that belief is not bulletproof. Even the most entrenched ideas can be questioned. And in that realization lies the deeper lesson: the same power that builds conviction can also unravel it. Change is always within reach. What follows are the pathways to that change—the cracks that form, the pressure points that break belief, and the way individuals can step out from under the weight of the systems that once held them.

Why Flat Earth Persists

Flat Earth belief is not simply the result of "bad science" or ignorance. It runs deeper. While misinformation might crack the door open, it is identity, belonging, and a deep-seated distrust of authority that hold it wide open.

Conspiracy theories do not thrive because they are convincing. They thrive because they are comforting. They offer a sense of certainty in a world that often feels chaotic—a clean narrative that explains away the messiness of complexity. The rhetoric behind them leans heavily on narrative framing, building a self-contained world where any contradictory evidence is reinterpreted as further proof of deception (Entman, 1993). It is not just misinformation—it is a kind of emotional architecture. The appeal to comfort is real. The message is clear: here, inside this belief system, things finally make sense.

And once someone steps into that space, confirmation bias takes over. People begin to seek out anything that supports what they already believe—ambiguous video clips, distorted facts, cherry-picked interpretations of science. Each one becomes a reinforcement, not a question. Anything that challenges the belief is either ignored or reframed as part of the conspiracy. In the Flat Earth world, contradictions do not dismantle belief. They feed it (Tversky & Kahneman, 1974).

But this is more than just flawed thinking. This is personal. Believing in a conspiracy theory is not just about accepting different facts—it is about accepting a different identity. "I know the truth," the believer tells themselves. "I am not like everyone else." That feeling of being in the know, of being part of an exclusive club that sees through the lies, becomes central to who they are. The belief fuses with their identity. And once that happens, letting go of the belief feels like losing a part of themselves.

This is why the ingroup/outgroup dynamic matters so much. According to social identity theory, the moment someone feels like they belong to a group, especially one defined in opposition to a larger "misled" public, it becomes harder to walk away (Tajfel & Turner, 1979). The group becomes not just a social circle but a defense system, one that frames doubt as betrayal and questions as weakness.

And that is what makes dismantling these beliefs so difficult. Facts alone rarely do the job. You can debunk the claims line by line—but unless you also address the emotional drivers beneath them, the belief holds firm. Fear, pride, belonging, mistrust—these are the real anchors. And until those are loosened, no amount of evidence will land.

The resilience of Flat Earth rhetoric—and that of most conspiracy movements—lies in this exact tension. It is not simply a misunderstanding of facts. It is a deeper need for stability, certainty, and identity. Facts can bend. Emotions and group loyalty do not.

Flat Earth theory does not gain traction because of the strength of its evidence. It gains traction because of the strength of its validation. For many, the phrase "You're not crazy, they're lying" is more than a slogan—it is a lifeline. It affirms what they already suspect: that their doubts are not irrational, that their mistrust is justified, and that they are not alone. That reassurance, that emotional hook, is what makes the Flat Earth narrative so magnetic. It is not just an invitation to question science—it is an invitation to feel seen.

The rhetoric at work here is deceptively simple. It casts the believer as someone who sees through the deception, someone brave enough to question what others blindly accept. It does not just explain the shape of the Earth. It offers moral clarity. The individual becomes more than just a skeptic—they become a rebel, a truth-seeker, a warrior against deception. This transformation provides something that many people crave: purpose. And in a world that often feels unstable, confusing, and unfair, that sense of purpose becomes deeply grounding. It becomes a kind of modern-day collective effervescence, a shared emotional high that comes from being part of a mission greater than oneself (Durkheim, 1912).

But the rebellion does not stop with the Earth's shape. It expands outward, aimed at science, education, government, media—any institution perceived as part of the system. The Flat Earth narrative becomes a vehicle for broader discontent, a catch-all for frustration, alienation, and mistrust. It is a big tent conspiracy, drawing in people who may not even care much about geography, but who resonate with the underlying suspicion. Whether it is fear of government control, anger at the media, or skepticism of experts, there is room in the tent. And once inside, everything that comes from "them" is viewed with suspicion. The story is not just that "they lied about the Earth." The story is that they lie about everything.

This is how a belief becomes an identity. The Flat Earth worldview offers a tribe, a cause, a sense of belonging. You are not just someone with a different opinion—you are one of the few who sees clearly. You are the person standing on the edge of the world, watching the rest of society follow blindly. The rhetoric reinforces that outsider identity, until it becomes central to how the believer sees themselves. It stops being about the model, and starts being about the moral. You are not just right—

you are righteously right. And that shift makes the belief incredibly resilient.

Because at its core, this narrative offers something more elusive: control. In a chaotic, overwhelming world, Flat Earth provides an explanation that makes everything click. No contradictions. No unanswered questions. No uncertainty. Every piece of the puzzle is in place. Everything makes sense. The theory, no matter how flawed, gives people a framework that feels solid. It replaces ambiguity with clarity. And clarity, in moments of fear or confusion, feels like truth.

What Flat Earth really offers is not science—but stability. Not logic—but meaning. And at the center of that meaning is the rhetoric of moral absolutism: the belief that your view is not just valid, but the only valid one. According to Moral Foundations Theory, this kind of thinking divides the world into good and evil, right and wrong, truth and lies (Haidt, 2012). It does not allow for ambiguity. That rhetorical posture elevates the believer above the masses, planting them firmly on moral high ground. And from there, it is a long way down.

The Flat Earth model is more than just an alternative theory—it is a visual narrative. Immediate. Intuitive. Accessible. For those who feel disillusioned or skeptical of authority, it offers a kind of clarity that feels like relief. No jargon. No complex models. No degrees required. In a world saturated with contradictions, expert disagreements, and technical language, the Flat Earth story feels like solid ground—simple, direct, and easy to grasp. That simplicity is not accidental. It is rhetorical. And it is effective.

The movement casts complexity as a tool of the elite. Scientific explanations, especially those that require abstraction or advanced education, are framed as intentionally confusing—designed to keep ordinary people in the dark. Flat Earth, by contrast, becomes a rebellion against that complexity. The claim is clear: "You do not need experts. You just need your own eyes." It is a populist message wrapped in the language of empowerment. And for those who already feel ignored or condescended to by traditional institutions, it lands hard.

This rhetorical move reframes expertise itself as suspicious. Scientists become gatekeepers, not guides. Educators become indoctrinators. The more intricate the explanation, the more likely it is to be dismissed as manipulation. In this dynamic, the complexity of the globe model becomes its own kind of disproof—not because the science is wrong, but because it is seen as inaccessible. According to framing theory, this is the power of narrative: to recast even valid information as part of a larger strategy of deception (Entman, 1993). It sets up a familiar social split—the experts versus the everyman—a textbook application of the ingroup/outgroup dynamic that underpins social identity theory (Tajfel & Turner, 1979).

In this light, Flat Earth rhetoric becomes a celebration of direct observation. The horizon looks flat. The Earth feels still. Therefore, it must be. This is naive realism at work—the psychological tendency to believe that what we perceive is how things truly are, unfiltered and objective (Ross & Ward, 1996). And when that perception clashes with expert claims, the rhetoric kicks in to resolve the tension: "Trust yourself, not them."

But the real shift happens when this simplicity becomes not just persuasive, but righteous.

Rejecting complexity is reframed as a moral act. The person who dismisses the globe model is not simply choosing an alternative theory—they are choosing to stand up against the system. The rejection of science becomes a kind of virtue signal. Ignorance, repackaged as independence, becomes a badge of honor. And this is where the danger lies. The Flat Earth model does not just oppose mainstream science—it redefines what it means to *know* something. It turns away from curiosity and replaces it with conviction. It elevates suspicion into a moral code.

In this world, doubt is no longer a tool for inquiry—it is the foundation of belief. And the simpler the explanation, the more trustworthy it seems. That inversion—where clarity signals truth and complexity signals deceit—creates a moral high ground that feels unshakable. The believer does not just *think* they are right. They *feel* they are righteous.

For many Flat Earthers, distrust is not just a side effect of belief—it is the foundation it stands on. And that distrust runs deep. It does not stop at science; it extends to politics, religion, media, and education. Within this worldview, these systems are not simply flawed—they are fundamentally corrupt, colluding to deceive the public. The belief rarely begins with "The Earth is flat." It starts with something more primal: "They are lying." That single idea becomes the bedrock of what scholars call an *epistemic bubble*—a self-reinforcing environment where trust in a limited set of sources grows stronger while outside voices are systematically dismissed (Nguyen, 2020).

This level of suspicion is not without historical precedent. Institutions have broken public trust before—sometimes with devastating consequences. But the digital age has accelerated everything. What might have once been a quiet doubt becomes, online, a shared identity. Through forums, comment threads, and livestreams, skepticism becomes communal. And once it becomes communal, it becomes profitable. Suspicion turns into content. Merch, conference tickets, livestream donations, and Patreon perks monetize that distrust, turning doubt into a brand.

One of the most powerful rhetorical tools in this ecosystem is deceptively simple: *If they lied about one thing, they could lie about everything.* It is a slippery slope that bypasses evidence in favor of emotional logic—a fallacy that turns any past failure, exaggeration, or injustice into a blank check to doubt everything else (Walton, 2008). It does not matter whether the "one thing" is about war, vaccines, or the moon landing. All that matters is the seed of doubt. Once that seed is planted, the rest does not need proof—it just needs a nudge.

At this point, Flat Earth stops being about the Earth at all. It becomes a broader rejection of authority, a symbolic no to institutions of power. Trusting the globe model is framed not as scientific literacy, but as blind faith—in governments, in scientists, in systems that the believer has already decided cannot be trusted. Rejecting it, then, becomes more than an intellectual decision. It becomes a declaration of freedom. It is an act of defiance. This is classic *psychological reactance*—a resistance that kicks in when someone feels their autonomy is under threat (Brehm, 1966).

And once that posture is adopted, the facts become almost irrelevant. The content of the argument does not matter nearly as much as the context: Who is saying it? Do they sound like part of the system, or outside it? Do they affirm the listener's identity, or challenge it? In the end, the belief is not held up by the strength of evidence. It is held up by the story—and the way that story is told.

Rhetoric, Not Evidence, Wins Hearts

Once trust breaks down, evidence stops standing on neutral ground. It is no longer judged by what it shows but by where it came from. In that kind of environment, persuasion does not work like a courtroom—it works like a storybook. And Flat Earth rhetoric knows exactly how to thrive in that kind of terrain. It does not win because it makes a stronger case. It wins because most people do not weigh evidence like a set of scales. They weigh it by how well it fits into the story they already believe. And when that story has become part of who they are, letting go of it feels like letting go of a piece of themselves.

This is where emotion leads the way. We like to think we process facts first and feelings second—but it is usually the other way around. A photo from space gets felt before it gets studied. If it comes from a distrusted source, it already smells like a lie before the pixels are even processed. But if it comes from someone you believe in, even a blurry shot can feel like the final piece of the puzzle. That is the affect heuristic at work: the brain leans on emotional cues to decide what something means before logic even enters the room (Slovic, Finucane, Peters, & MacGregor, 2002).

Flat Earth influencers understand this better than most. Their arguments do not depend on data. They depend on story. In their world, facts are not the foundation—they are accessories. Props in a much larger emotional drama where the believer is the brave truth-seeker and the skeptic is the brainwashed pawn. Within that frame, any new win is proof of progress, and any pushback is a sign that the enemy is scared. The players may change. The visuals may shift. But the plot never does.

Debunkers, on the other hand, often come armed with airtight logic and well-sourced facts, assuming those are enough. They build strong arguments. They explain where the thinking went wrong. They reach clear conclusions. But by the time they show up, the audience has often already made up its mind. The part of the brain that hungers for belonging, identity, and certainty already claimed the verdict. The argument, no matter how well made, gets filtered through that emotional lens and often does not make it through.

The Elaboration Likelihood Model explains this gap. When someone processes a message through the lens of belief or identity, they do not evaluate it carefully. They skim the surface, reacting to tone, familiarity, and gut instinct—not structure or substance (Petty & Cacioppo, 1986). So when a Flat Earth believer shows a flat horizon and says, "See? No curve," and the debunker responds with field of view explanations and distortion math, the audience often feels like the expert is dancing around what seems obvious. The science may be correct. But it feels evasive. It feels like an excuse.

That is why the rhetoric of simplicity often wins. "Just look with your own eyes" will always hit harder than "Let me walk you through this physics formula." Once logic becomes tied to identity, it stops being a way to change someone's mind. It becomes a tool to defend the mind already made up. That is why refuting a belief can actually make it stronger—a phenomenon known as the backfire effect (Nyhan & Reifler, 2010). A strong rebuttal does not always weaken the claim. Sometimes, it just confirms the belief that the system is desperate to keep the truth hidden.

To break through that, facts are not enough. You have to understand the scaffolding that holds the belief in place. You have to meet the story before you can challenge it. Because in these spaces, people do not just want to be right. They want to belong. They want to feel secure. And unless you speak to that first, they will never feel your facts—no matter how true they are.

The Emotional Architecture of a Lie

When a belief holds firm in the face of overwhelming evidence, it is rarely the facts themselves that give it staying power. What keeps it alive is the emotional scaffolding built around it. Flat Earth is not persuasive because its arguments are sound—it is persuasive because its message is wrapped in emotion, speaking directly to the need for meaning, identity, and belonging. At the center of that emotional structure are four recurring cues: betrayal, awakening, bravery, and persecution.

These are not just common themes. They are psychological triggers—shortcuts that bypass reason and tap straight into loyalty, purpose, and pride.

It begins with betrayal. The story starts with the idea that "they" lied—not just once, but consistently and deliberately. Governments, scientists, educators, media figures—all in on a grand deception. This is not framed as human error. It is painted as a vast, multi-generational conspiracy. The rhetoric is crafted to stir outrage, to awaken a sense of injustice. Once the premise of betrayal is accepted, trust in all official sources evaporates. It no longer matters what is being said—only who is saying it, and whether they are part of the lie. This emotional shift mirrors betrayal trauma, where a deep violation of trust by an authority figure or institution leaves lasting psychological wounds (Freyd, 1996). In this mindset, even the most verifiable evidence becomes suspect simply because of its origin.

From there, the story moves into awakening. The believer is cast in the role of the enlightened one—the person who has finally "seen through" the deception. This rhetoric flatters the listener, appealing to the desire to feel special, perceptive, and independent. It is a soft echo of a conversion story: once you know the truth, you cannot unsee it. There is a clear before and after, a transformation that gives meaning and direction to the believer's path (Clark, 1929). It does not just explain the world—it gives the believer a reason for being.

Then comes bravery. In this world, to believe something unpopular is not just an opinion—it is a moral stand. Holding the Flat Earth view, despite ridicule or rejection, is cast as an act of courage. Livestream debates, viral videos, and confrontations with mainstream science are more than outreach—they are public declarations of moral strength. This is a form of moral courage: the willingness to stand by one's beliefs despite social costs (Lennick & Kiel, 2005). Within the community, bravery is not defined by what is risked physically, but by what is endured emotionally. Every insult, every eye-roll, every banned account becomes another stripe earned in the name of truth.

Finally, persecution seals the frame. Criticism is not a threat—it is validation. The more they are mocked, censored, or "fact-checked," the more they believe they are over the target. Opposition is not taken as evidence that something might be wrong. It is proof that something must be right. This mindset reflects the dynamics of a persecution complex—where pushback is interpreted as direct assault on identity and belief, only strengthening group cohesion (Castelli, 2007). In this worldview, resistance from the outside world does not crack the foundation. It reinforces it. It tells the community: you are doing something important. Keep going.

Together, these four cues—betrayal, awakening, bravery, persecution—form an emotional loop that keeps belief insulated from contradiction. They do not engage the analytical mind. They activate the tribal one. And once those circuits are lit, the brain shifts its priorities. It favors loyalty over logic. It values safety over scrutiny. Neuroscience confirms this: when identity and emotion take center stage, factual accuracy often steps aside.

That is why every element of Flat Earth rhetoric—from memes to livestreams—is designed to tap into that emotional map. The jokes are not just for laughs; they are tribal markers. The conversations are not just about information; they are rituals of belonging. They build and reinforce the emotional structure needed to keep the belief intact.

And that is the key. If we want to understand why Flat Earth has staying power, we cannot just look at the claims. We have to look at the architecture holding those claims up. When betrayal is constantly invoked, when bravery is continually rewarded, when persecution becomes a badge of honor—it is no surprise that logic alone struggles to break through. But when you can recognize the beams, when you can see how and where these emotional cues are doing their work, you also start to see where the structure may eventually shift, crack, or give way.

The Theater of Certainty

In the world of persuasion, certainty is more than a mindset—it is a performance. And in Flat Earth spaces, that performance is finely tuned. It runs like stagecraft, complete with memorized lines, polished delivery, and an ironclad refusal to entertain doubt. The power of this performance lies in its contagiousness. Certainty, when delivered with conviction, spreads quickly. It moves through an audience like a spark through dry grass, igniting belief even in those who were on the fence. In that moment, the message itself takes a back seat. What sticks is not always what was said, but how confidently it was said.

Human beings are wired to mirror emotional states. When a speaker radiates absolute confidence, the audience begins to feel that same confidence—even before they have had time to evaluate the message. This response is not rooted in the truthfulness of the content. A speaker who sounds sure, who shows no hesitation, quickly earns a kind of perceived authority. And in the Flat Earth ecosystem, that authority is not accidental. It is intentional. It is part of the act.

This is where rhetorical fluency does its heaviest lifting. The ability to speak smoothly, pivot quickly, and wrap complex ideas in familiar language often matters more than scientific accuracy. Not because audiences have no interest in truth—but because our brains treat confidence as a stand-in for competence. A seamless delivery feels like mastery. And once that impression is set, the substance of the message is filtered through the speaker's perceived credibility rather than through the evidence itself.

Within this performance, hesitation is a liability. Silence is suspicious. Doubt is a weakness. So, the show must go on—fast, fluid, and unbroken. Flat Earth speakers flood the space with short, punchy statements, repeated slogans, and rehearsed refrains. These soundbites become the chorus lines of a movement, reinforcing the idea that the "truth" is self-evident. That only the blind—or the brainwashed—could miss it.

And here lies the mismatch. Science does not speak in absolutes. It pauses. It qualifies. It acknowledges uncertainty. A scientist might say, "The current data suggests…" A Flat Earther replies, "This proves it." One approach is careful, the other definitive. And in a rhetorical arena built on performance, the careful voice often sounds weak. The bold voice commands the stage.

Because in this theater, the crowd is not waiting for nuance. They are waiting for certainty. And the speaker who delivers that, without blinking, earns the standing ovation—not because they presented the most evidence, but because they performed the part best. The script does not allow for questions. Only declarations.

That is the lesson. In a world where persuasion often favors tone over truth, the performance of certainty can outshine the substance of science. And the one who never wavers—who never allows doubt even a second of air—wins the audience, even if they lose the argument.

Repetition as Identity Reinforcement

In Flat Earth spaces, repetition is not filler—it is the backbone of the entire persuasive system. Within just a few weeks inside the echo chamber, believers absorb a steady stream of the same slogans, catchphrases, and talking points. And at some point, those lines stop functioning as arguments. They become something else entirely—identity markers. "Water finds its level." "Show me the curve." "NASA lies." These phrases circulate like verbal passwords, granting access to a shared reality. Speaking them does not just signal belief; it signals belonging.

What gives repetition its power is the way it reshapes how truth is experienced. Outside these spaces, truth is something you test, verify, or compare against evidence. But inside a closed-loop system, truth becomes whatever feels familiar. This is the illusory truth effect in action—repeated statements are more likely to be believed, not because they make more sense, but because they sound more familiar (Begg et al., 1992). Familiarity breeds comfort. And over time, that comfort begins to feel like certainty. The brain stops asking whether a claim is true and starts treating it like furniture—always there, unquestioned, part of the scenery.

This is not a rhetorical accident. It is the strategy. The goal of repetition is not to sharpen the logic. It is to dull the instinct to question. Like the lyrics of a song that get stuck in your head, these repeated lines take root. And when doubt creeps in, they surface again—quiet, insistent, familiar. Each one becomes a small ritual, a reminder of what you believe and, more importantly, who you are. Repetition works not just as a persuasive tactic, but as a method of identity maintenance. Saying the phrase is like rehearsing your role in the group. And the more you say it, the more deeply you feel like you belong.

This is the engine of group cohesion. These shared lines are not just responses—they are glue. They hold the group together by reinforcing loyalty, solidarity, and shared purpose (Van Zomeren et al., 2008). They create a rhythm that is easy to follow, even when the outside world is shouting back in opposition.

And because the lines feel safe, they also feel strong. When challenged, the believer rarely pulls from a wide body of evidence. Instead, they reach for the phrases—short, practiced, smooth from use. These phrases become shields. The more intense the challenge, the tighter the grip on those familiar words. And when that happens, the conversation is no longer about finding truth. It becomes about surviving the encounter—about holding onto something that anchors the self.

If there is a path forward, it does not begin by attacking the slogans head-on. It begins by understanding what those slogans are protecting. Because beneath every repeated line is not just a claim about the shape of the Earth—it is a statement about identity. And when the self is fused that tightly to the language, any challenge to the words will land as a challenge to the person. The phrase defends the belief. But the belief defends the self.

Engaging Without Reinforcing

Repetition closes the circle. Each familiar phrase is more than a claim—it is a defense, a reinforcement, a cue to stay within the walls of the belief. In this closed loop, outsider voices rarely get in. And that makes the next move—whether to speak or stay silent—more consequential than it seems. In a world built to echo itself, even the act of engagement can become fuel.

In today's attention economy, visibility is currency. Every view, every comment, every share feeds the algorithms that decide what gains traction. And no fuel burns hotter than controversy. Flat Earth content thrives on friction. Every rebuttal, no matter how thoughtful or precise, risks triggering the very reward loops that push the content wider—into more feeds, more recommendations, more sidebars labeled "You might also like." The harder you push, the more the system rewards the pushback.

This is where good intentions can backfire. When a debunker steps onto a livestream to "set the record straight," or uploads a long-form response video, they might win on facts—but they risk losing the frame. Just by showing up, they give the impression of legitimacy. The Flat Earth creator spins it into a debate between equals. Suddenly, the point is not who was right. The point is that the conversation happened. That alone is validation. This is the backfire effect in motion—when an attempt to correct misinformation ends up reinforcing it instead (Nyhan & Reifler, 2010).

At that point, it is not a debate—it is theater. And in that theater, the goal is not understanding. It is performance. A debate for correction tries to inform. A debate for performance tries to rally. Flat Earth content thrives in this second mode. It is not about idea exchange—it is about confidence, loyalty, and spectacle. It is framed to win before the first sentence is spoken. And that framing matters. Framing theory tells us that how a message is presented shapes how it is understood (Entman, 1993). When the debate is framed as "the truth versus the establishment," the believer wins simply by standing on stage.

So before entering that stage, the question must change. It is no longer "Can I win this argument?" It is "Who am I really speaking to?" Because the target is almost never the person across the screen. It is the audience—the quiet watchers, the bystanders, the undecided. Sometimes, the most powerful move is to aim not at the core but at the edges. To speak with clarity without amplifying the center. And sometimes, the smartest move is silence. Not surrender. Strategy.

Because in the world of algorithms, silence is not weakness—it is starvation. And no rhetoric, no matter how rehearsed, can echo without an audience to catch the sound.

Even with the best intentions, engagement often builds a stage you never meant to stand on. Social media threads, livestream chats, YouTube comments—none of these are neutral spaces. They are theaters. And in Flat Earth circles, the audience is rarely watching with an open mind. For the influencer, a reply from a skeptic is not a threat. It is an opportunity. It is the opening act.

These platforms reward performance. A Flat Earth creator responding to criticism is not just defending a claim—they are shaping an image. Calm under pressure. Quick with comebacks. Framed by the interface itself—split screens, threaded replies, pinned comments—they step into the role of the unshaken truth-teller. Even if the critic lands every point, the optics favor the one who controls the tempo. It is not just what is said—it is how and where it is delivered. That is the power of framing. The context becomes part of the message (Entman, 1993).

And the stage extends far beyond the moment. Clips get trimmed. Stumbles get looped. Complex points, mid-explained, get cut off and labeled "meltdowns" or "fails." These segments get re-uploaded, reshaped, and sent back into circulation—not as counterpoints, but as trophies. Proof that "the globe defenders are cracking." These edits are not made for accuracy. They are made for effect.

Then comes the echo. Algorithms do not care about who is right. They care about who is being watched. Every comment, every share, every reaction adds fuel. And whether the engagement is outrage or applause, the signal sent to the system is the same: boost it. Push it to more screens. Promote the friction.

The result? The critic who meant to dismantle the message ends up amplifying it. Not by intention, but by proximity. Just showing up can be spun as validation. The influencer does not have to win the argument. They just have to keep the spotlight on.

That is the trap. Because in these spaces, the real question is not "What will I say?" It is "Whose audience will I be saying it to?" Without that clarity, the risk is simple but devastating: you walk into the frame and become a character in someone else's story. And once the edit is rendered, the context is gone—but your cameo remains.

Not every challenge to misinformation needs to meet it head-on. In fact, the more forcefully a false claim is confronted, the more likely it is to harden in the mind of the person defending it. This is psychological reactance in action—the instinct to push back when one's sense of freedom feels threatened (Brehm, 1966). It is why direct confrontation often strengthens belief rather than weakens it. The key is to shift the focus—not toward the claim itself, but toward the structure holding it up.

Think of it as rhetorical judo. You do not attack the bricks. You examine the scaffolding. Instead of arguing over what is "true" or "false," you look at how the argument is framed. What assumptions is it built on? What emotions does it target? What does it ask the listener to fear, admire, or reject? This shift—from content to form—turns the spotlight onto the tactic itself. And once you can see the tactic, the spell starts to break.

This is the terrain of informal logic. It is not about swapping facts—it is about asking whether the reasoning makes sense, whether the moves are valid, whether there is a pattern of fallacies hiding inside a persuasive story (Walton, 2008). Instead of chasing each talking point, you slow the conversation down and ask: *What would count as convincing evidence for you? How would you know it was real?* These are not rhetorical traps. They are invitations to reflect on process—on how conclusions are formed.

That is where naive realism begins to wobble. The belief that our perception is objective truth—and that disagreement signals ignorance or bias—loses its grip when we are asked to step outside our own lens (Ross & Ward, 1996). Not to abandon it. Just to examine it.

This is where rhetorical inoculation comes into play. You teach the audience to spot the trick before it is used on them. Repetition, persecution narratives, black-and-white framing—once named, these tactics are easier to resist. The goal is not to flip the believer. It is to give the quiet observers—the ones watching the exchange from a distance—the tools to hold their ground.

And how that message is delivered matters. Ridicule may feel gratifying in the moment, but it rarely opens minds. Curiosity does. A calm question can reach further than a sharp retort. The aim is not to win the moment. It is to give doubt just enough air to breathe. Because once planted, doubt works slowly—but it works.

In some battles, the strongest move is to leave the field entirely. Choosing not to engage is not always avoidance. Sometimes, it is a deliberate form of rhetorical resistance. In the digital landscape, where attention is the oxygen that fuels visibility, withholding that oxygen can be a powerful act. Low engagement means low algorithmic priority—and without reactions to feed on, even the loudest message can start to fade.

Silence, in this sense, is not passive. It is strategic. On platforms built around clicks, comments, and watch time, every interaction signals value—whether it is praise or pushback. By refusing to respond, you withhold those signals. The content still exists, but it begins to sink beneath the surface, reaching only the already-convinced. This tactic echoes the idea of strategic silence: a purposeful refusal to engage as a way to shift power, reclaim control, or interrupt the cycle of performative discourse (Comouche, 2021).

There is also the quieter force of shadow suppression—when algorithms demote content without removing it, burying it in the feed's undercurrent. While controversial, this tactic reflects a principle that silence can function as containment. When rebuttals stop amplifying the message, the conflict no longer fuels growth. The argument loses its wings. These dynamics fall under what is known as algorithmic curation or platform governance, where companies use opaque systems to shape what rises and what sinks in the stream of public discourse (Gillespie, 2022).

Still, silence is not without risk. When false claims go unanswered, it can be seen as neglect—especially in public spaces where onlookers may be undecided or vulnerable to influence. There is always a tension between letting an idea wither and allowing it to take root. The choice to stay silent must be intentional, weighed carefully against the risk of allowing harm to spread unchecked.

But silence is not surrender. It is one tool—one option—in the broader work of persuasion, resistance, and rhetorical judgment. Knowing when to speak and when to step back requires more than knowledge of the facts. It demands a clear read of the moment, the message, and the audience. Sometimes, the most effective move is to make space for doubt to grow—not by challenging the noise, but by refusing to feed it.

Breaking the Spell: Case Studies in Doubt and Departure

In tightly sealed worlds, doubt is not just a harmless question—it is a threat to the entire structure. When someone steps outside and comes back with a story that does not match the script, the reaction is swift and familiar. Within days of one insider's public departure, the defenses lit up: claims that he had been bought, misled, or planted from the beginning. Even the firsthand observations that had shaken his belief—things he had seen for himself—were recast as part of the deception. The very account that broke the spell was folded back into the conspiracy.

The mental gymnastics required to absorb a contradiction and reframe it as deeper confirmation is a textbook display of cognitive dissonance—where conflicting ideas must be resolved, not by changing the belief, but by reshaping the facts (Festinger, 1957). And in Flat Earth spaces, that reflex is telling. It reveals less about the one who walked away, and more about the strength of the spell itself.

In communities where identity is fused with belief, doubt is treated as betrayal—and betrayal must be neutralized quickly. The rhetorical response is not just defensive—it is preventative. It is meant to send a clear signal to anyone watching: Do not follow. The content of the departure hardly matters. What matters is preserving the boundary. The wall must hold. This reaction maps directly to social identity theory, where in-group loyalty is maintained by casting out those who threaten the shared belief system (Tajfel & Turner, 1979).

And yet, the break still happened. In a world where belief is reinforced through endless repetition, someone who had carried the slogans and lived the arguments stepped away— because of something he saw. Something he could not unsee. That shift reveals something important: real-world contradiction can pierce rhetorical armor. But only for some. Others will absorb the same contradiction and twist it into further proof that the world is lying to them.

The difference is not in the evidence—it is in the readiness. A firsthand account can be powerful, but only if the listener is in a place where it can land. If not, it bounces off. This is what the elaboration likelihood model helps explain: a strong message only works when the audience is both motivated and able to process it. Otherwise, they fall back on peripheral cues—

the speaker's tone, their identity, or how well they fit into the expected narrative (Petty & Cacioppo, 1986).

So the challenge is not just to show the cracks. It is to understand how doubt works from the inside. When it finally takes root, it can unravel years of belief. But before it can break the spell, it has to survive the storm of defenses built to keep it out.

Belief does not usually collapse in one dramatic moment. More often, it unravels slowly—thread by thread—until the contradictions can no longer be held together. Doubt begins quietly, not as a bold announcement, but as a private unease. Something does not fit. An answer feels too rehearsed. A pattern that once felt solid now seems a little too perfect. This tension can build over months, even years, invisible to everyone but the person carrying it.

The triggers are rarely dramatic. Sometimes it is simple exhaustion—the drain of constantly defending a belief against a world that refuses to agree. Sometimes it is a contradiction that just will not go away, no matter how many times it gets explained. And sometimes, it is silence from the influencers themselves—those once-commanding voices that suddenly have no answer. That kind of hesitation hits hard. The erosion of trust in a figure once seen as reliable is a clear example of a breakdown in source credibility, a key factor in whether someone accepts or rejects a message.

In moments like these, the belief does not collapse from external pressure—it begins to shift from within. A trusted voice stumbles. An explanation rings hollow. The familiar slogans still come, but now they feel mechanical, less alive. None of this feels like a turning point in the moment. But taken together, these small breaks accumulate. The scaffolding moves. And at some point, it cannot hold.

That tipping point, when it finally arrives, can feel like stepping out of a fog. What once seemed airtight now feels paper-thin. What once inspired certainty now inspires questions. But even here, the change is not always visible. Some keep their doubts to themselves, running quiet tests of their new thoughts before ever speaking them aloud. Others never speak them at all, choosing instead to drift silently away from a belief they once held with conviction.

From the outside, it might look like everything changed in an instant. But from the inside, it is the end of a long, private unraveling—a quiet, personal reckoning with a story that no longer holds together.

Why Doubt Is Both Fragile and Powerful

Doubt lives in a precarious space. Inside a tightly sealed belief system, it does not just raise questions—it threatens identity. The first instinct is to hide it, even from oneself. To acknowledge it openly risks far more than being wrong. It risks the friendships, family ties, and shared purpose that belief has built. Suppressing doubt becomes a way to stay safe—not because the question is weak, but because the cost of asking it aloud feels too high. This fear of isolation is central to the spiral of silence theory, which suggests that when people feel their views are in the minority, they are less likely to express them for fear of ridicule or rejection (Noelle-Neumann, 1974).

But when doubt does break the surface, the impact is immediate. These communities rely on the illusion of certainty—a shared assumption that everyone is on the same page. To voice uncertainty is to crack that illusion. The group's rhetorical defenses snap into place fast. The doubter may be met with challenges, shame, or even outright rejection. This is textbook groupthink, where the desire for harmony overrides honest inquiry and dissent is suppressed to preserve unity (Janis, 1972).

And yet, that same rejection reveals doubt's quiet power. Once spoken, it cannot be unheard. The group may dismiss it, but the words have already entered the room. For someone listening—someone who is already carrying questions of their own—that small fracture can become a doorway. A single deviation from the script, posed without anger or drama, can echo louder than the slogans that surround it.

For the person who voices it, the fallout can be real. Community ties may fray. Criticism may come. Doors may close. But something else opens, too: a sense of freedom. Once the need to maintain perfect agreement is broken, the mind is free to explore. There is room again for curiosity.

That is the paradox. Doubt is delicate—but also contagious. It spreads quietly, not by winning arguments, but by lingering. It survives in whispered questions, in second thoughts, in the silence that follows rehearsed lines. And once it awakens curiosity, it becomes very hard to put back to sleep.

Lessons for Communicators

When belief is tightly fused to identity, trying to tear it down directly often backfires. The harder you push, the more unshakable it becomes. This is the heart of psychological reactance—the instinct to resist when people feel their autonomy is under threat (Brehm, 1966). What works better than a head-on challenge is something quieter: creating space. A pause. A moment where the believer can reflect without feeling attacked. Those moments may be small, but they open doors.

Empathy and rhetorical humility are key to making that happen. Empathy does not mean agreeing—it means understanding what emotional scaffolding is holding the belief in place. That scaffolding is often invisible from the outside. But moral psychology teaches us that beliefs are not built on pure logic alone—they are rooted in emotion, intuition, and social connection (Haidt, 2012). To approach someone with rhetorical humility means resisting the urge to win. It means stepping into the conversation not to dominate it, but to invite dialogue. The goal is to make leaving the belief feel possible—not humiliating.

That possibility matters. Many people stay inside a belief system not because they are convinced, but because walking away would cost them too much—relationships, status, a sense of purpose. Social identity theory reminds us that belonging shapes how we see ourselves (Tajfel & Turner, 1979). If leaving means isolation, people will often choose to stay. But if the exit feels safe—if there is another path, another community, or even just one person who will not shame them for changing their mind—then doubt has a chance to take root and grow.

Helping someone see doubt as strength, not failure, is one of the most generous moves a communicator can make. It affirms their agency, their ability to think for themselves. It reframes uncertainty as an opening, not a threat. This is the spirit of epistemic humility: recognizing the limits of one's own knowledge and being open to change—a trait at the core of critical thinking (Ward & Brewer, 2020).

Most transformations do not happen in public. They happen quietly, in the privacy of thought, when the slogans start to sound hollow and the story starts to lose its grip. As communicators, we may never see that moment happen. But we can shape the conditions that make it possible. And in that, we hold real persuasive power—not in forcing belief to break, but in making room for something new to take its place.

The Risks of Underestimating Persuasive Language

Every tool of persuasion carries a risk. The same rhetorical moves that can open minds, build trust, and spark insight can just as easily distort reality, harden falsehoods, and erode public trust. Rhetoric itself is neutral—it does not come with a moral label. Its impact depends entirely on the intention behind it and the skill with which it is used. A tool is only as virtuous—or as dangerous—as the hands that wield it.

This is one of the most sobering realizations from studying Flat Earth spaces: their most effective strategies are not exotic or fringe. They are familiar. These techniques appear every day in marketing campaigns, political speeches, and even well-meaning educational materials. Consider repetition, for instance—a core element of the propaganda model (Herman & Chomsky, 1988), which shows how repeated messages grow more credible simply through frequency. Or framing theory (Entman, 1993), which demonstrates how the way a question is posed can guide an audience toward one answer while obscuring others. There is also narrative transportation, where information embedded in a story becomes more persuasive than data standing alone. And of course, there is imagery, metaphor, and the polished use of language—devices that turn abstract ideas into something you can feel.

These tools work not because they are manipulative by nature, but because they target something deeper than raw information: identity. A campaign slogan, a classroom example, and a Flat Earth meme might serve very different ends, but they run on the same mechanics—create familiarity, build emotional trust, and link the message to the listener's sense of self. That sense of self is not incidental; it is the engine. The illusion of truth effect, a cognitive bias where repeated statements feel more believable, and social identity theory (Tajfel & Turner, 1979), which explains how group belonging shapes personal belief, both underline this reality. If an idea becomes part of who you are, defending it feels like defending yourself.

The danger is not in the tool—it is in assuming the tool is always safe. Familiarity can numb us to consequence. Marketing can promote wellness or sell addiction. Political speech can foster solidarity or incite division. Education can nurture critical thinking or silence dissent. The technique remains the same; only the aim and impact change.

This is where the double edge becomes clear. A skilled communicator can galvanize resistance against injustice—or guide a crowd toward it. They can tell stories that bridge divides—or ones that burn those bridges behind the listener. The rhetorical machinery does not care. It sharpens to the same point either way. The responsibility falls on both sides: the speaker to use it with care, and the audience to recognize when care has not been taken.

Seeing rhetoric as a tool—not a virtue in itself—is the first step toward using it wisely. The same arc that makes a scientific breakthrough compelling can also make a conspiracy sound inevitable. A confident voice may be a signal of understanding—or a cover for its absence. Once you see the blade for what it is, you are far less likely to mistake its shine for safety.

In high-emotion environments, the delivery of a message often matters more than the message itself. Charisma, confidence, and polish can eclipse content, shaping how a claim feels before its truth is ever tested. A well-paced voiceover, clean editing, a sharp slide deck—these are not just aesthetic choices. They become cues of credibility, shortcuts our minds use to judge trustworthiness before engaging with substance. This is ethos in its most streamlined form: perceived authority based not on evidence, but on presentation (Aristotle, c. 350 BCE).

Flat Earth influencers understand this instinctively. A confident delivery projects mastery. High production value suggests professionalism. In online spaces, these signals often substitute for actual credibility. A clean visual aesthetic can make a lie feel like a lecture. This is the attractiveness heuristic in motion—our tendency to equate visual appeal or charisma with competence (Chaiken, 1979).

The effect grows stronger in emotionally charged spaces. When a speaker mirrors the audience's feelings—whether anger, alienation, or curiosity—it builds connection before a single claim is examined. This is pathos, the emotional appeal. And in these contexts, style becomes its own kind of proof: If they sound this sure, if they look this polished, surely they must be right.

But this is not a failure of intelligence. It is a feature of how human beings process trust. We are social animals. We rely on cues—intonation, confidence, aesthetics—as a first test of credibility. And that is precisely where the danger lies: persuasion and manipulation use the same tools.

The same charisma that makes a powerful teacher can also power a demagogue. The same design sense that sells public health can also sell pseudoscience. When style is mistaken for substance, rhetoric stops being a vessel for truth and becomes a substitute for it.

This is the line where persuasion ends and manipulation begins. Persuasion seeks to amplify what is true. Manipulation seeks to obscure what is not. Both operate with polish, presence, and rhetorical grace. The difference is in purpose.

In emotionally primed environments, that purpose can be hard to detect. And that is why awareness matters—not to strip the style from speech, but to remind us that polish and confidence are not proof. They are, at best, the packaging. At worst, they are the performance that keeps the truth offstage.

One of the most potent tools in persuasion is the appearance of expertise. Rhetoric can simulate authority by borrowing the external signals of mastery—specialized jargon, rapid-fire explanations, confident simplifications—without ever delivering the depth of knowledge those signals are meant to represent. This is false fluency: the smooth delivery of claims that sound informed but often collapse under scrutiny (Unkelbach & Greifeneder, 2018).

The effect works because we are wired to respond to certain cues when deciding whom to trust. We assume that someone who speaks without hesitation must understand the subject. We associate complex language with advanced knowledge. We equate the ability to explain something simply with having mastered it. These mental shortcuts—known as heuristics—help us process information quickly, but they also leave us vulnerable when the cues are hollow (Meinert et al., 2022). In the right hands, these are real signs of expertise. In the wrong hands, they are props in a performance.

Flat Earth discourse is saturated with this technique, especially among what might be called *Visual Rationalists*—influencers who use diagrams, 3D models, and "sciency" aesthetics to sell their arguments. A digital grid stretched across a flat plane, an animation of the sun sweeping over a circle, labeled angles and axes in clinical blue—these are not mere illustrations. They are rhetorical armor. They borrow the look and feel of scientific communication, even when the logic beneath them does not hold (Rice, 2009). To an untrained eye, they resemble educational materials. And that resemblance is the point.

Confidence completes the illusion. In livestreams and video presentations, complex-sounding explanations are delivered in long, unbroken streams—fast, dense, and without pause. There is no room to question, no space to catch your breath. The rush of words creates the illusion of depth: if you cannot keep up, the assumption becomes that the failure is yours. This is how rhetorical authority sidesteps credentials. The delivery becomes the qualification.

The danger is not just in being persuaded by someone without expertise—it is in internalizing their performance as the new standard. Once these cues are mistaken for proof, genuine experts may be dismissed for speaking plainly, or for taking time to unpack complexity. False fluency thrives in that gap, where speed and polish masquerade as understanding.

The remedy is awareness. When a message leans heavily on performance, ask: What is actually being said beneath the jargon? Do the visuals *demonstrate* the claim—or just *decorate* it? Would the argument still hold if stripped of its polish? These are not just questions of content. They are questions of integrity. And asking them pulls back the curtain on authority that exists only in appearance.

The most effective persuasion often works in silence. It unfolds not with a clash of arguments, but with a whisper of familiarity—so seamlessly woven into our perception that we do not even realize persuasion is happening at all. We are far more likely to trust messages that feel fluent, familiar, and emotionally aligned with what we already believe. That fluency—how easy a message is to absorb—creates the illusion of objectivity. We think we are evaluating the message on its merits, but what we are really responding to is how easily it fits into the mental framework we already carry.

This is the *illusory truth effect,* a cognitive bias where repeated statements are judged as more truthful than unfamiliar ones, regardless of their accuracy (Hasher, Goldstein, &

Toppino, 1977). It is not the strength of the evidence that convinces us—it is the ease with which we process it.

And that is the blind spot. When rhetoric works invisibly, we are less likely to question it. A well-timed pause, a resonant metaphor, a familiar aesthetic—each can pass beneath conscious notice while shaping how we interpret a claim. The more natural it feels, the more likely we are to assume the conclusion was our own. And when we believe we arrived there independently, we defend it with greater conviction.

Flat Earth rhetoric thrives in this unnoticed space. Its memes, slogans, and talking points are not structured as formal arguments—they are designed for smooth entry. They are short, repeatable, emotionally primed, and deceptively simple. They *feel* like common sense. This is why repetition, covered earlier, pairs so effectively with identity reinforcement: the more we hear something in a form that feels intuitive, the less likely we are to question its content.

The real danger is not in the strength of these messages—it is in how easily we dismiss their power. We imagine persuasion only works on *other* people—on the uninformed, the gullible, the easily swayed. This is the *third-person effect*, a bias that leads us to believe others are more vulnerable to influence than we are (Davison, 1983). But rhetorical influence is not a flaw in reasoning—it is part of how human cognition functions. We are all susceptible to messages that are emotionally resonant, fluently delivered, and in sync with our values. The question is not whether we are influenced, but whether we notice it when it happens.

This is where awareness becomes a form of defense. *Inoculation theory* suggests that attitudes can be made resistant to persuasion by exposing people to a weaker form of the persuasive tactic before they encounter the full force of it (McGuire, 1964). In practice, that means learning to recognize the signals: spotting the repetition, noticing the framing, questioning the source, and identifying when style is being used to distract from substance. When we name the technique, we weaken its hold.

Persuasion loses much of its force when it is dragged into the light.

The paradox of rhetoric is that even when we use it to expose manipulation, we are still using it ourselves. There is no way to communicate without shaping language, tone, and structure in ways that influence how a message lands. Rhetoric is not optional—it is always present. The difference is not whether it is being used, but how. The real question is whether it is deployed with transparency, honesty, and respect for the audience's ability to decide for themselves (Dubov, 2015; Number Analytics, 2025).

Ethical persuasion rests on more than technique. It rests on intention. It requires the discipline to resist exaggeration, distortion, or emotional shortcuts—even when the cause feels justified. In this way, skill without ethics can be more dangerous than ignorance. The better one becomes at moving people, the greater the responsibility for where those people are being moved (Number Analytics, 2025). Mastery without conscience turns persuasion into manipulation.

This chapter—and this book—have used rhetoric to illuminate rhetoric. Metaphors, pacing, repetition, and narrative structure were chosen deliberately. Not to obscure, but to reveal. The same tools that draw someone toward belief have been used here to pull back the curtain on belief itself. That is not contradiction—it is recognition. Rhetoric cannot be removed from communication. It can only be directed.

The danger is not in rhetoric itself, but in forgetting that it surrounds us. Every headline, every ad, every viral clip and comment thread is a crafted message. Someone made choices—about what to emphasize, what to leave out, and how to make you feel. Learning to see those choices is the first defense against manipulation. It is how we begin to recognize persuasion not as magic, but as craft.

Rhetoric cuts both ways. It can chain us to illusion, or it can break the chains. The difference lies in whose hands hold the blade—and whether they choose to cut with care. This dual nature of persuasion, as both tool and weapon, has been understood since antiquity (Richter, 2014). But it has never been more urgent to remember it than now.

Holding the Thread

If there is one lesson to carry forward, it is this: belief and persuasion are rarely settled by facts alone. They are shaped by identity, emotion, repetition, and the stories we tell to make sense of our world (Slovic et al., 2002; Tajfel & Turner, 1979). These forces do not live only on the fringe. They run through our politics, our advertising, our media feeds, and even our conversations at the dinner table (Herman & Chomsky, 1988).

The goal is not to fear rhetoric, but to see it. Once you begin to recognize how messages are crafted—what they emphasize, what they omit, and how they make you feel—you gain something invaluable: choice. That clarity helps guard against the traps of surface polish. It makes you less likely to confuse confidence for truth, style for substance, or repetition for proof (Petty & Cacioppo, 1986). This is the core of media literacy. This is how critical thinking begins—not by rejecting persuasion, but by learning to navigate it with your eyes open (Entman, 1993).

And here is the quieter truth: none of us are immune. Persuasion works because it mirrors how we think. It speaks in the language of familiarity, it rides the currents of emotion, and it echoes through the voices of people we trust. Strength is not found in pretending we are beyond influence. It is found in recognizing when it is happening—and choosing how to respond (Begg et al., 1992; Rokeach, 1968).

Rhetoric is the thread that runs through every belief, every argument, every movement. Some use it to weave connection and insight. Others use it to bind, blind, and divide. The challenge is not to cut the thread, but to hold it—to see it for what it is—without letting it tie your hands.

Epilogue: On Transparency, Doubt, and the Use of Tools

If a Flat Earther reads this book—and some inevitably will—the response may follow a familiar script. They will say this is a manual for psychological manipulation, just another tool of "the system." They will claim every citation, every rhetorical breakdown, and every psychological insight is part of a coordinated effort to gaslight truth-seekers and keep the public comfortably indoctrinated.

Let us take that claim seriously, if only for a moment.

This book does not conceal its methods; it lays them bare. The strategies are on display. The framing is explained, not hidden. Every chapter has shown not only what the argument is, but how it was constructed. That is not manipulation. That is transparency.

The Flat Earth movement often claims to stand against cherry-picked data and curated narratives. And yet, it relies on exactly those practices. Sources are mined for fragments, stripped of context. Historical quotes are pulled from obscurity, presented without scrutiny. Science is invoked—but only when it flatters the conclusion already chosen.

This book could have done the same. It could have stacked quotations, blurred citations, and leaned into emotional appeal. Instead, it modeled the opposite. Where Flat Earth content performs evidence, this book processed it. Every rhetorical move has been named. Every psychological mechanism has been introduced—not to weaponize, but to understand. And when the final page arrives, there is a bibliography. Not as an afterthought, but as a blueprint. This is how research is done when the goal is comprehension, not control.

This is not a book that tells you what to believe. It is a book that shows how belief is built—and how it can be bent. Rhetoric is a double-edged sword. That is not an accusation; it is an admission. The difference lies in the disclosure. Tools become dangerous when they are disguised.

To those inside the Flat Earth community, this book may still feel like an attack. Not because it mocks, but because it names the frame. It exposes the mechanisms usually left in silence: the emotional incentives, the community bonds, the power of repetition. It does not just challenge the claims—it challenges the machinery that makes the claims feel real.

This book was never written for the hardened believer. It was written for the quiet skeptic, the curious observer, the person caught between doubt and certainty. It was written for those who sense something persuasive at work but cannot yet name it. It is not an argument to be won—it is a lens to be used.

Belief is not the enemy. But the tools that shape it must not go unexamined.

The Lens We Choose

By the time you reach the end of a book like this, it is fair to ask: What now?

This was never meant to be a takedown. It was not a final word, or a victory lap. It was an invitation to step behind the curtain and see how belief is built—how language, emotion, and repetition work together to make something feel true, even when it is not. Flat Earth was the case study, but the tools extend far beyond it.

The truth is, most people do not choose their beliefs based on raw facts alone. Belief is shaped by presentation. A well-placed word can make a flawed idea sound reasonable. A steady tone can make it feel real. And when enough people around you start echoing that message, it begins to feel shared—and shared belief feels safe.

But once you start spotting the patterns—the framing choices, the emotional hooks, the deliberate repetition—you begin to see belief for what it often is: constructed. You hear more than the message. You hear the machinery behind it.

This book was not written to mock, nor to argue. It was written to slow the rhythm just long enough for you to notice it. To make the invisible tools visible. To train the ear to hear not only what is said, but how—and why—it is said that way. The aim was never to help you win arguments. The aim was to make you less likely to be swept away by them.

Belief is not the enemy. Belief is human. But when belief is shaped by tools we do not even recognize, we become easier to move, to market, and to manipulate. This is where awareness becomes power.

So next time you encounter a polished claim, a compelling voice, or a video that lands just a little too perfectly—pause. Ask yourself: What feeling is this trying to stir? What identity is it inviting me to adopt? What story is being left out?

We live in a world saturated with crafted voices and precision messaging. The question is no longer whether we will be persuaded. The question is whether we will recognize how.

Stay skeptical. Stay curious. And remember—every belief carries a story about how it got there.

Glossary

Algorithmic Amplification - A process where content is boosted by social media algorithms based on how engaging it is, not how accurate or informative it may be.

Appeal to Tradition - A fallacy that claims something is true or correct simply because it has been believed or practiced for a long time.

Belief Perseverance - The tendency to continue believing something even after the original basis for the belief has been discredited.

Cherry-Picking - A tactic where only select facts or data are presented to support an argument while ignoring evidence that contradicts it.

Cognitive Dissonance - A psychological discomfort experienced when a person holds two or more conflicting beliefs, values, or ideas at the same time.

Confirmation Bias - The tendency to search for, interpret, and remember information in a way that supports one's existing beliefs or expectations.

Echo Chamber - An environment where people are only exposed to opinions, information, or beliefs that reinforce their own, while alternative views are ignored or dismissed.

Either/Or Fallacy - A logical fallacy that falsely presents two opposing options as the only possible choices, ignoring alternatives or nuance.

Enargeia - A rhetorical technique that uses vivid, detailed language to create a strong mental image, making the audience feel as if they are experiencing something directly.

Ethos - A rhetorical appeal based on the speaker's credibility, character, or authority, used to gain the audience's trust.

False Dichotomy - A logical fallacy that presents two options as the only possibilities when other alternatives exist.

False Dilemma - A type of false argument that limits a situation to two opposing choices, ignoring other viable options or complexities.

Filter Bubble - A digital environment where algorithms selectively present information that aligns with a user's past behavior, limiting exposure to diverse perspectives.

Firmament - An ancient concept describing a solid dome or vault that was believed to cover the Earth, separating the heavens from the Earth below.

Flat - A descriptive term for a surface with no noticeable curvature or elevation change; in scientific contexts, it does not imply a large-scale geometric shape.

Flat Cosmology - A belief system or model that describes the Earth as a flat, stationary plane, often surrounded by a dome and based on non-scientific interpretations of observation or scripture.

Framing – The way information is presented or structured to influence how people interpret and respond to it.

Geocentric - A model of the universe that places the Earth at the center, with all celestial bodies—including the sun and stars—revolving around it.

Groupthink – A psychological phenomenon where the desire for group harmony or conformity leads people to suppress doubts and go along with the majority.

Heliocentric - A model of the solar system in which the sun is at the center, and the Earth and other planets orbit around it.

Identity Protection - The tendency to defend beliefs that are closely tied to one's sense of self, even when those beliefs are challenged by strong evidence.

Level - A surface where all measured points are at equal height relative to a consistent reference established by a plumb line or calibrated instrument.

Literalism - The interpretation of texts, especially religious or historical ones, in their most direct and surface-level meaning, without considering metaphor, symbolism, or cultural context.

Logos - A rhetorical appeal to logic, reason, and evidence, used to persuade through clear thinking and structured argument.

Motivated Reasoning - A cognitive process where people form or evaluate arguments in a way that supports their existing beliefs or desired conclusions.

Narrative Coherence - The degree to which a story or explanation makes internal sense, with events, characters, and claims fitting together in a logical and consistent way.

Narrative Fidelity - The extent to which a story or message aligns with a person's values, experiences, and sense of what feels true or familiar.

Paradox of Ridicule - The idea that mocking or dismissing a belief can sometimes strengthen it, by reinforcing group identity or making followers feel persecuted and validated.

Pathos - A rhetorical appeal that targets emotion, aiming to persuade by evoking feelings such as fear, hope, anger, or sympathy.

Proof by Parroting - An illusion of truth created by repeating a claim so often that it begins to seem believable, regardless of whether it is supported by evidence.

Purity Appeal - A rhetorical strategy that presents a belief or action as morally superior by framing it as pure, untainted, or more faithful than alternatives.

Purity Culture - A belief system or social framework that emphasizes moral or spiritual purity, often through strict rules, conformity, and avoidance of perceived corruption.

Purity Spiral - A social or ideological dynamic where members of a group compete to show greater purity or loyalty, often leading to increasingly extreme positions and the rejection of moderation or nuance.

Rhetorical Construct - A deliberately shaped idea, phrase, or framework designed to influence how people think, feel, or respond.

Rhetorical Identity - A sense of self or group belonging that is formed or reinforced through language, symbols, and persuasive narratives.

Rhetorical Sleight of Hand - A persuasive technique that distracts or misleads by shifting focus, redefining terms, or manipulating language to obscure the real issue.

Scriptural Inerrancy - The belief that sacred texts are completely accurate and free from error in all their teachings, including historical or scientific claims.

Social Proof - The tendency to assume something is true or correct based on the number of people who believe, endorse, or repeat it.

Stacking the Deck - A fallacy or tactic where only supporting evidence is presented while ignoring or leaving out any counterarguments or opposing facts.

Straw Man - A fallacy where someone misrepresents or oversimplifies an opposing argument to make it easier to attack or dismiss.

Virality - The rapid spread of content, ideas, or messages—especially online—driven by sharing, emotional impact, and algorithmic promotion.

Zetetic - An approach to inquiry that emphasizes personal observation and skepticism of established knowledge, often rejecting traditional scientific methods.

Appendix A: The Scientific Method and Proper Research — A Primer

Introduction: Why This Matters

This book is about rhetoric — how language persuades, how belief spreads, how performance can replace proof. But beneath all of that lies a deeper question: how do we know what is real?

That is where this appendix comes in.

Because persuasion is not just about how something is said. It is about whether it holds up. And if you do not understand how reliable knowledge is built — how real research works, how science checks itself — then you are left judging everything by tone, confidence, and emotional appeal. You become vulnerable to performance dressed up as evidence.

That is exactly what many misinformation campaigns rely on. They do not just use words. They use the illusion of method. They say "I did my own research." They say "we ran an experiment." They speak the language of inquiry while sidestepping the process entirely.

This appendix is here to slow that down — to explain what proper research actually looks like. Not in theory. Not in slogans. But in practice. Because real research does not start with a conclusion. It starts with a question. And it is built on method — not on how convincing something sounds in a video, or how confident someone looks behind a microphone, or how neatly selective evidence seems to support the claim.

That is the key here: method. Evidence without process is not persuasive — it is performance. Rhetoric, for all its power, still has to answer to reality.

So think of this appendix as a practical lens. It will not turn you into a scientist overnight, but it will give you the tools to tell the difference between someone doing science and someone dressing it up in costume. And that difference matters — especially when belief gets packaged, monetized, and sold.

Let us start where science itself starts: not with answers, but with method.

Understanding the Scientific Method

Science is not a slogan. It is a process — a way of asking questions, testing them, and adjusting when the answers surprise you.

At its heart, science is about building models that explain how the world works. Not perfect ones, not final ones — just ones that work better over time. The goal is not to be right from the start. The goal is to keep checking.

Here is how the process typically unfolds:
- Observation — Notice something in the world.
- Question — Ask why or how it works.
- Hypothesis — Make an educated guess.
- Experiment — Test the guess under controlled conditions.
- Data — Gather results from the test.
- Analysis — Look for patterns and meaning.
- Conclusion — Decide whether the hypothesis holds up.
- Replication — Let others test it again.

It begins with observation. Something catches your attention. You notice a pattern or something that does not quite add up. So you form a hypothesis — a guess about what might be happening and why.

Then you test it. That means a controlled experiment: something that isolates variables and lets you measure results.

Once the test is done, you gather the data. You do not cherry-pick. You look at all of it.

If the results support the hypothesis, great. If they do not, even better. Now you know what does not work — and that moves you closer to what does.

But science does not stop there. Other people need to test it too. That is what peer review and replication are for. If it only works once, it might be a fluke. If it works again and again, under different conditions, then you are onto something.

That is where falsifiability comes in.

A real scientific claim has to be testable. And not just testable — disprovable. If there is no way to show it could be wrong, it is not science. It is belief. Saying "and that is a fact" might sound confident, but it shows a fundamental misunderstanding of how the scientific method works.

Flat Earth rhetoric avoids this on purpose. The claims change shape as soon as they are questioned. The terms get redefined. The goalposts move. Answers are ignored if they do not fit. That is not research. That is performance.

Science expects to be wrong sometimes. That is what makes it reliable. It learns. It adjusts. It moves forward. That is the difference.

Inside a Real Experiment

Understanding the scientific method is one thing. Seeing how it plays out in a real experiment is another. This is where the process becomes hands-on — where ideas get tested, data gets recorded, and the difference between science and storytelling becomes impossible to ignore.

There is a difference between testing something and just doing something that looks like a test. A real scientific experiment is not about proving yourself right. It is about checking if your idea holds up — and building the test so that it could fall apart if it does not.

That is the key: an experiment must be able to fail. That is what makes it honest.

Too often, especially in Flat Earth circles, the word "experiment" is used to describe whatever someone just did on camera — usually with no controls, no documentation, and no clear idea of what is being tested. That is not how science works.

A real experiment is carefully designed. Each part has a purpose. You need a testable hypothesis, clear variables, a consistent setup, and a method anyone else could repeat. You are not just pointing a camera at the sky or shining a laser across a lake. You are building a process — and the structure of that process matters.

Here is what that structure looks like:

- Hypothesis — A specific, testable statement about what you expect.
- Variables — Define what you are changing and what you are measuring.
- Controls — Set a baseline so you know if your results mean anything.
- Procedure — Write clear, repeatable steps that others could follow.
- Data Collection — Gather results carefully, not selectively.
- Analysis — Look at the data honestly and see what it actually shows.
- Conclusion — Decide whether your hypothesis held up — and be willing to revise.
- Replication — Let others run the same test and compare results.

If you skip steps, bend the rules, or ignore outcomes that do not fit — it is not an experiment. It is a performance. And science is not theater.

What Proper Research Looks Like

You have heard the phrase everywhere: "Do your own research." It sounds reasonable. Empowering, even. It hints at independence — a kind of intellectual self-reliance. And in the right context, it can be. But more often than not, the phrase is used to shut down questions, not explore them. It gets thrown into conversations as if it ends the debate — as if personal belief, backed by hours of scrolling, now holds the same weight as disciplined inquiry.

That is the problem.

Real research is not a scavenger hunt for the thing that proves you right. It is not clicking through search results until you find a video that agrees with you. It is not watching six hours of conspiracy content and calling yourself informed. Research — proper research — is a process. And like science, it starts with a question, not a conclusion.

Doing Research — Not Just Reinforcing a Story

When done honestly, research begins with curiosity. You do not start by trying to prove something. You start by trying to understand it — even if that means finding out you were wrong.

That is a mindset, not a method. It requires the ability to sit with uncertainty and the willingness to be corrected. It means taking in more than one viewpoint and not treating evidence like a buffet where you only grab what looks good.

Real research does not aim to reinforce a story you already like. It asks whether the story even holds up. It pushes past repetition, resists convenience, and forces you to test your own assumptions — not just someone else's.

It also means resisting the urge to win. You are not arguing. You are learning.

Research Looks Different Depending on the Field

There is no single blueprint for research. It depends on what you are trying to understand. What works in a lab will not work in a library. What works in a newsroom will not work in a telescope array. But even though the methods vary, the discipline behind them does not.

Scientific Research

In science, research is about testing — building hypotheses, designing experiments, analyzing data, and refining models based on results. It demands structure: variables, controls, peer review, and repeatability. It is about asking questions in ways the natural world can answer.

Historical Research

History relies on primary sources — letters, journals, official records, firsthand accounts — and interprets them in context. It is not about guessing what people might have thought or retrofitting modern views onto the past. It is about piecing together a picture from what was actually left behind, while being honest about what we can and cannot know.

Journalistic Research

Journalism investigates events and issues in real time. It depends on verifying facts, checking sources, triangulating claims, and exposing gaps. Good reporting asks who benefits from the story being told — and who gets left out. It is not about being first. It is about being accurate.

Each discipline uses a different toolkit, but they all share the same backbone: honesty, transparency, and accountability. If someone tells you they are "doing research," but everything they cite comes from the same kind of source — the same platform, the same worldview, the same rhetorical style — then they are not researching. They are recycling.

Evaluating Sources

Not all information is created equal. Just because something is written down, filmed, or said with confidence does not make it trustworthy. Research is not only about finding information — it is about knowing what to trust, why, and where it came from.

That means asking a few hard questions:
- Who is the source?
- Do they have relevant expertise or firsthand knowledge? A scientist explaining a phenomenon is not the same as a social media influencer reacting to it. Credentials do not guarantee truth, but ignoring them completely is not critical thinking — it is self-flattery.
- What is their motive?
- Is the source trying to inform, persuade, sell, or convert? Everyone has bias. The question is whether that bias is acknowledged, managed, or hidden. If a source sounds too sure, too dramatic, or too certain that everyone else is lying, stop and ask why.
- How transparent is the process?
- Can you trace where their information comes from? Do they cite sources, show methods, explain their reasoning? If the claims are bold but the evidence is thin — or hidden — you are not dealing with research. You are dealing with storytelling.
- Research is not about trusting no one. It is about trusting carefully — based on patterns of accuracy, openness, and accountability over time. If a source shuts down questions or frames disagreement as proof of conspiracy, that is not research. That is a red flag.

Primary vs. Secondary Sources

One of the easiest ways to spot weak research is to ask: Where is this coming from? And more importantly: Is it coming straight from the source, or being filtered through someone else's lens?

Primary sources

These are firsthand materials — original data, direct observations, eyewitness accounts, official documents, transcripts, and recordings. In historical research, this could mean letters, speeches, or newspapers from the era being studied. In science, it means published studies with full methods and raw data. In journalism, it means direct quotes, live reporting, or interviews.

Secondary sources

These interpret, comment on, or summarize the primary material. A textbook, a blog post about a study, a documentary about an event, or a podcast breaking down the news — these all count as secondary. That does not make them worthless. But they are one step removed, and that distance matters.

The more someone leans on secondary sources without ever showing the primary ones, the more you should ask what got left out. Good research does not avoid the source material — it starts there.

And if a video, blog, or podcast confidently tells you what a source says — but never actually shows it — they might be relying on your trust instead of evidence.

Research Red Flags

If someone tells you they are "doing research," but what they are actually doing is assembling content that confirms what they already believe — that is not research. That is curation. Here are some common signs that someone is performing belief, not practicing inquiry:

- Cherry-picking
- Only including the data that supports their view while ignoring everything that contradicts it. Real research does not skip the inconvenient parts.
- Quote-mining
- Pulling a line out of context to make it sound like an expert agrees. If you are not reading around the quote — before and after — you are not checking. You are repurposing.
- YouTube as a primary source
- If the only place a claim shows up is a video with dramatic music, a glitchy voiceover, and no citations — stop. That is a performance, not a paper trail.
- No original sources at all
- Copy-paste content with no links, no citations, and no clear trail back to where the information came from is not research. It is repetition.
- Confidence without transparency
- The more certain someone sounds while refusing to show methods, sources, or data, the more skeptical you should be. Confidence is not evidence.
- Ghost citations
- Phrases like "scientists now believe" or "experts say" without names, credentials, or links are not proof. If you cannot trace the claim, question it.
- Wikipedia without the footnotes
- Wikipedia can be a decent starting point. But if someone treats it like a final authority — or skips the citations at the bottom — they are browsing, not researching. Scroll down. Follow the links. See where it came from.
- Framing Questions Well

- Good research does not start with a conclusion. It starts with a real question — one that you do not already know the answer to, and one you are willing to be wrong about. That is harder than it sounds.

If your question is designed to funnel you toward a single answer, you are not researching — you are reinforcing. If your question is built on an assumption, a conspiracy, or a loaded premise, you are stacking the deck before the cards are even dealt.

"Why is NASA hiding the truth?"

"How can the Earth be a globe if I do not see curvature?"

"Why do scientists ignore this evidence?"

These are not honest questions. They are leading lines meant to narrow the field, not expand it. They assume dishonesty and demand submission.

Real questions are open-ended. They are curious. They create space to discover something — even if it is not what you expected.

Patience and Process

Proper research takes time. Not just time to gather information — time to sit with it, sort it, cross-check it, and sometimes start over. It is not about speed. It is about clarity.

This is what separates real research from a content binge.

The goal is not to "find the answer" as quickly as possible. It is to ask better questions — and keep asking them, even after you think you know. Because most misinformation survives on urgency: Look at this now. Wake up. They do not want you to see this. It rushes you past the part where reflection should happen.

Good research slows that down. It makes room for doubt. It leaves space for change.

And that — more than any search term or citation — is what separates truth-seeking from belief-polishing: the willingness to wait, and the courage to revise.

Final Thoughts

Rhetoric works best when it feels like truth. That is what makes it powerful — and what makes it dangerous. Because if you do not understand how real research works, you cannot always tell the difference between a persuasive performance and an evidence-based claim.

This appendix was never just about science. It was about structure. About knowing when a message is built on process, and when it is built on persuasion. If someone is asking the right questions, showing their methods, and opening their claims to scrutiny, that is one thing. If they are dressing belief in the language of research, that is something else entirely.

Rhetorical analysis is not just about words. It is about the weight behind them — and whether that weight comes from knowledge, or just the sound of certainty.

Appendix B: Eric Dubay's "200 Proofs" — A Rhetorical Analysis

Introduction

Eric Dubay's *200 Proofs Earth is Not a Spinning Ball* is one of the most widely circulated documents in Flat Earth circles. At first glance, it appears exhaustive — a dense wall of claims, ready-made for rapid-fire reposting. To the casual reader, the sheer quantity of "proofs" can seem overwhelming, even persuasive.

But a closer look tells a different story.

This appendix does not attempt to refute all 200 claims. That has already been done thoroughly by others. What this analysis aims to show is how the structure of the list — not just its content — is built to impress rather than inform.

It is a performance of volume: a list that appears vast but relies heavily on repetition, rhetorical sleight of hand, and scientific misrepresentation. It is not 200 unique pieces of evidence. It is far fewer ideas, recycled, reshaped, and repackaged to give the illusion of weight.

By analyzing the **patterns**, **themes**, and **presentation tactics** behind Dubay's list, we can better understand how rhetorical strategy can substitute for genuine substance — and how repetition can be used not to reinforce truth, but to simulate it.

The Illusion of Quantity

Dubay frames his document as a definitive blow to the globe model — *two hundred* distinct proofs, all neatly numbered, often cited as if their volume speaks for their validity.

But quantity is not quality. And in this case, it is not even quantity.

A structural analysis of the full list reveals that many of the 200 "proofs" are not proofs at all, and more than half are not even distinct. Ideas are repeated, reworded, and repositioned — sometimes just a few entries apart. The result is not a cumulative case. It is a rhetorical stacking of similar claims to give the appearance of overwhelming evidence.

Breakdown of the 200 "Proofs"

Claim Type	Number	Percentage
Unique Claims	89	44.5%
Semi-Duplicates	69	34.5%
Full Duplicates	42	21.0%
Total	200	100%

Note: Claim classification was based on internal structural review, identifying repeated phrasing, duplicated themes, and trivial variations across Dubay's list. The purpose was to examine rhetorical construction, not to scientifically verify or debunk individual claims.

In other words, **more than half (55.5%) of the list is recycled** — with no added information or evidence. Many items differ only in phrasing, emphasis, or rhetorical angle.

This is not argumentation. It is list inflation.

When a list presents 200 items but repeats itself more than half the time, what it really proves is how easily volume can become illusion. And when the goal is to impress rather than inform, **repetition becomes the tool — not evidence.**

Thematic Repetition and Claim Recycling

A closer look at Dubay's list reveals something even more telling than duplicated entries: **thematic loops**. Most of the 200 so-called "proofs" fall into just a handful of recurring categories. The language may change, the order may shift, but the core content stays the same.

This repetition creates the illusion of breadth. It makes the list seem wide-ranging and thorough — when in fact, it is the same handful of misunderstandings, cycled through again and again with minor variations.

Here are some of the most commonly recycled themes:
- Optical Misunderstandings
- Horizon appears flat
- Ships do not disappear "over the curve"
- Sunlight and shadow behavior
- Crepuscular rays, visual scaling, camera zoom effects

Dubay treats everyday perception as absolute, ignoring known limitations of human vision and optics. These claims rely on what *looks* right, not on how light, distance, and perspective actually work.

- Misinterpretation of Gravity
- Water "clinging" to a spinning ball
- Airplanes not "dipping their nose"
- Rivers "flowing uphill" on a globe

These entries rest on cartoon logic — treating gravity as though it were optional, misunderstood, or suspicious simply because its effects are not intuitive.

- Astronomical Misconceptions
- Polaris visibility from southern latitudes
- Phases of the moon and moonlight being "cold"
- Stars "moving" in ways that seem inconsistent with Earth's motion

These claims confuse relative motion, line-of-sight, and celestial geometry — often by ignoring scale or context entirely.
- NASA and Space Conspiracies
- CGI accusations
- "Clouds behind the Sun"
- Astronauts on wires and green screens
- Claims of no real photos of Earth

Rather than address evidence, these entries attempt to discredit the source — often relying on familiar conspiracy tropes and recycled internet myths.
- Rhetorical Slogans
- "We do not feel the Earth move"
- "No one has ever seen the curve"
- "Water finds its level"
- "Show me real pictures"

These are not testable claims — they are talking points. Most rely on oversimplified language meant to be repeated, not examined.

When viewed thematically, Dubay's 200 proofs collapse into fewer than a dozen actual ideas. What fills the space between them is repetition, restatement, and rhetorical styling — not new information.

Padding the List with Tricks, Not Evidence

At a glance, *200 Proofs Earth is Not a Spinning Ball* gives the impression of a carefully constructed argument — long, detailed, and meticulously researched. But that impression depends more on **presentation tactics** than on substance.

Much of the list is padded with rhetorical tricks. These are not mistakes in logic so much as **deliberate choices in framing** — choices that make weak claims sound stronger and repetition feel like reinforcement.

Here are some of the techniques most frequently used:

Rewording as Repetition

Dubay often presents the same idea two or three times, changing only the phrasing or angle. A claim about horizon flatness might be followed by another about boats not disappearing — then another about zoom lenses proving the same thing. Different words, same argument.

Emotional Framing

Several "proofs" lean on emotional appeal: suggesting that people who believe in the globe are asleep, blind, or victims of lies. These entries rely more on **tone** than on evidence, encouraging readers to feel betrayed rather than evaluate a claim.

Anecdotes as Data

Some entries rely on personal or historical anecdotes — quotes from sailors, diary fragments, or outdated maps — presented as if they carry the weight of scientific data. In a few cases, these anecdotes are taken out of context or cannot be verified at all.

Science by Dismissal

Instead of building an argument, many of the claims are framed as *"That does not make sense to me, so it must be false."* There is no exploration — only a rejection of known explanations, followed by a leap to an unproven alternative. This is not evidence. It is objection as proof.

Conspiratorial Shortcuts

Where claims are difficult to explain or rely on misused science, the fallback is almost always the same: *"They are lying."* NASA, scientists, textbooks, and pilots are accused broadly, without evidence. The goal is to erode trust, not to establish facts.

The net effect is not 200 facts — it is 200 lines of rhetorical scaffolding, propped up by recycled themes, emotionally loaded language, and deliberate distortion of how evidence works.

Dubay does not build a case. He builds **a structure that looks like a case** — and relies on volume, tone, and repetition to keep it standing.

Why This Matters

Someone flipping through *200 Proofs* might not read every line. That is part of the design. The long scroll gives a sense of authority. The repeated themes create rhythm. The numbered format makes it feel official, documented — even scientific.

This is rhetorical performance disguised as research. And it works.

It works because most readers are not looking for formal validity. They are looking for confidence. They are looking for something that feels bigger than a single claim. And when an idea shows up in list form — numbered, repeated, bolded, underlined — it begins to feel real, even before it is understood.

That is how rhetorical padding becomes persuasive. Not through substance, but **through volume, tone, and formatting**.

And that is why this analysis matters. It is not just about Dubay's list. It is about **how bad ideas are dressed up to look like airtight arguments** — and how repetition, emotional framing, and a high word count can do more work than evidence ever could.

The power of *200 Proofs* is not in what it proves. It is in how many people **think** it proves something — and never stop to check.

Final Thoughts

This appendix was never about debunking Flat Earth through scientific evidence. That work has been done many times over by those with a stronger command of the physical sciences. What this analysis focuses on is something different — and just as important. It looks at **how** the argument is delivered. Not what it claims, but how it convinces.

What Dubay offers is not evidence. It is **structure masquerading as substance** — a carefully crafted performance that leans on repetition, emotional triggers, and rhetorical sleight of hand to create the illusion of overwhelming proof.

By breaking apart that performance, we are not just analyzing one document. We are pulling back the curtain on a broader pattern: the way **style can overpower content**, and how formatting can mimic authority even when the ideas themselves do not hold up.

Understanding that distinction — between argument and appearance, between rhetoric and reason — is one of the most important skills a critical thinker can develop. Especially in a world where **belief can go viral faster than truth** ever could.

Appendix C – Visual Rhetoric and Flat Earth Media

Why the Visual Works

When people think about rhetoric, they often imagine only words: speeches, slogans, arguments, and debates. But rhetoric is not just spoken or written. It is **anything used to persuade** — and that includes images, colors, layouts, and camera angles. Visuals are not separate from rhetoric. They are part of it. In fact, they are often more powerful than the words themselves.

The Flat Earth movement understands this — deeply. Its persuasive power is not built on textbooks or peer-reviewed journals. It is built on **thumbnails, zoomed-in videos, horizon snapshots, and memes wrapped in emotion**. These visuals are not neutral. They are carefully selected, edited, and framed to provoke doubt, stir outrage, or imply secrets hidden in plain sight.

Now you are looking at visual rhetoric.
You are not reading it. You are not hearing it. You are seeing it. A well-framed photo can make a point. A meme can carry an entire argument in eight words and a stock image. A YouTube thumbnail can set the emotional tone before the video even begins. This is how persuasion slips in through the eyes — long before logic even catches up.

Understanding Flat Earth rhetoric means looking beyond the script. It means seeing how persuasion happens even when no one is talking. And it starts by asking a deceptively simple question: **what is this image trying to make me believe?**

Common Visual Tactics

Flat Earth visuals are not random. They follow patterns. The same image types, color schemes, angles, and framing choices show up again and again — not because they are *true*, but because they *work*. They evoke emotion, suggest contradiction, and imply hidden knowledge. Below are some of the most common visual tactics used to persuade without evidence.

Tactic 1: Flat Horizon Photos

The image is simple: a photo taken from a beach, a plane window, or a drone. The horizon looks straight, so the Earth must be flat.

That is the intended message — and it lands easily. Most viewers have not studied optics or perspective. They do not know that the Earth's curve is subtle over short distances, or that wide-angle lenses can flatten it out. They just see flatness, and flatness *looks* like confirmation.

But the image is doing more than showing. It is framing. The camera is placed low, the zoom tight, the lighting often dramatic. There is no context — no altitude, no lens type, no comparison. Just a slice of the world, chosen for how it feels, not for what it proves.

This tactic works because it **leverages expectation** — the unspoken idea that if Earth were curved, the curve should be visible all the time, from everywhere. It also **frames absence as evidence**, implying that because something is not seen, it must not exist. That is not science. It is suggestion dressed up as demonstration.

Tactic 2: Extreme Zoom Footage

This one always comes with a twist of revelation. A boat disappears over the horizon — then, with a high-powered zoom, it "reappears." The message is clear: "See? It never went over a curve. It was just distance."

But this tactic hides as much as it reveals.

First, the optics are misunderstood. Zoom does not cancel curvature; it compresses distance and amplifies mirage effects. Atmospheric distortion, lens compression, and refraction can all bring an image "back" in ways the eye alone cannot. What looks like reappearance is often just artifact.

Second, the setup is selective. Videos often skip the part where the boat slowly vanishes hull-first — a telltale sign of curvature. They jump straight to the "magic" of reappearance, reinforcing the illusion that science has been fooled by a camera.

This is **visual sleight of hand**, and it works because it mimics revelation. It feels like catching someone in a lie. But what it actually catches is a misunderstanding — or worse, a manipulation — of how light and lenses work.

Tactic 3: Meme Logic

This is where persuasion shrinks to a single square.

Meme logic is not about building a case — it is about **skipping the argument entirely**. One image. One phrase. Usually something smug, snarky, or loaded with false confidence:

"If Earth spins, why can I see the same stars every night?"
"Water finds its level."
"Still waiting for real photos of Earth."

These are not questions. They are traps. They are designed to **sound obvious**, to feel like common sense — and to **shame you for not agreeing**. Add a photo in the background, a red circle, a laughing emoji, and the message is not just made, it is reinforced by tone.

Memes flatten nuance. They reward repetition, not research. And in Flat Earth spaces, they are everywhere. That is not by accident. It is by design. Because if belief can be condensed into a meme, it can be shared, repeated, and performed — without ever being examined.

Tactic 4: Side-by-Side Image "Proofs"

This is comparison as accusation.

A NASA photo on the left. A different one on the right. Maybe the colors are off. Maybe the continents are sized differently. The caption usually says something like: *"Which one is real?"*

The trick here is framing **inconsistency as deception**. It plays on the assumption that any difference must mean fabrication — not lens variation, not processing differences, not mission context. Just fraud.

These images ignore everything except visual mismatch, and then invite the viewer to distrust everything based on that alone. It is a classic **false equivalence** — contrasting two things as if they should be identical, when they were never meant to be.

Tactic 5: "Spot the Curve" Challenges

This one comes with a dare.

A panoramic view from a mountaintop or a drone. A flat skyline. The caption:
"Where's the curve?"

It seems like a challenge, but it is really a trick — one rooted in **scale manipulation**. The curve of the Earth is vast. You do not see it unless you are looking far enough, from high enough, with the right tools. The human eye was never meant to detect that kind of geometry unaided.

This tactic banks on a misunderstanding: that if we lived on a sphere, the curve should be obvious from anywhere. It is not just wrong — it is persuasive *because* it feels like it should be right.

Tactic 6: Dark Thumbnails & Dramatic Fonts

This is emotional priming, pure and simple.

Flat Earth videos often feature black backgrounds, neon outlines, and font choices straight out of horror movie posters. Add a fearful face, a satellite image in shadow, or the word "EXPOSED" in red, and the stage is set.

These design choices are not mistakes. They are **psychological cues**, meant to spark distrust and adrenaline before the content even begins. They suggest danger, secrecy, urgency — not information.

When you feel something before you know something, your guard drops. That is the goal.

Tactic 7: Pick the Right Image — or Pick the Right Gasp

Sometimes the image itself is not persuasive — it is the *reaction* it gets.

Flat Earth spaces often crowdsource awe. A user posts a snapshot: the sun seeming too close, a cloud pattern that looks suspicious. The comments supply the gasp:
"Wake up!"
"They are hiding it in plain sight!"
"This PROVES it!"

This is **performance disguised as discovery**. The image is bait. The reaction is the hook. And before long, the sense of personal revelation replaces actual investigation.

You are not just seeing a picture. You are seeing a moment scripted for agreement — an emotional cue wrapped in a visual one.

Spot the Trick

When you know what to look for, it becomes harder to be fooled.

That is the core idea behind this section. Flat Earth visuals are rarely neutral. They are carefully crafted to guide interpretation — often without the viewer realizing it. A cropped image that hides context. A repeated phrase that builds false familiarity. A misleading scale that distorts what you are seeing.

These are not just design choices. They are rhetorical tactics.

Here, we will break down some of the most common ones. Not to ridicule them — but to understand how they work. Because once you can name the trick, you can start seeing it everywhere.

1. The Crop-and-Claim

What is not shown is just as important as what is.

Flat Earth visuals often rely on strategic cropping. A wide-angle photo might be trimmed to remove surrounding context — no horizon line, no landmarks, no indication of elevation. The result is an image that looks ambiguous, or even flat, until you realize what has been cut out.

This is not just lazy editing. It is rhetorical framing — shaping interpretation by removing inconvenient details.

2. The Misleading Scale

Size is easy to manipulate — especially when there are no reference points.

Whether it is a distant skyline, a distant ship, or the moon, Flat Earth visuals often distort scale. Without context like distance markers, focal length, or altitude, your brain fills in the blanks — and often gets it wrong. The result is an illusion of closeness, flatness, or distortion that feels real, even when it is not.

3. The Freeze Frame

Pause at the right moment, and almost anything looks suspicious.

Flat Earth videos love to stop at the exact frame where a visual glitch, lens artifact, or momentary blur appears. These single-frame "anomalies" are then presented as evidence of deception — even though they vanish when the video runs normally. It is a tactic built on selective stillness, not sustained observation.

4. The Visual Echo

If one image suggests a message, twenty of the same image can make it feel like truth.

Flat Earth spaces often repeat the same type of image — a flat horizon, a zoomed-in skyline, a level lake — until they blur together into a visual mantra. The repetition creates an illusion of abundance. It is not proof. It is saturation.

5. The Comparison Trap

Side-by-side images look authoritative — but they are rarely equal.

These visuals pair two photos to imply contradiction or deception: a NASA Earth image next to a Flat Earth diagram, or different satellite views shown to suggest inconsistency. But the images are often taken under different conditions, at different scales, with different tools. They are not equals — and the comparison is not neutral.

6. The Thumbnail Trick

Before the video even plays, you have been primed.

Flat Earth thumbnails are often packed with dramatic fonts, red arrows, and shadowy filters. They are not just eye-catching — they are emotionally suggestive. A thumbnail with dark clouds and bold accusations hints at hidden truth or danger. It sets the tone before a single argument is made, nudging the viewer toward suspicion before any evidence appears.

It is not just decoration. It is preloading the message.

7. The Emotional Filter

Sometimes, what makes a visual persuasive is not what it shows — but how it feels.

Certain colors, lighting choices, and compositions are used repeatedly across Flat Earth media: dim backdrops, fiery skies, slow zooms, or sepia tones. These choices evoke emotion

— awe, dread, rebellion — and help shape the viewer's perception of credibility. It is rhetoric without words, designed to be felt, not questioned.

Final Thoughts

Always ask: Who framed this shot—and what story is it trying to tell?

Visual rhetoric is not about what is seen. It is about how we are shown to see it. Every crop, every contrast, every zoom is part of the argument—whether that argument is spoken aloud or whispered through design. Flat Earth media excels at this kind of nonverbal persuasion. It shapes belief not by presenting evidence, but by framing experience.

That is why this appendix exists. A rhetorical analysis cannot stop at language. Words are only one part of how persuasion works. The Flat Earth movement has learned to communicate through aesthetic, through emotional staging, and through carefully engineered visuals that feel intuitive rather than intrusive. The trick is that they rarely declare their intent—they just *look* true.

This is rhetoric without a microphone. And if we do not learn to read it, we risk being moved by it without ever realizing why.

So stay alert. Look at the picture, yes—but do not forget to examine the frame.

Appendix D: Cognitive Biases and Psychological Influences

Why We Believe — Even When It Makes No Sense

Some of the most powerful forces in persuasion never get named in a debate. They do not come from evidence or logic, and they are not always part of the message itself. They come from us—from how we process, react, and protect what we already believe.

When people talk about being "fooled," they often imagine someone else doing the fooling. A con artist, a cult leader, a movement. But just as often, the mind is fooling itself—and doing a very convincing job of it. Not out of stupidity or weakness, but out of a natural, human tendency to seek shortcuts, protect our identity, and hold onto beliefs that feel safe.

The Flat Earth world knows this well. It plays to emotions first, then dresses them up in logic. It leans on certainty, on gut feeling, and on patterns that feel obvious—even when they are not. And once that feeling of certainty sets in, it becomes harder and harder to challenge, because it feels like it came from within. It feels earned.

Not all traps are laid by others. Some are set by the mind itself. And in these next pages, we are going to walk through some of the most common ones—how they work, why they matter, and how rhetoric can quietly trigger them without ever saying a word.

The Biases Behind the Belief

We like to think of ourselves as rational creatures. We imagine our beliefs are carefully thought through, our choices grounded in logic, our judgments fair. But the brain is not wired for perfect reason. It is wired for speed, efficiency, and survival. And that means it takes shortcuts—mental habits that help us make fast decisions, even when they are not the most accurate ones.

These shortcuts are not flaws. In fact, we need them. They help us function in a world full of noise, complexity, and contradiction. But when persuasion tactics tap into them—especially without our awareness—those same shortcuts can lead us straight into false certainty.

Here are just a few of the cognitive patterns that play an outsized role in belief, especially inside echo chambers like Flat Earth spaces:

1. Pattern Recognition Bias

The brain is always looking for patterns—it is how we learn, predict, and survive. But sometimes, it sees patterns where none exist. Flat Earth arguments often rely on visual claims ("the horizon looks flat") or numerical alignments ("33 times in the Bible") that feel significant. But feeling is not evidence. Not every coincidence has a meaning. Not every pattern is a plan.

2. Confirmation Bias

This is the big one—the gravitational pull of belief. Once we form an opinion, our mind starts looking for proof. Not just passively, but actively. We ignore what challenges us. We highlight what agrees. Flat Earth influencers know this, and they feed their audiences exactly what they already suspect, reinforcing belief with each scroll, video, or meme.

3. Attribution Error

We are quick to assign motive. If a scientist says the Earth is round, some Flat Earthers will assume they are part of a conspiracy. But when a Flat Earther makes a claim, it is taken as honest truth-seeking. This double standard is not just a rhetorical move—it is a mental one. We tend to excuse our in-group and question the out-group. It is tribal, emotional, and often invisible.

4. The Dunning-Kruger Effect

The less we know about a subject, the more confident we tend to feel. It sounds backwards, but that is exactly the point. Without enough knowledge to recognize gaps or complexity, everything seems simple. And simplicity feels like truth. Flat Earth claims thrive in this space—offering certainty in a world that is actually full of nuance.

5. Illusory Truth Effect

Repeat something often enough, and it starts to sound true. This is how slogans like "Water finds its level" or "You cannot see the curve" lodge themselves into the mind. It does not matter that they are flawed or oversimplified. What matters is repetition. And inside an echo chamber, repetition is not just common—it is the structure.

These are not just isolated quirks. They are the very architecture of belief. And while they affect everyone, they become especially powerful when coupled with persuasive tactics designed to trigger them.

The Levers They Pull

If belief is the engine, bias is the fuel. Every tactic Flat Earth influencers use runs on something already in the brain — instincts, shortcuts, emotions, habits. They do not have to invent new mechanisms of persuasion. They just have to reach for the ones already built in.

These are the five psychological levers most commonly pulled:

- **Social Proof**
  When many people appear to believe something, it begins to feel more true. Influencers exploit this by showcasing follower counts, comment sections, likes, testimonials, and livestream activity to create the illusion of consensus. "So many people can't be wrong" becomes a silent, persuasive chorus.
- **Manufactured Urgency**
  Deadlines, collapsing systems, and hidden truths "they don't want you to know" stir panic and reactive thinking. This urgency short-circuits reflection and makes impulsive belief feel like brave resistance. It is not about time; it is about pressure.
- **Identity Fusion**
  Belief becomes fused with self-worth. To question the claim is to question the self. Flat Earth rhetoric often rewards loyalty and casts doubt as betrayal, making belief not just something you hold — but something you *are*. In-group signaling becomes survival.
- **The Illusion of Mastery**
  Complexity is flattened into slogans and diagrams. The user feels like they "get it" — more than scientists, more than experts. Simple visuals, confident speech, and faux-experiments combine to create an inflated sense of comprehension that is hard to surrender.
- **Rejection of Outside Authority**
  Preemptively dismissing scientific institutions, mainstream media, and academic consensus clears the field. Now, only "insiders" and "truth-tellers" remain. This manufactured distrust ensures that outside information is not just ignored — it is weaponized as proof of suppression.

Tactics That Tap into Bias

Each of the following is more than a rhetorical strategy. It is a psychological lever—pulled not to discover truth, but to reinforce belief. These moves are designed to bypass critical thinking by appealing directly to emotional, cognitive, and social instincts. Some will sound familiar. That is no accident.

Moving the Goalposts

It shows up early and often — a belief fortified not by answers, but by shifting demands. Once one challenge is addressed, another takes its place, always just out of reach. What might seem like intellectual rigor is often just a clever escape hatch. The rules keep changing, not to clarify truth, but to protect the claim.

Gish Gallop (Rapid-Fire Questioning)

We have seen this one before — the performance of argument through sheer density. It floods the room with fragments, half-claims, and misquoted questions so quickly that no single point can be pinned down. It is not about persuasion. It is about pace — staying ahead of scrutiny by staying shallow.

JAQing Off (Just Asking Questions)

A favorite tool of denial masquerading as curiosity. By phrasing a claim as a question, the speaker avoids taking responsibility for the assertion—while still planting the seed. It is plausible deniability dressed up as open-mindedness.

Weaponized Ambiguity

Precision is the enemy of conspiracy. Vague claims—half-defined, loosely framed, and flexible—allow believers to retrofit the details to whatever comes next. The less clear a claim is, the harder it becomes to falsify. Ambiguity becomes armor.

Fractal Conspiracies

These are beliefs that expand to absorb contradiction. The more you challenge them, the larger they grow. Every piece of debunking becomes proof of the cover-up. These frameworks are self-sealing—impossible to falsify, because every disproof is reclassified as evidence.

Playing the Underdog

A classic appeal to emotion and identity. Casting oneself as the outsider, the brave voice in a sea of silence, turns criticism into oppression. It makes fact-checking look like censorship and grants rhetorical immunity to those who claim persecution.

Exploiting Skepticism Language

Words like "independent thinker" or "do your own research" are used not to invite inquiry but to inoculate against it. The moment you push back, you are dismissed as a sheep. True skepticism requires effort. Here, it is simply a label worn like armor.

Echo Chamber Reinforcement

Say it often enough, and it becomes real. Inside tightly sealed groups, repetition creates familiarity, and familiarity becomes truth. The illusion of consensus is constructed one shared post at a time. What matters is not accuracy—it is agreement.

Emotional Appeals to Children and Safety

These tactics bypass logic altogether. The image of a child, the invocation of safety, the call to protect — these short-circuit analysis by triggering moral panic. If you question the claim, you are accused of endangering the innocent. That is the point.

Why It Works So Well

Cognitive bias is not a flaw in reasoning; it is the structure of it.

The human mind is designed to simplify, not to calculate everything with clinical precision. We look for patterns, rely on familiarity, and lean into what feels true. These mental shortcuts—biases—are not signs of failure. They are survival tools. But that same efficiency can be exploited.

Flat Earth rhetoric does not win through evidence. It wins by echoing certainty, rewarding agreement, and flooding the system with questions that sound insightful but dodge responsibility. It speaks to how we are wired to think quickly, emotionally, and socially.

Each tactic pulls a lever in that system—appealing to group identity, triggering skepticism of outsiders, or anchoring belief through sheer repetition. Over time, these tools do not just persuade; they reinforce. They turn exposure into acceptance, and familiarity into conviction.

That is why belief can stick even when the facts do not. It is not about logic. It is about how the story is framed, delivered, and repeated. And once it feels familiar, it feels true.

Final Thoughts

Belief builds over time. It draws from emotion, repetition, group loyalty, and the stories we grow comfortable retelling. Flat Earth rhetoric does not succeed because of its evidence—but because it taps into those familiar patterns of thought and feeling.

This was never about diagnosing pathology or labeling people irrational. It was about spotting the structure behind persuasion. When you understand which levers are being pulled—identity, fear, familiarity, distrust—you begin to see why facts alone rarely change minds.

That is why rhetorical analysis matters. It does not just explain *what* is said—it helps reveal *why* it works, *how* it sticks, and *where* our reasoning can be quietly redirected without us even noticing.

Once you see the structure, you can start to question it. And from there, real doubt—the kind that leads forward—can begin.

Appendix E: How to Talk to a Flat Earther Without Losing Your Mind – A Quick Reference Guide

Before You Begin

Some conversations do not start with curiosity — they start with conviction. And when belief is worn like armor, facts alone will not get through. This quick-reference guide is not a script, but a map. It is here to help you keep your footing, protect your sanity, and recognize the rhetorical terrain before you walk into it. Whether you are talking with a friend, a stranger, or someone halfway lost to the echo chamber, these points offer a way to engage without getting pulled under.

1. Know the Terrain

Flat Earth is not just a theory — it is an identity. Before you speak, understand what it really means to them. You are stepping into a belief system, not a debate. The emotional and social stakes are high. Learn the lingo: globehead, sheep, NASA lies, cognitive dissonance. And study their "greatest hits" — 200 Proofs, Antarctica gatekeeping, infinite plane theory. You cannot respond to a language you do not speak.

2. Know What You're Talking About

If you do not understand the topic, do not try to debate it. Flat Earth arguments twist science and bend logic, so learn the basics they distort — gravity, perspective, motion, and scale. Understand how they use rhetoric, not just what they claim. Skip the NASA memes. Bring real-world logic. And most of all, speak plainly. Jargon does not persuade — clarity does.

3. Choose Your Moment

Not every setting is built for real conversation. Public threads invite performance. Group chats trigger defense. Private, calm spaces open the door. Do not rush it — timing is persuasion's quiet partner. A well-placed question in the right moment goes further than a dozen facts shouted into a crowd.

4. Ask, Do Not Tell

Do not walk in with a stack of facts and expect a mic-drop moment. That almost never works. Instead, ask open-ended questions like **"How would this work on a curved Earth?"** or **"What would actually prove the globe to you?"** These questions shift the weight back onto their reasoning and make space for reflection.

Let them talk. Most Flat Earth arguments collapse under their own contradictions. Use their terms carefully—but only to clarify, not to validate. And unless you are aiming to entertain, skip the sarcasm. You are not trying to win a point—you are trying to open a door.

5. Spot the Deflection

Flat Earth arguments rarely stay in one lane. Ask about curvature, and suddenly it is about NASA. Mention gravity, and you are redirected to ancient maps. This is not always bad faith—it is often a defense mechanism.

Recognize when the topic shifts. Bring it gently back: **"Let's stick with what we were just talking about—curvature."**

If every question gets answered with a new claim, that is not a conversation—it is a smoke screen.

6. Use Rhetoric Without Being Rhetorical

Facts alone will not save you. Flat Earth belief is not built on data—it is built on doubt, identity, and performance. If you have not set the emotional ground, quoting equations will not move them.

So lean into rhetoric that works:

- **Use analogies** Storytelling creates mental pictures—much harder to dismiss than numbers alone.

- **Appeal to shared values**: honesty, protecting children, curiosity, the desire to understand. Common ground opens doors.
- **Repeat core truths calmly**—repetition is not just their tool. It works both ways.
- **Debate the method, not the map.** Do not get lost arguing coastlines. Focus on how they know what they know.

Persuasion is not just logic—it is timing, tone, and delivery.

7. Protect Your Sanity

Flat Earth conversations can drain you—mentally, emotionally, even physically. Know your limits.

- **Set boundaries**. It is okay to say, "Let's pause this for now."
- **Take breaks**. Step back before frustration turns into mockery or sarcasm.
- **Do not fall into the performance trap**—arguing just to win a crowd.
- **Reflect on your own triggers**. Are you trying to persuade—or prove something to yourself?
- **Know when you are too tired to keep your cool.** Walk away with grace, not with a slam.

You are not obligated to win. You are obligated to stay sane.

8. Final Reminder: You're Not Just Talking to *Them*

Online or in public, your conversation has an audience—silent readers, curious lurkers, people on the fence.

- **Speak for the bystanders**. Many are listening, even if they never comment.
- **Model respectful engagement**. How you respond teaches more than what you say.
- **Leave a trail of clarity**. The Flat Earther may never shift—but someone else might start to wonder.

- **Resist the urge to "win."** Instead, plant seeds of doubt, curiosity, or a better way to think.
- The loudest voice is not always the most persuasive. Sometimes it is the calmest.

Every word you say might be the one that someone else needed to hear.

Final Thought

You are not here to win a debate. You are here to stay sane, stay grounded, and maybe—just maybe—leave behind a better question than the one you found.

Some conversations are not about changing minds in the moment. They are about offering a different rhythm, a pause in the noise, a glimpse of what honest curiosity looks like.

Flat Earth belief is not just about facts. It is about fear, identity, and control. Your job is not to dismantle someone's worldview in one conversation. Your job is to protect your own clarity while offering a more honest lens.

Walk in with patience. Walk out with peace. And remember: someone else might be watching, waiting for a reason to rethink.

Appendix F: Suggested Readings and References

Introduction: Keep Learning

The story of Flat Earth rhetoric is more than a quirky footnote in history — it is a case study in persuasion, belief, and the human mind's need for meaning.

If you would like to explore the topics in this book more deeply — from the psychology of conspiracy theories to the art of rhetoric to the history of Flat Earth itself — the following books and resources are a good place to begin.

Books on Rhetoric and Persuasion

I. Foundational Rhetoric & Persuasion

Thank You for Arguing – Jay Heinrichs
A lively and accessible introduction to classical and modern persuasion.

The Elements of Eloquence – Mark Forsyth
A playful breakdown of rhetorical devices and figures of speech.

Influence – Robert B. Cialdini
Seminal work on psychological triggers of persuasion.

Made to Stick – Chip & Dan Heath
What makes ideas memorable and how to craft messages that last.

Amusing Ourselves to Death – Neil Postman
Cultural commentary on media, narrative, and distraction.

II. Scholarly Rhetoric & Persuasion

The Rhetoric of Science – Alan G. Gross
Explores how even science relies on persuasive structures.

Rhetoric in Popular Culture – Barry Brummett
Analyzes rhetorical patterns in everyday media and entertainment.
The Only Authentic Book of Persuasion – Richard E. Vatz
Challenges the "information model" by emphasizing salience, agenda-setting, and framing in persuasive communication.

III. Critical Thinking & Skepticism

Calling Bullshit – Carl T. Bergstrom & Jevin West
How to spot manipulation in statistics, data, and arguments.
The Demon-Haunted World – Carl Sagan (removed as per user request)
(Removed from list)
A Field Guide to Lies – Daniel J. Levitin
Helps readers detect misleading claims in media and conversation.
The Believing Brain – Michael Shermer
Why we believe things first—and then rationalize afterward.

IV. Psychology of Belief & Conspiracy

The Conspiracy Theory Handbook – Stephan Lewandowsky & John Cook
Compact guide to understanding the structure of conspiratorial thinking.
Suspicious Minds – Rob Brotherton
Psychological deep dive into why people believe in conspiracy theories.
The Knowledge Illusion – Steven Sloman & Philip Fernbach
Explores how little we actually know—and how much we rely on others.

V. Propaganda, Language, & Media Manipulation

Propaganda – Edward Bernays
Classic text on public opinion engineering by the father of modern PR.

Words Like Loaded Pistols – Sam Leith
A historical and analytical look at rhetorical power across ages.

Trust Me, I'm Lying – Ryan Holiday
Insider's account of manipulating modern media ecosystems.

References

Arkes, H. R., Boehm, L. E., & Xu, G. (1991). Determinants of judged validity. *Journal of Experimental Social Psychology, 27*(6), 576-607.

Aristotle. (c. 350 BCE). *On rhetoric: A theory of civic discourse.* (G. A. Kennedy, Trans.). Oxford University Press.

Aristotle. *Rhetoric.* (W. Rhys Roberts, Trans.).

Arvidsson, A. (2006). *Brands: Meaning and value in media culture.* Routledge.

Balakrishnan, J., & Al-Aswad, A. (2021). Deceptive marketing practices in the digital age. In *The Routledge Companion to Digital Media and Advertising.* Routledge.

Barbour, I. G. (2000). *When science meets religion: Enemies, strangers, or partners?* Harper San Francisco.

Barkun, M. (2003). *A culture of conspiracy: Apocalyptic visions in contemporary America.* University of California Press.

Bartlett, F. C. (1932). *Remembering: A study in experimental and social psychology.* Cambridge University Press.

Begg, I. M., Anas, A., & Farinacci, S. (1992). Dissociation of processes in a feeling-of-knowing task. *Journal of Experimental Psychology: Learning, Memory, and Cognition, 18*(3), 431–441.

Begg, I., Anas, A., & Farinacci, S. (1992). Dissociation of processes in belief: Source attribution, memory for content, and receipt of plausible messages. *Journal of Experimental Psychology: General, 121*(4), 446–458.

Bem, D. J. (1972). Self-perception theory. In L. Berkowitz (Ed.), *Advances in experimental social psychology* (Vol. 6, pp. 1–62). Academic Press.

Benkler, Y., Faris, R., & Roberts, H. (2018). *Network propaganda: Manipulation, disinformation, and radicalization in American politics.* Oxford University Press.

Berger, P. L., & Luckmann, T. (1966). The social construction of reality: A treatise in the sociology of knowledge. Doubleday.

Bernstein, D. M., & Branscombe, N. R. (2018). *Introduction to social psychology*. Oxford University Press.

Brehm, J. W. (1966). *A theory of psychological reactance*. Academic Press.

Bruner, J. (1990). *Acts of meaning*. Harvard University Press.

Burgoon, J. K., Buller, D. B., & Woodall, W. G. (1996). *Nonverbal communication: The unspoken dialogue*. McGraw-Hill.

Burke, K. (1966). Language as symbolic action: Essays on life, literature, and method. University of California Press.

Burke, K. (1969). *A rhetoric of motives*. University of California Press.

Campbell, J. (2008). *The hero with a thousand faces*. Princeton University Press.

Cappella, J. N. (1987). Interpersonal communication. In C. R. Berger & S. H. Chaffee (Eds.), *Handbook of communication science* (pp. 377-414). Sage.

Castelli, L., De Dea, C., & Nesdale, D. (2007). The development of ingroup favoritism and outgroup derogation. *Advances in child development and behavior* (Vol. 35, pp. 247-285). Elsevier.

Chaiken, S. (1979). Communicator physical attractiveness and persuasion. *Journal of Personality and Social Psychology, 37*(8), 1387–1397.

Chong, D., & Druckman, J. N. (2007). Framing public opinion in competitive democracies. *American Political Science Review, 101*(1), 101–116.

Cialdini, R. B. (1984). *Influence: The psychology of persuasion*. William Morrow.

Cialdini, R. B. (2001). *Influence: Science and practice* (4th ed.). Allyn and Bacon.

Clark, K. B. (1929). The church and the Negro. *The Crisis, 36*(7), 229–231.

Collins, F. S. (2006). *The language of God: A scientist presents evidence for belief*. Free Press.

Comouche, J. (2021). The framing of COVID-19 in the media. *International Journal of Communication, 15*, 223–242.

Conley, T. M., & Cain, C. (2006). *Rhetoric in the European tradition*. University of Chicago Press.

Cook, J., & Lewandowsky, S. (2011). *The debunking handbook*. Skeptical Science.

Coulton, S. (1997). *A history of the world*. Penguin Books.

Davison, W. P. (1983). The third-person effect in communication. *Public Opinion Quarterly, 47*(1), 1–15.

Dillenberger, J. (1988). Protestant thought and natural science: A historical interpretation. University of Notre Dame Press.

Douglas, K. M., & Sutton, R. R. (2011). Does identifying with a conspiracy theory predict greater endorsement of other conspiracy theories? *European Journal of Social Psychology, 41*(4), 512–524.

Douglas, K. M., Sutton, R. M., Callan, M. J., Fincham, F. D., & Taglang, C. (2017). The social psychology of conspiracy theories. *Current Directions in Psychological Science, 26*(6), 538–544.

Dubay, E. (various works/statements).

Eliade, M. (1959). The sacred and the profane: The nature of religion. Harcourt Brace Jovanovich.

Entman, R. M. (1993). Framing: Toward clarification of a fractured paradigm. *Journal of Communication, 43*(4), 51–58.

Festinger, L. (1957). *A theory of cognitive dissonance*. Stanford University Press.

Fishbein, M., & Ajzen, I. (1975). Belief, attitude, intention, and behavior: An introduction to theory and research. Addison-Wesley.

Fisher, W. R. (1987). Human communication as narration: Toward a philosophy of reason, value, and action. University of South Carolina Press.

Frankfort, H., Frankfort, H. A., Wilson, J. A., & Jacobsen, T. (1949). *Before philosophy: The intellectual adventure of ancient man.* Penguin Books.

Freyd, J. J. (1996). Betrayal trauma: The logic of forgetting childhood abuse. Harvard University Press.

Galilei, G. (1957). Letter to the Grand Duchess Christina. In S. Drake (Trans. & Ed.), *Discoveries and Opinions of Galileo* (pp. 175-219). Doubleday Anchor Books. (Original work 1615).

Garwood, C. (2007). Flat earth: The history of an infamous idea. Macmillan.

Giles, H., Coupland, J., & Coupland, N. (1991). *Contexts of accommodation: Developments in sociolinguistics.* Cambridge University Press.

Gillespie, M. R. (2022). The impact of social media on political polarization. *Journal of Media Studies, 12*(3), 112–130.

Girard, R. (1986). *The scapegoat.* (Y. Freccero, Trans.). Johns Hopkins University Press. (Original work published 1982).

Goffman, E. (1959). The presentation of self in everyday life. Doubleday.

Gould, S. J. (1999). Rocks of ages: Science and religion in the fullness of life. Ballantine Books.

Green, M. C., & Brock, T. C. (2000). The role of transportation in the persuasiveness of narratives. *Journal of Personality and Social Psychology, 79*(5), 701–721.

Haidt, J. (2012). The righteous mind: Why good people are divided by politics and religion. Pantheon Books.

Hart, G. (1990). *Egyptian myths.* University of Texas Press.

Hasher, L., Goldstein, D., & Toppino, T. (1977). Frequency and the conference of referential validity. *Journal of Verbal Learning and Verbal Behavior, 16*(1), 107–112.

Hatfield, E., Cacioppo, J. T., & Rapson, R. L. (1994). *Emotional contagion*. Cambridge University Press.
Heath, C., & Heath, D. (2007). Made to stick: Why some ideas survive and others die. Random House.
Heidel, A. (1949). The Babylonian genesis: The story of creation as told in Iraq. University of Chicago Press.
Herman, E. S., & Chomsky, N. (1988). Manufacturing consent: The political economy of the mass media. Pantheon Books.
Hofstadter, R. (1963). *Anti-intellectualism in American life*. Vintage Books.
Horton, D., & Wohl, R. R. (1956). Mass communication and para-social interaction: Observations on intimacy at a distance. *Psychiatry*, *19*(3), 215–229.
Janis, I. L. (1972). Victims of groupthink: A psychological study of foreign-policy decisions and fiascoes. Houghton Mifflin.
Kahneman, D. (2011). *Thinking, fast and slow*. Farrar, Straus and Giroux.
Kahneman, D., & Tversky, A. (1979). Prospect theory: An analysis of decision under risk. *Econometrica: Journal of the Econometric Society*, *47*(2), 263–291.
Kelly, H. A. (1978). The problem of anachronism in literary history. *New Literary History*, *10*(1), 69–80.
Kepler, J. (1997). *Harmonies of the world* (E. J. Aiton, A. M. Duncan, J. V. Field, Trans.). American Philosophical Society. (Original work published 1619).
Kitcher, P. (1993). The advancement of science: Science without legend, objectivity without illusions. Oxford University Press.
Kruglanski, A. W., & Webster, D. D. (1996). Motivated closing of the mind: "Seizing" and "freezing." *Psychological Review*, *103*(2), 263-283.
Krupp, E. C. (1997). Beyond the blue horizon: Myths and legends of the sun, moon, stars, and planets. HarperCollins.

Lakoff, G. (2004). Don't think of an elephant!: Know your values and frame the debate. Chelsea Green Publishing.

Lawson, T. E. (2004). *Theories of religion*. Cambridge University Press.

Leary, M. R., & Kowalski, R. M. (1990). Impression management: A literature review and two-component model. *Psychological Bulletin*, *107*(1), 34–47.

Lemaître, G. (1950). *The primeval atom: An essay on cosmogony*. D. Van Nostrand Company.

Lennick, D., & Kiel, F. (2005). Moral intelligence: Enhancing business performance and leadership success. Pearson Prentice Hall.

Lewandowsky, S., Ecker, U. K. H., Seifert, C. M., Schwarz, N., & Cook, J. (2012). Misinformation and its correction: Continued influence and successful debiasing. *Psychological Science in the Public Interest*, *13*(3), 106–131.

Lewin, K. (1947). Frontiers in group dynamics: II. Channels of group life; Social planning and action research. *Human Relations*, *1*(2), 143–153.

Livingstone, D. N. (2007). Adam's ancestors: Race, religion, and the politics of human origins. Johns Hopkins University Press.

Loewenstein, G. (1994). The psychology of curiosity: A review and reinterpretation. *Psychological Bulletin*, *116*(1), 75–98.

Long, J. B. (2011). *Introduction to ancient Mesopotamia*. Oxford University Press.

Malinowski, B. (1923). The problem of meaning in primitive languages. In C. K. Ogden & I. A. Richards, *The meaning of meaning* (pp. 296–336). Harcourt Brace Jovanovich.

McGuire, W. J. (1964). Inducing resistance to persuasion: Some contemporary approaches. In L. Berkowitz (Ed.), *Advances in experimental social psychology* (Vol. 1, pp. 191–229). Academic Press.

Mehrabian, A., & Ferris, S. R. (1967). Inference of attitudes from nonverbal communication in two channels. *Journal of Consulting Psychology*, *31*(3), 248–252.

Meinert, E. (2022). Associations between behavior. *Journal of Medical Internet Research, 24*(1), e34538.

Messaris, P., & Abraham, L. (2001). The role of visuals in persuasion. In R. E. Rice & C. K. Atkin (Eds.), *Public communication campaigns* (3rd ed., pp. 245–258). Sage.

Nardo, D. (2004). *The ancient mesopotamians*. Gale Group.

Nickerson, R. S. (1998). Confirmation bias: A ubiquitous phenomenon in many guises. *Review of General Psychology, 2*(2), 175–220.

Noelle-Neumann, E. (1974). The spiral of silence: A theory of public opinion. *Journal of Communication, 24*(2), 43–51.

Numbers, R. L. (2009). Galileo goes to jail and other myths about science and religion. Harvard University Press.

Nyhan, B., & Reifler, J. (2010). When corrections fail: The persistence of political misperceptions. *Political Behavior, 32*(2), 303–330.

Paivio, A. (1986). Mental representations: A dual coding approach. Oxford University Press.

Patterson, J., & Johnson, A. (2022). *The rhetoric of conspiracy theories*. Routledge.

Perelman, C., & Olbrechts-Tyteca, L. (1969). *The new rhetoric: A treatise on argumentation*. (J. Wilkinson & P. Weaver, Trans.). University of Notre Dame Press.

Petty, R. E., & Cacioppo, J. T. (1986). Communication and persuasion: Central and peripheral routes to attitude change. Springer-Verlag.

Petty, R. E., & Cacioppo, J. T. (1986). Communication and persuasion: Central and peripheral routes to attitude change. Springer.

Pfau, M., & Wan, H. (2006). Persuasion theories. In J. F. Nussbaum & J. Coupland (Eds.), *Handbook of communication and aging research* (2nd ed., pp. 301–322). Lawrence Erlbaum Associates.

Pierce, J. L., Kostova, T., & Dirks, K. T. (2001). Toward a theory of psychological ownership in organizations. *Academy of Management Review, 26*(2), 298-310.

Pinch, G. (2004). Egyptian mythology: A guide to the gods, goddesses, and traditions of ancient Egypt. Oxford University Press.

Plato. (1997). *Republic*. (G. M. A. Grube, Trans., Rev. C. D. C. Reeve). Hackett Publishing Company.

Polkinghorne, D. E. (1988). *Narrative knowing and the human sciences*. State University of New York Press.

Polkinghorne, J. (1998). *Belief in God in an age of science*. Yale University Press.

Reber, R., & Schwarz, N. (1998). Effects of perceptual fluency on judgments of truth. *Journal of Experimental Psychology: General, 127*(3), 303–311.

Reber, R., & Schwarz, N. (1999). Effects of perceptual fluency on judgments of truth. *Memory & Cognition, 27*(2), 338–342.

Rice, R. (2009). Visual rationalism and the politics of science. *Journal of Visual Culture, 8*(3), 253–272.

Ritzer, G., & Jurgenson, N. (2010). Production, consumption, prosumption: The nature of capitalism in the age of the digital prosumer. *Journal of Consumer Culture, 10*(1), 13-36.

Rokeach, M. (1968). Beliefs, attitudes, and values: A theory of organization and change. Jossey-Bass.

Rosenberg, T. (2017, December 6). The Purity Spiral. *The New York Times*.

Ross, L., & Ward, A. (1996). Naive realism: Implications for social conflict and misunderstanding. In E. S. Reed, E. Turiel, & T. Brown (Eds.), *Values and knowledge* (pp. 103-135). Lawrence Erlbaum Associates.

Ross, L., & Ward, A. (1996). The fundamental attribution error. *Psychological Bulletin, 119*(2), 223–236.

Russell, J. B. (1991). Inventing the flat earth: Columbus, scholars, and modern historians' fabrication of an ancient flat earth. Praeger.

Sargent, M. (2018). Flat earth clues: The book.

Simons, H. W. (1971). Persuasion: Understanding practice, and analysis. Random House.

Slovic, P., Finucane, M. L., Peters, E., & MacGregor, D. G. (2002). The affect heuristic. In T. Gilovich, D. Griffin, & D. Kahneman (Eds.), *Heuristics and biases: The psychology of intuitive judgment* (pp. 397-420). Cambridge University Press.

Smith, H. (1991). *The world's religions*. HarperOne.

Stahlberg, D., & Frey, D. (1988). Belastungen, Fehlbeanspruchungen und ihre Folgen. In D. Frey, C. Graf Hoyos, & D. Stahlberg (Eds.), *Angewandte Psychologie: Ein Lehrbuch* (pp. 427-?). Psychologie Verlags Union.

Staw, B. M. (1976). Knee-deep in the big muddy: A study of escalating commitment to a chosen course of action. *Organizational Behavior and Human Performance, 16*(1), 27-44.

Swann, W. B., Jr., Jetten, J., Gómez, Á., Whitehouse, H., & Bastian, B. (2012). The psychology of feeling at one with a group: Social fusion and the consequences for collective action. *Journal of Personality and Social Psychology, 103*(5), 789–803.

Swire, B., Ecker, U. K. H., & Lewandowsky, S. (2017). The role of misinformation in the communication of science. *Journal of Applied Research in Memory and Cognition, 6*(1), 104-114.

Tajfel, H., & Turner, J. C. (1979). An integrative theory of intergroup conflict. *Organizational Behavior and Human Performance, 23*(1), 7–24.

Tajfel, H., & Turner, J. C. (1979). An integrative theory of intergroup conflict. *The social psychology of intergroup relations, 33*, 47.

Thorndike, E. L. (1920). A constant error in psychological ratings. *Journal of Applied Psychology, 4*(1), 25–29.

Toulmin, S. (1958). *The uses of argument*. Cambridge University Press.

Tversky, A., & Kahneman, D. (1974). Judgment under uncertainty: Heuristics and biases. *Science, 185*(4157), 1124–1131.

Unkelbach, C., & Greifeneder, R. (2018). Experiential fluency and declarative advice jointly inform judgments of truth. *Journal of Experimental Social Psychology, 76*, 162–171.

Unkelbach, C., & Greifeneder, R. (2018). Experiential fluency and declarative advice jointly inform judgments of truth. *Journal of Experimental Social Psychology, 79*, 78–86.

Van Zomeren, M., Postmes, T., & Spears, R. (2008). Toward an integrative social identity model of collective action: A quantitative research synthesis of predictors of collective action. *Psychological Bulletin, 134*(4), 504–535.

Walton, D. (1989). Informal logic: A handbook for critical argumentation. Cambridge University Press.

Walton, D. (1996). *Arguments from ignorance*. Pennsylvania State University Press.

Walton, D. (2008). *Informal logic: A pragmatic approach*. Cambridge University Press.

Walton, D. (2008). *Informal logic: A pragmatic approach* (2nd ed.). Cambridge University Press.

Walton, D. N. (1992). *Plausible argument in everyday conversation*. State University of New York Press.

Walton, D. N. (1996). *Arguments from ignorance*. Pennsylvania State University Press.

Walton, D. N. (1992). *Plausible argument in everyday conversation*. State University of New York Press.

Walton, G. M. (2008). Mere belonging: The power of social connection. *Journal of Personality and Social Psychology, 94*(4), 573–585.

Walton, J. H. (2009). Ancient Near Eastern thought and the Old Testament: Introducing the conceptual world of the Hebrew Bible. Baker Academic.

Ward, L. M., & Brewer, M. (2020). *The psychology of media and popular culture*. SAGE Publications.

Wason, P. C. (1960). On the failure to eliminate hypotheses in a conceptual task. *Quarterly Journal of Experimental Psychology, 12*(3), 129–140.

Weber, M. (1947). The theory of social and economic organization. Free Press.

White, D. M. (1950). The "gate keeper": A case study in the selection of news. *Journalism Quarterly, 27*(4), 383–390.

Witte, K. (1992). Putting the fear back into fear appeals: The extended parallel process model. *Communication Monographs, 59*(4), 329–349.

Young, R. (1995). *The Bible and the flat earth*. Christian Literature Publications.

Zajonc, R. B. (1968). Attitudinal effects of mere exposure. *Journal of Personality and Social Psychology, Monograph Supplement, 9*(2, Pt. 2), 1–27.

www.ingramcontent.com/pod-product-compliance
Lightning Source LLC
Chambersburg PA
CBHW020531030426
42337CB00013B/811